FOOTBALL ITALIA

FOOTBALL ITALIA

THE OFFICIAL COMPANION TO THE 1993/94 SEASON

RAY DELLA PIETRA & GIANCARLO RINALDI

Virgin

Half-title page: José Altafini celebrates Milan's 1962 *Scudetto*.

Title spread (left): Marco Van Basten, Ruud Gullit and Jean-Pierre Papin in self-congratulatory mood.

Title spread (right): A balcony view for Sampdoria fans.

This page: Omar Sivori and Cesare Maldini exchange pleasantries before Milan-Juventus, 24 November 1963.

First published in Great Britain in 1993 by Virgin Books, an imprint of Virgin Publishing Ltd, 332 Ladbroke Grove, London W10 5AH

Art direction: Peter Jackson

Page design: Paul Kime

For Virgin Publishing

Project editor: Carolyn Price

Publisher: Philip Dodd

Printed and bound by Bath Colour Books, Glasgow

Acknowledgments

Many thanks to my family, Kate, Margaret, all at Chrysalis and Keir Radnedge – and a special tribute to Diego Maradona, the greatest player in soccer history.
Ray Della Pietra

My sincere thanks to Mario Risoli for all the help and advice he provided, and of course to my family for all their support, patience and understanding throughout the time I was working on this book.
Giancarlo Rinaldi

contents

introduction

After my first season in Italy, I can see just how different life in Serie A is to the Premier League back home. Over here the fans and the press make 'calcio' a completely different ball game to the one we play in England.

Living in Rome and playing for Lazio has been a tremendous experience – especially when I scored that goal in the Derby match with Roma – and this season we'll be in Europe in the UEFA Cup too. I'm sure we're going to be challenging for the *Scudetto*. Anyone who watched our matches on Channel 4 will have seen just what we are capable of.

I know that many fans who've been following *Football Italia* every week have been crying out for more information on the game – this is the book you've been waiting for. Ray Della Pietra and Giancarlo Rinaldi have written a superb guide to the game. There's a profile of each of this season's Serie A clubs, a look back at last season, a history of Italian football, some great photos and a ton of stats. There's even some facts I didn't know. Unbelievable.

I hope you enjoy reading the book and that it helps you to enjoy *Football Italia* even more than you do already. Ciao!

Paul Gascoigne

FOOTBALL ITALIA
taking it to the screens

Foreign football – live on British television? 'It will never catch on' was the jaundiced view of a few sports pundits when Channel 4 announced their plans to cover the 92/93 season of Serie A football from Italy. A year later, the experts had been forced to eat their words, after a regular and loyal audience of nearly 4 million viewers had tuned in to each weekend's serving of the best league football in the world.

But it wasn't just the audience figures that delighted everyone involved at Channel 4 and Chrysalis TV (who produce the coverage). It was the general impact the Italian game made on the consciousness of every sports fan in the country.

At a time when Premier League football was tucked away on satellite, and the only other regular live football was being drawn from the lower leagues, Italian football was suddenly readily available and able to parade its talent in front of an appreciative audience. Long-term connoisseurs of the game have revelled in the skills of the world's greatest striker Marco Van Basten, the finishing ability of Lazio's Beppe Signori, and the creative magic of Roberto Baggio. And a totally new public – many of them women, and many of them younger viewers – started following the unfolding drama.

If anyone remained unconvinced that they were watching the highest level of football around, then the near total domination of Serie A clubs in Europe settled the argument. Juventus won the UEFA Cup in supreme style; Parma surprised everyone by lifting the Cup Winners' Cup. And Milan were magnificent in the European Cup, until they finally ran out of steam at the very last hurdle against Bernard Tapie's Marseille. Milan – all-conquering in the 91/92 Serie A – faltered, stumbled and were very nearly caught by Inter at the end of the season, sustaining the attention of *Football Italia*'s audience, an attention that had first been grabbed by the Gazza factor.

Paul Gascoigne is a character. Full stop. Love him or not, no one could deny that his impact on the TV audience was immense during the season. Whatever scrapes he got into during the week, he was always there on screen every Saturday morning in *Gazzetta Football Italia* (well nearly every Saturday!) to explain it all away in his own disarming manner.

A hero when he scored the vital equalizer in his first Rome Derby. A villain when he got sent off a few weeks later. Castigated for noises 'on camera' and an earlier four-letter verbal volley. Praised for his brave comeback from injury. Dubbed 'Phantom of the Opera' for wearing his famous mask. Gazza was never out of the headlines – and nor was coverage of Italian football.

Out in Italy, James Richardson became a regular fixture, on a balcony overlooking Rome, or out on location talking to the players, coaches and owners in the news. The commentary team of Peter Brackley and Gary Bloom, backed up by Ray Wilkins, Liam Brady, Glen Hoddle, Paul Elliott, Joe Jordan and Luther Blissett and the unmistakable timbre of Kenneth Wolstenholme, became fully established. And the cry of 'Golaccio!' was left ringing in everyone's ears.

The combination of great football, Gazza and the *Football Italia* team (including Ray Della Pietra, co-author of this book) had an impact beyond viewing figures and publicity. Cottage industries sprang up, supplying Italian soccer watches, strips, sweaters, pennants, tracksuits and T-shirts. Italian football fanzines like *Rigore!* (edited by Ray's co-author Giancarlo Rinaldi) found a new, larger and more informed readership. Travel companies responded by organising regular trips to the San Siro and the other top stadia. Suddenly, *Football Italia* had become a part of everyday life for a large section of the British public.

Other TV companies realised that Channel 4 had made a shrewd decision. BBC Sport bought the Italian Cup highlights from Chrysalis TV; ITV regularly featured Serie A goal highlights and Milan loomed large in their European Cup packages. Newspapers began printing regular columns on Italian football in general and not just on the British players abroad.

We have established a large and faithful audience. That's why this book has been produced, to give you more background on the whole phenomenon of Italian football – the clubs, the history, the stats and the way of life. And we look forward to bringing you even more *Football Italia* in the coming months.

Buona Fortuna, from the *Football Italia* team.

Left: Match commentator Peter Brackley and Ray Wilkins prepare for another Sunday of Football Italia.

CALCIO!

Football has a special place in Italian life and the league programme represents a mere part of the intriguing and sometimes eccentric world the Italians call *'Calcio'*. With its own cast of heroes and villains, Italian football has developed into a long running soap opera. Drama, love affairs, and scandal add to the glamour that has made *calcio* the Hollywood of football.

Italian football is played on Sunday, the day of rest, granting the majority of the country's aficionados the opportunity to follow their favourite teams. Each Sunday is referred to as 'la Giornata', the Day, hence 'la Prima Giornata' for the opening day of the season, 'la Seconda Giornata' for the second round of matches and so forth. However, the events that take place during the week preceding the Sunday can be as memorable as those which develop inside the stadia.

Although football *is* only a game, the different elements encompassing the sport often overshadow the developments on the field of play, making football in Italy more than just a game. It is a ruthless and affluent business which stands tall among the top ten industries in the country's economic table, proudly positioned alongside major companies such as Olivetti and Pirelli. More than 1,000,000 spectators, watching from Serie A to semi-professional football, pass through the turnstiles every Sunday (approximately one in 40 of Italy's population) while 25,000,000 fans follow the day's events by television or radio. Despite Italy's bleak economic climate, calcio is flourishing, generating revenue in the region of £2.5 billion a year. Television rights, gate receipts, sponsorship, merchandise sales, refreshments and more produce the wealth which allows players to earn collective annual salaries of £150 million in Serie A alone.

Milan, who invested a record £13 million for Gianluigi Lentini from Torino, incur the highest wage bill. Inevitably, Lentini reaps the largest salary, closely followed by Marco Van Basten and Franco Baresi. Indeed, in the 92/93 season, Milan accounted for six of the top seven best paid players in Italy – Gianluca Vialli of Juventus was the only representative from a different club. Astonishingly, Roberto Baggio and Paul Gascoigne, two of the finest players in the world today, are not included in the league of highest earners. Lentini's extravagant price tag is matched by his lifestyle. He drives a pricey sports car, wears Italian designer clothes, notably Gucci, and owns a luxurious apartment valued at more than £1 million. For all the creature comforts Lentini now enjoys, however, his

transfer from Torino was not entirely plain sailing. The announcement of his departure caused outrage among home fans who rioted in the city streets before besieging the club's headquarters in protest. Even the Vatican disapproved of such a costly transaction at a time of recession – the Pope claimed the sum of money involved was 'immoral'.

The man responsible for creating the formidable Milan dream team is the television supremo, Silvio Berlusconi. He owns three television networks, in addition to 'pay TV' channels and has investments in a host of other ventures including property and publishing. The Italian media have awarded him the title of *Il Suo Emittenza*, literally meaning 'His Excellency of Transmission'. Milan were on the brink of bankruptcy when Berlusconi took over as the club president in 1985 and he has spent his riches wisely, constructing a team which has dominated both domestic and European football throughout the last six years.

Following a disastrous period in the early 1980s, he has restored the honour of a prestigious club which seemed destined to years of obscurity. In 1980, the unthinkable happened when Milan were relegated from Serie A for the first time in their history and their demotion was not only an embarrassment but highly ignoble. Serie A comprised 16 teams in this era and of the three that were relegated only Pescara did so as a result of accumulating an insufficient number of points. Both Milan and Lazio, who finished the 1979/80 season third and thirteenth respectively, were punished by the Italian football federation for their part in the infamous bribes scandal.

Milan were then in the greedy hands of President Colombo, who successfully bribed Lazio to lose a Serie A fixture at their majestic San Siro Stadium. Players and coaches involved were punished with suspensions and hefty fines when the scandal was uncovered. The former Italian international Enrico Albertosi, the goalkeeper beaten four times by the unforgettable Brazilian team in the 1970 World Cup Final in Mexico and Lazio's Bruno Giordano, who later went on to win

Left: Italian fans know how to make their presence felt.
Above: Giuseppe Signori enjoying a little light lunch.

the *Scudetto* alongside Diego Maradona at Napoli, were two distinguished names to fall from grace. Games had also been thrown by other teams in Serie A. Paolo Rossi, who became the toast of Italy in 1982 for scoring six goals which virtually captured the World Cup for Italy, received a three year ban while playing for Perugia for his part in the swindle, later reduced to two. Rossi always claimed his innocence and in a bizarre twist had one year deducted from his suspension in time to lead the *Azzurri*'s Cup-winning attack in Spain.

President Farina followed in Colombo's tainted footsteps at Milan but ultimately fled to South Africa to escape from his falling empire and tax problems. Milan fans have been given little cause to worry by Silvio Berlusconi. The billionaire television and media mogul seems content to invest his vast fortune into the club in exchange for success and nothing less. It's worked so far.

In nearby Turin breathes Juventus patron, Gianni Agnelli, Berlusconi's primary antagonist. The Agnelli name has been associated with Juventus since the 1920s when Gianni's father, Edoardo, became the club president. Edoardo Agnelli lost his life in a freak air accident off Genoa in 1935 and Juve were starved of success for more than a decade until Gianni Agnelli was handed the reins in 1947. The FIAT controller has been a part of the famous 'Old Lady' ever since. His relationship with Silvio Berlusconi remains one of Italy's most fascinating. Agnelli, for so long Italy's number one football tycoon, came up against this younger man with an insatiable hunger for success. Silvio Berlusconi has enjoyed a larger return on his ventures over the past few seasons and success on both domestic and European fronts have swelled his club's coffers beyond comparison. A fruitful campaign in the Champions Cup rakes in around £25 million for Milan. The club also held a record-breaking number of season ticket holders in the 92/93 season, the 73,000 tickets sold yielding an exorbitant income even before a ball was kicked.

The omnipotent duo's rivalry is not confined to Italian football. The two impresarios have associated on the business circuit for more than a dozen years, though on opposite sides in recent times. Agnelli's influence was the key to Berlusconi's progress in the business world. The FIAT president himself set the wheels in motion for Berlusconi's takeover of the Milan based newspaper, *Il Giornale*, in 1978 and Agnelli continued to collaborate with his young counterpart through to the mid-80s. But, as Berlusconi's importance to the Italian economy increased, his rapport with Agnelli deteriorated.

Agnelli and Berlusconi were both interested in the £13 million acquisition of Gianluigi Lentini in the summer of 1992. Berlusconi was the first to act and optioned his purchase with a down payment of £3 million. However, the intrepid Juventus patron was not to be outdone. In a move worthy of the most outlandish of television dramas, the two presidents attempted to lure the bemused player to their respective teams by holding banquets in his honour. Lentini was unimpressed and refused a transfer from his hometown team. The threat of intervention from the Italian Football Federation eventually brought down the closing curtain before the whole affair could turn into absolute farce. Torino accepted Milan's £13 million offer and despite Lentini's declaration of love for his club he signed on the dotted line, hence Juve's submission.

'Berlusconi has lost his sense of proportion,' said an irritated Agnelli. 'I wouldn't have paid that much for him!'

Instead, the silver-haired billionaire signed Gianluca Vialli from Sampdoria for one million less.

Although Agnelli and Berlusconi gain the majority of publicity, other wealthy industrial figures also enjoy a healthy share of the limelight. Inter's Ernesto Pellegrini, market leader of the refreshments industry, Sampdoria's oil baron Paolo Mantovani and Napoli owner Corrado Ferlaino have invested huge amounts towards building championship-winning sides and all have been successful. The three clubs shared the *Scudetto* between 1989 and 1991.

Ferlaino has been running a Serie A club longer than any other current Italian president and in 1984 he presented Napoli's fans with the ultimate gift in the shape of a robust little Argentinian with the world at his feet. Diego Maradona emerged as the most talented player ever to perform in Europe and in 1987 he delivered the league championship to the passionate Neapolitan fans for the first time in the club's 61-year history. Ferlaino approached three banks for the loans necessary to entice Maradona from Barcelona in Spain and repaid the £5 million within a year as Maradona's arrival filled Napoli's San Paolo Stadium. The Argentine's skills were remarkable and never before witnessed in Italy. Maradona had the fans spellbound. He lived the life of a king in Naples, yet his behaviour was unworthy of such a title and he rejected his role model status. Even so, the citizens of Naples worshipped the little man and would have forgiven him anything.

Maradona's well publicized cocaine indulgence met with a fifteen month ban from the Italian Football Federation, which soccer's governing body, FIFA, extended worldwide. Perhaps his demise would have been averted had Napoli agreed to release him in 1988, when the Argentine insisted that the pressure in Naples had become overbearing. Maradona meant too much to Napoli financially, so President Ferlaino refused to let go of his most prized possession. Maradona was always stretching his fans' allegiance to its limit, and went as far as trying to turn the Neapolitan public against the Italian national team before the 1990 World Cup semi-final showdown with Argentina. He declared that the prosperous north of Italy had never accepted Naples as part of the country and never would, therefore the public should support and remain faithful to him as the city's chief ambassador, despite the fact he was playing for another country. At the San Paolo stadium, the fans' reply, in the form of a banner, was simple and poignant. '*Maradona Napoli ti ama,*

ma l'Italia è la nostra patria' – 'Maradona Naples loves you, but Italy is our motherland'. Although the majority of Napoli's fans stayed loyal to their country, some were not prepared to desert Maradona. However, as the Italian national anthem blared around the stadium, cries of 'Diego, Diego' were immediately muted by the sounds of 'Italia, Italia'.

28 million Italians witnessed Argentina eliminate their national team on penalties on television and Maradona led his team to Rome's Olympic Stadium to play West Germany in the World Cup Final. The showpiece turned into a personal disaster for Maradona as Argentina were beaten 1-0 and the stocky genius left the stadium sobbing to a chorus of jeers. His outburst prior to the semi-final in Naples had finally exhausted the Italians' patience. Their contempt could not have been illustrated better during the Gulf War when the Italians held a poll to find out which man they most hated. Saddam Hussein came a distant second!

The rivalry between northern and southern teams has always been intense. Of the 90 league championships played since 1898, only six have been captured by clubs from the south – Napoli and Roma twice, plus Lazio and Cagliari – which highlights the belief that football reflects its times and society. The impoverished south has constantly struggled to keep up with its rich neighbours. The unfriendly relationship between north and south is typified by the hostilities experienced by Napoli, who are seldom welcome in the north and in Verona in particular. Recently, the Veronese demonstrated their dry sense of humour when they greeted the Neapolitan players and fans alike with a shameful banner which read 'Welcome to Italy'. The enmity extended to Milan in the late eighties, evidently fuelled by Napoli's rise to the top of the Italian game. In 1990, Maradona inspired them to their second *Scudetto,* but that achievement was tarnished by controversy. During an Atalanta-Napoli contest, Napoli's Brazilian midfielder, Ricardo Alemao, collapsed on the borders of the pitch after he was struck by what was claimed to be a one hundred lire coin. The fixture ended goalless, although Napoli were

and Vittorio Cecchi Gori, are the latest to find that spending shameless sums of money does not automatically bring success. Their dismissed coach, former TV soccer pundit, Aldo Agroppi, once said that success starts at the top and in football that can only mean with the President and his ability to forge a sound structure in which to build a strong side. Players are generally signed to enhance a club's quality and ambition, but a club also needs a productive youth policy. During the last dozen years, the first team places of talented young players have been taken up by an increasing number of foreigners. The Italian league re-opened its frontiers to overseas players in 1980, lifting an embargo which had lasted fifteen years. The Serie A clubs were then allowed one import per team, an allocation which rose steadily up to 1992, when the Football Federation took away all remaining restrictions. This paved the way for players from outside Italy to seize the places once reserved for the most talented youngsters.

This is not to say that the players of the future have been abandoned. At the last count, three thousand soccer schools are recognised by the Italian football federation, while five thousand kids are already associated with the eighteen Serie A clubs. Inevitably, Milan have the largest youth programme in the country, with sixteen teams comprising three hundred and fifty players! Last year the club invested more than £2 million in its minor ranks. In addition, almost another 30,000 schools provide tuition for aspiring children eager to follow in the footsteps of their idols. The federation holds half a million young members, which shows one in six Italian boys between the ages of eight and sixteen play football. The statistic is all the more staggering when you consider that just ten years ago only one in sixteen played the national pastime. Eighteen of the 3,000 soccer schools affiliated with the Football Federation are run by former professionals, including the World Cup hero from 1982 Antonio Cabrini. The ex-Juventus defender has eighty youngsters on his books, but his target is to enrol a thousand children starting from the age of five. He offers the basic principles behind the game and, with

awarded the victory as a result of the rebellious behaviour shown by the Atalanta fans. This, according to the Milan faithful, virtually clinched Napoli's second title and pushed Milan down into the runners-up spot. To rub salt into the wound, Napoli's fans mocked Milan's sorrow and in typical Neapolitan fashion went on to sell miniature bottles of water labelled 'Berlusconi's Tears'! Milan's president was only able to bear his disappointment after his club's second consecutive European Champions Cup victory in the same month.

Winning means everything to Italian clubs and requires prudent investment by club presidents. Alas, so many have squandered their fortunes in failing to fully examine the demands of a championship-winning side. Fiorentina's father and son team, film producers Mario

five psychologists on the staff, also concentrates on the development of a young footballer's behaviour. Cabrini also runs a summer camp in San Marino called Summer Green, which clashes with those conducted by professional clubs, but he rejects claims that they disrupt the plans of Serie A clubs.

'Everybody knows that we take great care in what we do,' he said. 'Besides, the main purpose of our course in San Marino is for the children to treat it like a holiday, naturally with a lot of football.'

Once Italian children enter the ranks of a club or a soccer school, they are then categorised according to age, starting from the class of six to eight year olds aptly named, '*Primi calci*' (First Kicks). This is followed by the group of eight to ten year olds called '*Pulcini*' (the Chicks), who play seven-a-side matches on smaller pitches than the full-sized fields used by professional teams. From ten to twelve years the children are classed as '*Esordienti*' (the Rookies), and those playing in the twelve to fourteen bracket are known as '*Giovanissimi*' (the Juniors). If the young talents survive the junior ranks, their chances of becoming professionals increase and from the ages of fourteen to sixteen they are then known as '*Allievi*' (the Cadets). The coach of Italy's national youth side, Sergio Vatta, believes that only the players who go on to represent Italy at under-16 level

stand a chance of making it as a professional in Serie A. Approximately 350 *Allievi*, selected by their respective professional clubs at the age of fifteen, arrive each year for the national trials. Ultimately, the number is whittled down to twenty as the best players compete for a place in the starting line up. Vatta states that even then only 70 per cent of the first team squad eventually go on to play Serie A football. From sixteen to eighteen, the players enter the '*Primavera*' class, meaning Spring to denote the boys are just a touch away from joining the bright lights of first team football. The jump from the *Primavera* to the first team is naturally the most difficult to achieve.

Professional clubs are permitted to buy minors once they reach the *Giovanissimi*, the Junior class. Prices average at around £70,000 for those under sixteen, but clubs are normally only allowed to purchase under-16s who live in their regions. There are always exceptions, however, and in 1990, Juventus signed Luigi Sartor, a 14 year-old defender from Padova, for half a million pounds. Sartor broke into the Juventus first team in the 92/93 season, but was unfortunate in scoring an own goal during his one and only league appearance. Sartor has the ability and more importantly the resolve to bounce back from his disappointment and the country's foremost experts believe he has a long future at the very top of his chosen profession. Sartor has said 'I have made sacrifices to play for

Juventus, but they have been repaid. I don't feel like I'm working – kids of my age already work in factories. I believe I'm very privileged.'

The wealthy northern clubs constantly explore the country's playing fields in search of young talent and once found, they do not hesitate in relocating the child's entire family to city of the club concerned. The boys combine their studies with training, while their parents are also 'looked after'. In 1992, Juventus lured

Clockwise from bottom left: The personal fortunes of Gianni Agnelli and Silvio Berlusconi help fund the youth programmes which can enable the very best of young Italian players to achieve the lifestyles of Serie A stars like Franco Baresi and Paolo Maldini.

CALCIO!

13-year-old twins, Lorenzo and Maurizio Bedin, to Turin from Reschigliano, a small town on the outskirts of Padova. Juve already held their older brother under contract. The boys' mother travelled the short distance to Turin with her sons, but their father stayed in Reschigliano to keep their family business open, visiting his sons on weekends. Lorenzo and Maurizio train with the *Giovanissimi* for two hours a day, four days a week, their school studies taking up the rest of their time.

The system has its critics, but the man responsible for Juve's youth programme, former player Beppe Furino, is more concerned with the attitudes of the boys' families. They dream of stardom for their kids and are often motivated by the fortunes which accompany the lives of top-class professional players. The parents are usually quite willing to uproot from their homes. Michael Rea, a 13-year-old American boy who originates from Pescara, travelled the thousands of miles from Conneticut in order to pursue his ambition of becoming a professional footballer in Italy. His parents have agreed to move from the United States if their son fulfills his dream.

'Money isn't everything,' says Furino. 'I only hope the parents learn to understand this more than the boys themselves. Because it's the families who create the most problems. It's not all hard work for the boys: we give them the chance to enjoy themselves. We begin to play closer attention to the players once they are over sixteen years of age.'

Coaches pay careful attention to both the technique and physical fitness of professional players. Ball skills are taught early and even an unknown Serie A defender may develop superior technique to his counterpart from a different country. Ray Wilkins, one of the most acclaimed and successful British exports to have experienced Serie A football, playfully recalls the apprehension he felt during his first training sessions with Milan. 'I was amazed. Even the defenders had better technique than I had. I felt like catching the first plane back to England before I ruined my reputation.'

Needless to say, the former England captain stayed in Italy and enjoyed a fruitful three year spell in Milan. Other imports haven't been as fortunate. Some have made notable contributions to *calcio's* multi- billion lira industry, earning considerable wealth *en route*. But a stream of foreigners have failed to live up to their reputations and, although greeted with euphoria on arrival, many have been long since forgotten. Only a fraction of approximately 200 foreigners have fulfilled their promise since the barriers were lifted in 1980.

Certain players will always be remembered for the excitement they each brought to Italy. The Brazilian Zico, the elegant Frenchman Michel Platini, and of course the inimitable Diego Maradona have become legends of the world game. The Dutch pair Marco Van Basten and Ruud Gullit will doubtless join them in Serie A's Hall of Fame once their Italian escapades come to an end. Their success has camouflaged the failings of lesser known imports. Players like the Uruguayan Waldemar Victorino, Mika Aaltonen from Finland and the Dane Soren Skov have left the memory of their colourful names, though little else. Countless others, from as far away as Australia to the Ivory Coast, have met similar fates.

Perhaps the culture shock encountered by players from different parts of the world has often proved too great a burden. In many respects, the quality of Italian football has also exposed the mediocrity of numerous renowned players. David Platt's former Bari teammate, the Australian Frank Farina, arrived from the Belgian league and provides the most recent example of a player who failed to live up to his superstar billing. A celebrated striker in Belgium is not guaranteed equal acclaim in Italy.

The Italians call Serie A 'The most beautiful league in the world' and with all its dazzling performers, stadia and colourful fans they have good reason to feel proud. The game pioneered by Englishmen has been enriched by *calcio*. Players from abroad have been seeking their fortunes in Italy since the pre-war days of Raimondo 'Mumo' Orsi, the legendary Juventus forward who arrived from Argentina and went on to play for the Italian national team due to his Italian heritage. Orsi scored one of Italy's two goals that defeated Czechoslovakia in extra time in the 1934 World Cup Final staged in Rome.

Vittorio Pozzo, once a language teacher in England, coached the national team to World Cup glory in 1934, and again four years later when they defeated Hungary 4-2 in Paris. His soccer roots sprouted in his homeland, but he moved abroad after guiding the *Azzurri* in the 1912 Olympic games before returning to Italy, where he coached the national team for more than twenty years. In Italy, tactics have changed considerably from those Pozzo had adopted from the pre-World War I Manchester United team he so admired. From the zonal system, which involves defenders patrolling areas of the field rather than an opposing player and allows for a more attacking philosophy, the Italian game was sucked into the almost paranoid defensive game called the *Catenaccio*, literally meaning 'to bolt up' the defence. An extra defender, playing behind the others, acted as the spare man, the *'libero'* or sweeper, who picked up an opponent or a pass which had escaped his teammates. Defenders would mark designated opponents rather than zones of the field.

Catenaccio started to appear in the Italian league in the 1950s and by the end of the following decade, most of the Serie A teams, and indeed the national team, deployed the tactic established by the Austrian, Karl Rappan, the coach of the Swiss national team from the 1940s. Inter, who were coached by the Argentinian Helenio Herrera, enjoyed the most success with *Catenaccio* in the Sixties, winning three league championships and two European Cups in the space of four years. Since then, most of Italy's championship-winning sides have used the man-for-man marking system. In the most recent past, many clubs have reverted to the zonal system and Milan have mastered the art to the extent that the former coach of their *Scudetto*-winning team from 1988, Arrigo Sacchi, was given the task of leading the national team to the 1994 World Cup Finals.

The Italian league has seen its pendulum of power swing from club to club since its inauguration in 1898, and a half dozen sides have dominated the capture of the *Scudetto* – the tricolour shield worn on the playing jerseys of the league Champions. Being the founder members of *calcio,* Genoa predictably dominated the early years, but the true picture of Serie A began to take shape in the 1920s once the fierce rivalry surfaced among the big city teams. Juventus captured five championships in a row from 1930 to 1935 and their stranglehold on Serie A was disrupted by (the now struggling) Bologna, and Inter. In the 1940s, the city of Turin continued its reign as the footballing 'capital' of Italy with the rise of the magical Torino side, which captured four consecutive league titles. Only World War II and the fatal Superga air disaster, which cost the lives of the entire squad on its return from a testimonial friendly in Lisbon on 4 May 1949, prevented Torino from monopolizing the *Scudetto*. History reveals the extent of their tragedy – Torino have captured only one league championship, in 1976, since that grisly day. Other than intermittent *Scudetto* wins by less fashionable clubs like Fiorentina and Cagliari, the Serie A title has been dominated by the 'Big Three': Inter, Juventus and Milan.

Only the three richest clubs have the coveted gold star on their playing jerseys; Juventus have two. The prestigious emblem is awarded when a Serie A team collects its tenth league title and the Milan giants have each won the *Scudetto* on 13 occasions, while Juventus are way ahead with 22 Championship wins. In 1982, the Turin club added its second gold star to the first it had obtained in 1958.

Juve's 20th league championship victory was a contentious affair and their race for the title with Fiorentina wasn't resolved until the very last day of the season. Juve were one point clear of the Florentines on the eve of their trip to Catanzaro, who are currently in Italy's third division, and Fiorentina travelled to Sardinia, where Cagliari needed to avoid defeat in order to preserve their Serie A status. Fiorentina failed to break down Cagliari's resilient defence, but to this

Above: Sandro Ciotti.

Top middle: Bruno Pizzul, Italy's premier TV commentator.

Bottom right: Sandro Ciotti presenting *La Domenica Sportiva* with his 'assistant', Simona Ventura.

day believe their third *Scudetto* was robbed from them after the referee ruled out a goal they claim was valid. To add fuel to the fire, Fiorentina's appeals for a penalty were turned down late in the game. At the same time in Catanzaro, Juventus, who had the master playmaker Liam Brady in their ranks, were awarded a disputed penalty late in their match. The Irishman, who was making his final league appearance in Juve's black and white colours to make way for the arrival of Michel Platini, calmly stroked Juve to their twentieth league title. The day's incidents were endlessly scrutinized on the many football television programmes which fill Italy's broadcasting timetable. Of course, once the final whistles are blown television evidence can do little to alter the day's events, but the Italians love to analyse their national sport to its finest detail.

Today, there are no fewer than thirteen regular transmissions dedicated to *calcio* on three national networks and the pundits continue to review the Sunday matches right up to the ensuing Tuesday. The week kicks off with 'Dribbling' on Saturday afternoons, which is broadcast by the state network RAI, Radiotelevisione Italiana. The show is transmitted from Rome where the affable presenter, Gianfranco De Laurentis, is accompanied by the knowledgeable Antonella Clerici. Generally, female sports presenters are employed just to sit pretty and read the scores, but Signorina Clerici combines her good looks with an admirable command of the game. With the assistance of a studio guest, the match of the day is previewed and the main personalities are interviewed, usually at a team's training ground, while the rest of the week's news is reviewed in the latter part of the half-hour programme.

It's a no-nonsense and calm build-up to the drama which unfolds on the following day. Italia 1, which is a part of Silvio Berlusconi's company Fininvest, starts the ten hour marathon coverage on a Sunday with its *Guida al Campionato* (the Guide to the Championship) which begins two hours before the matches start. Again, the key fixtures are previewed. There are no live transmissions of Serie A matches, so the millions of fans who fail to travel to the stadia switch to their radios for *Tutto il calcio minuto per minuto*, which literally means 'All the football minute by minute'.

Commentators are positioned at every ground of the day's nine fixtures, in addition to the venue of the most important game in Serie B, Italy's second division. Each contest is covered in an inexorable sequence lasting anything from thirty seconds to three minutes depending on the game's importance to the Championship race. It's a riveting and thrilling production and the commentators' excitable tones can sometimes conceal the fact the match is being heard and not seen. The end of the radio's broadcast is immediately followed on RAI television by the aptly named *'Novantesimo Minuto'*, the 'Ninetieth Minute', which shows a concise two-minute edit of each Serie A match with a reporter's summary from every ground. This is only the beginning of a scrupulous examination of the day's football and there are usually enough talking points to take into the following week.

Novantesimo Minuto has competition from the private network, Telemontecarlo, which has its equivalent, *Domenica Stadio*, 'Sunday Stadium', televised at more or less the same time. By the end of these programmes, those wishing for an extra fix of *calcio* tune into RAI's forty minute highlights programme of Serie A's game of the day, strangely called *Calcio Serie* A. It's a little bit like calling the BBC's *Match of the Day* 'Football Premier League'. At eight o'clock, Gianfranco De Laurentis and Antonella Clerici return with *Domenica Sprint*. This hour-long production includes a regular studio guest and also a former referee, Bruno Longhi, who, with the trusted aid of his companion *La Moviola*, a fancy name for a tape machine which basically shows the action in slow motion, examines the day's most contentious issues.

Telemontecarlo again runs a similar programme called *Galagoal* simultaneously, while Berlusconi's Italia 1 channel shares its 10.30 time slot with the more popular Sunday evening programme, RAI's *La Domenica Sportiva*. The latter is conducted by the

gravel-voiced Sandro Ciotti, who makes his way to the Milan studio following his earlier stint as a radio commentator.

The late night shows are the most intriguing and are sometimes explosive, where players, coaches and soccer pundits gather to exchange views. Aldo Agroppi gave up his position as a soccer pundit to return to coaching and was sacked within four months by Fiorentina, but perhaps his polemic style was more suited to his television role. During the 91/92 season, Agroppi excelled on one particular edition of *La Domenica Sportiva* when he crossed swords with the president of the football federation, Antonio Matarrese. Agroppi has never witheld his contempt for the haughty president, in particular for sacking the former national team coach, Azeglio Vicini, and he took his opportunity to humble the man from Bari with the full sting of his venomous tongue. Agroppi had his questions continually rebuked by the president, which ultimately played right into his hands.

'I don't have to answer any of your questions,' said Matarrese pontifically.

'Well, what the hell are you doing here? Why don't you get on the first plane back to Bari,' replied Agroppi to euphoric applause from the studio audience. Matarrese hasn't appeared on the programme since.

Just when you thought it was all over, RAI delivers its late evening Monday show, *Il Processo del Lunedi*, which alarmingly means 'The Monday Trial'! Italia 1 broadcasts a satirical show the same evening called *Mai dire Gol*, 'Never Say Goal', which takes a welcome light-hearted view of the game. The next day, Berlusconi's channel follows with its *L'Appello del Martedi*, 'The Tuesday Appeal', which again sounds distinctly like a courtroom drama, but is in fact another football show and arguably the most controversial. The programme allows for more heated discussions and, considering the show takes place two days after the matches have been played, it needs the added spice to draw a large television audience. *L'Appello del Martedi* even has an agitator on its panel, who is paid simply to be controversial. Football on television doesn't stop here. On Wednesday and Thursday RAI and Fininest share the midweek cup coverage, while Telemontecarlo transmits *Mondocalcio*, dedicated to worldwide soccer. RAI has exclusive rights on the national team's contests, while Fininvest deliver the Italian Cup, the *Coppa Italia*. When the European action reaches the screens, both networks divide the matches between them. Obviously, Berlusconi televises all Milan's European games. Friday is the only day a television set can be switched on without a football in sight, unless, of course, you have Silvio Berlusconi's pay TV channel ...

Fans are able to compensate for anything they may have missed on TV with an abundance of newspaper coverage. Italy has three national sports dailies and they are each based in different major cities. Milan publishes *La Gazzetta Dello Sport*, Rome *Il Corriere dello Sport* and Turin *Tuttosport*. The bias towards their city's individual teams (there are two in each) is always evident and an example was provided in

CALCIO!

1992/93 by the differing reports on Paul Gascoigne's performance against Milan. In the Monday edition after the match, the Rome-based *Il Corriere dello Sport* eulogized Gascoigne's display. In contrast, *La Gazzetta* from Milan played down Gazza's achievements.

Italian football fans do not necessarily need to buy a sports daily to satisfy their hunger for latest news. There are at least six major quality newpapers that cover sport, ranging from Rome's *La Repubblica* to Turin's *La Stampa*, not to mention the 75 or so regional papers. A weekly colour magazine, *Guerin Sportivo*, also has a high circulation and further still, the clubs' official magazines are widely available, such as *Forza Milan*, ('Come on Milan') or Inter's creatively named *Inter Football Club*.

Italian journalists are not always popular with players and coaches alike. They are the first to condemn them when things go wrong and by the same token bestow excessive praise when, on occasions, a simple pat on the back would suffice. The media had little or no confidence in the Italian national team prior to the 1982 World Cup Finals in Spain and after the *Azzurri's* opening matches, they launched scathing attacks on Enzo Bearzot's side following three disappointing draws. Italy qualified for the second phase by virtue of having a better goal difference than Cameroon, but the players issued a *silenzio stampa*, the customary press ban Italian players resort to when all is not well. Dino Zoff, the legendary goalkeeper and captain of the *Azzurri* was elected speaker and knowing that Zoff was hardly the most talkative of men, the press were far from charmed. Italy surprised everybody when they eventually lifted the World Cup for the third time after defeating West Germany with a convincing 3-1 scoreline. Still the newspapers were ready for them and lavished the team with infinite praise, *CAMPIONI DEL MONDO* read the oversized headline in *La Gazzetta Dello Sport* the next day.

Italian fans do not need a great deal of encouragement when it comes to exhibiting their euphoria and the celebrations on that warm July night lasted through to the next day. Football is a sacred pastime in Italy and its followers represent the full spectrum of the country's society. Students, housewives, doctors, bankers or MPs all share an equal passion for the game, which is illustrated by a recent survey conducted by Abacus, one of Italy's foremost research institutes in Milan.

The study revealed that Juventus are the best supported club in Serie A with an overwhelming seven million *tifosi*, two million of whom reside in Southern Italy. Milan aren't too far behind with five million, followed in order by Inter, Napoli and Fiorentina. Despite the fact that Juventus have failed to win the *Scudetto* for the last seven years, the club's fans are essentially young, which is symptomatic of the weight the name carries due to Juve's glorious past. In contrast, their city rivals, Torino, enjoy a larger percentage of older support, albeit through having the smallest quota of young fans out of all the clubs in Italy's top flight. Football is renowned as a predominantly male domain, which is exemplified by Napoli with 80 per cent of its support coming from male *tifosi* and, in addition, the club has the largest number of adolescent fans. But the most surprising findings centred around Genoa and Sardinia where two clubs were represented by a vast number of female supporters. In Cagliari, the men are outnumbered by almost two to one, while in the city of Genoa, women account for more than half of Sampdoria's support. According to the survey, Sampdoria also boast the largest number of intellects. If so, why they don't follow a more successful side such as Milan or Inter remains a mystery!

Supporting a Serie A club is an expensive hobby and ticket prices range from around ten pounds to the extortionate one hundred pounds for the best seats in the house. The association of Italian football fans, the FISSC, have campaigned long and hard for the prices to be reduced, yet the expense has failed to deter the lion's share of supporters from travelling to Italian games. In Naples, one of the poorest Italian cities, a home fixture regularly attracts sixty thousand devotees. Even this season, when Napoli suffered a decline in fortune, their fans did not abandon their beloved team. Napoli broke its gate receipt record for their confrontation with Juventus in October 1992, which attracted close to 80,000 spectators. Unfortunately, the Neapolitans, who have regularly suffered the effects of prejudice in the North, characterized the ill feeling between the two regions by launching missiles, mainly in the form of bottles, at the Juventus players. Crowd disturbances persist in spite of the many recent tragedies witnessed in stadia all over the world. Lazio's two factions of supporters, the Eagles and the *Irriducibili* have even been known to contest the battle for territorial control in Rome's Olympic Stadium.

The majority of names relating to different groups of supporters stem from the English language and are generally selected to produce an aura of power and intimidation. The Lions, Tigers, Commandos, and Rangers are in constant confrontation with one another. Names are also bestowed upon sections of the club's respective grounds reserved for home support. Sampdoria's Bulldogs enter Milan's Lion's Den, *La Fossa Dei Leoni,* at their peril.

The FISSC believes that the only way to rid Italian football of its hooligan element is by introducing a membership scheme, which was rejected by English clubs and supporters not so long ago. The system suggested would enforce the registration of each fan, who would then be handed a membership card. The plastic card would be inserted into a computer-operated turnstile entry system at the ground. The idea is to eliminate troublemakers by withdrawing their membership cards when they are caught misbehaving, so ruling out their chances of gaining future access into the stadium. The FISSC convened in Venice in a meeting labelled 'The Supporter's Maastricht' to discuss this proposal, amongst others, together with representatives from clubs and the police. The association has taken giant steps in order to make a football match a trouble-free occasion. The FISSC parade anti-violence banners at most major grounds displaying the simple message *'Violenza è stupido'*, a slogan chosen from hundreds submitted by children in a recent competiton run by Unicef.

Violence is not solely reserved for the prestigious arenas of Serie A. Football can lead to bizarre events in the amateur leagues too, especially in Italy's youth leagues. In a small town outside Naples, shootings were reported at a seemingly low key Under-11 fixture. The matches are vitally important to the town's residents who go to extraordinary lengths to ensure their team's victory. Pity the little goalkeeper who, like a genuine veteran, announced that he was about to retire from the game after he had received death threats from the parents of a player from an opposing team.

There are positive aspects to *tifoşi*. The *gemellaggio* which exists between the fans of rival Italian clubs, where fans from one city are twinned with those from another, is uncommon in most countries. During the 91/92 season, leaders of the *Ultras,* the name given to the most fervent Italian fans, from Verona and Inter marched arm in arm across the pitch at Verona's Bentegodi Stadium displaying banners that depicted the respect they each have for one another. Napoli and Genoa fans also share a *gemellaggio.*

The pageantry paraded at a stadium is customary and, on occasions, may border on the extreme. Fluorescent cards, flags, scarves, banners, streamers, balloons, ribbons, and fireworks are all ingredients that go towards making a top Serie A fixture the most colourful of spectacles. On derby day in Genoa, the fans are free to enter the Luigi Ferraris Stadium and prepare the setting as early as seven o'clock in the morning. The decorations will have been made from anything up to two weeks before the festive occasion. There is certainly no love lost between the two rival sets of supporters, but they have rarely allowed their sporting differences to extend to violence. The current holders of Italy's Fair Play award for having the best behaved supporters are Parma.

Fans will sometimes resort to vandalism in protest. They can be fickle and feelings of adoration towards their respective clubs can soon change to feelings of resentment. In Foggia, in south-east Italy, the team's supporters were far from happy with President

Top : **Napoli fans celebrating their last**
Scudetto.

Above: **Law and order, Italian style.**

Right: **Genoa fans upstaging their rivals**
from Sampdoria.

Casillo's running of the club and vandalised the VIP section of their Pino Zaccheria Stadium, before digging up segments of the playing surface. Only a few months earlier, the same Foggia *tifosi* had placed a sizable placard on the centre circle of the pitch with words of affection for the club which read '*Una Domenica Dio creò il calcio, chiamò il Foggia e gli disse: Vai per il mondo e insegnalo a tutti*' – 'One Sunday God created football and summoned Foggia and said: Go all over the world and teach it to everyone'.

Many have compared football to religion, but an incident in Castellamare di Stabia in southern Italy married the two. Sister Stefania Iorio had always dreamed of watching Napoli play at their San Paolo Stadium. However, the hapless nun has been forbidden to set foot inside the ground despite her strong allegiance to the *Azzurri*. Her disappointment was compounded by the knowledge that a priest, Father Fedele, was given permission to watch his team, Cosenza, 'just because he's a man'. The Bishop of Castellamare, Monsignor Felice Cece, claimed the issue

was not a matter of sexual discrimination, but that of a nun's stricter regime which requires a greater dedication to a contemplative life. A photograph of Sister Stefania was published by leading newspapers depicting her with a Napoli flag neatly positioned by her side. An autographed photo of Diego Maradona also takes pride of place in her room, as does a poster of his replacement, the midfield genius, Gianfranco Zola, alongside the sacred cross! Her Mother Superior, Madre Maria Candida Starita denied any knowledge of the decision prohibiting Sister Stefania from realizing her 'vision', saying 'It is a question of decorum, just like smoking. Nobody forbids a nun to smoke, yet has anyone ever seen a nun smoke? If Sister Stefania had wanted to watch football in a stadium, she should never have become a nun.' It wouldn't be surprising if the Catholic church lost a loyal servant to football. Sister Stefania shall go to the match.

Season Review 92/93

On the opening day of the 1992/93 Serie A championship the *Rossoneri* of Milan had much to live up to after a superlative unbeaten season. The question on everyone's lips was whether they would cruise on unchallenged, or whether one of the chasing pack of challengers would finally bring the superstars down to earth.

This review of the season includes a month by month commentary on the events on and off the pitch, and follows the unfolding story at the top - and the bottom - of Serie A, plus the results of every match and the league positions as they stood at the end of each month.

Serie A stars in action in 1992/93:
Gianluca Vialli (far left), Nicola Berti and
Paolo Maldini (left).

settembre

The anticipation and sheer excitement generated by the opening day of the Serie A calendar is unrivalled by any other European League. Still, all the hype, speculation and eccentric predictions were quickly cast aside as the league's 18 clubs got down to business. From every club president down to every fan, hopes for a successful campaign ran high.

Billions of lira had been invested by Italy's megalomaniac money men, while the hard-core fans relinquished a sizeable portion of their annual salaries in order to buy the costly season tickets. Of course, this did not apply to the British public, who, for the first time, were able to follow the world's most glamorous league on terrestrial television.

The Serie A calendar was kind to Channel 4 and to the producers of *Football Italia*, Chrysalis Television, as the season kicked off with a showpiece match – Sampdoria versus Lazio. The absence of Paul Gascoigne, who was still recuperating after treatment for his much publicized knee injury, provided the only blemish on an otherwise auspicious start to the live Sunday coverage. There was to be no battle royal, but Des Walker's selection in the Sampdoria line-up, following his transfer from Nottingham Forest, sustained British interest.

The contest more than lived up to expectation and produced the season's opening goal, albeit an own goal, courtesy of Lazio's midfielder Diego Fuser! By the 20-minute mark, a relatively unknown striker catapulted Lazio into a 2-1 lead.

The first of Giuseppe Signori's two strikes – the first 'authentic' goal of the league season – was rewarded with 700 bottles of wine from a company based in Pescara. Paul Gascoigne looked from the sidelines and was particularly stirred by Signori's contribution.

'I'd never heard of him before I arrived in Rome,' Gazza confessed. 'But after I watched him play, I began to think he was one of the best footballers I'd ever seen!'

Sampdoria and Lazio kept the spectators enthralled throughout the course of the game and Sampdoria held the edge close to full-time, leading 3-2. Another own goal scored by Renato Buso, in almost identical fashion to Fuser's opener, provided a thrilling final twist to the match. The plethora of goals witnessed in Genoa's Luigi Ferraris Stadium was to set a precedent for the rest of the month.

Meanwhile, Milan and Juventus, the title favourites, were still dusting off the cobwebs after the summer break. An own goal by Foggia's left-back, Gualtiero Grandini, earned a 1-0 victory for the Champions. Juve's players returned from the holiday island of Sardinia with little more than improved sun tans following a goalless draw in Cagliari. Both Milan and Juventus dominated the summer transfer season. Milan's acquisitions included the £10 million Frenchman, Jean-Pierre Papin, from Olympique Marseille, Dejan Savicevic, who was signed from Red Star Belgrade, and the most expensive player in soccer history, £13 million Gianluigi Lentini from Torino. Juventus didn't stand on ceremony and lured Italy's golden boy, Gianluca Vialli, from Sampdoria in a deal worth £12 million, as well as acquiring England's David Platt from relegated Bari.

Inter, another pretender to the Serie A throne, unexpectedly came unstuck at newly promoted Udinese, while Roma and Napoli departed from their respective stadia with the jeers of their fans ringing in their ears. Both southern clubs were expecting comfortable victories against two other promoted sides. Instead, Roma suffered a 1-0 defeat at home to Pescara and Napoli's clash against the previous season's Serie B champions,

LEAGUE TABLE

AT THE END OF WEEK 4

		P	Pts
1	Milan	3	6
2	Torino	4	6
3	Sampdoria	3	5
4	Fiorentina	4	5
5	Juventus	4	5
6	Inter	4	5
7	Napoli	4	4
8	Roma	4	4
9	Genoa	4	4
10	Lazio	4	4
11	Parma	4	4
12	Brescia	4	4
13	Atalanta	4	4
14	Pescara	4	3
15	Cagliari	4	2
16	Udinese	4	2
17	Foggia	4	2
18	Ancona	4	2

DANIEL FONSECA

(b: 13/09/69 Montevideo, Uruguay) The Uruguayan international striker has a rare talent for goalscoring. He established a record for an Italian club when he scored all five goals in Napoli's UEFA Cup victory in Valencia. At the age of just 20, Fonseca arrived in Italy from Nacional of Montevideo and joined Cagliari. Two promising years in Sardinia culminated in a transfer to Napoli, where he formed one of Serie A's most powerful partnerships with the Brazilian Careca.

Brescia, ended scoreless. In summary, the events of Week One promised the closest Championship race in years.

A combination of early season jitters from Serie A's defenders and sharp finishing delivered more goals in Week Two, when seven of the nine Serie A fixtures produced four or more *reti*. Pescara's commendable assault on Milan's supremacy almost brought the *Rossoneri* crashing down to earth. Pescara were leading 4-2 before naively surrendering their advantage in a nine goal carnival. The goalscorer supreme, Marco Van Basten, spared Milan coach Fabio Capello's blushes with a hat-trick.

David Platt made his first league appearance in Juve's black and white striped shirt a week later in Genoa. The England midfielder's 77th minute equalizer, pulling back a 2-1 deficit, might conceivably have secured his place in the starting line-up for the weeks ahead, but Platt was to be dropped a fortnight later. Significantly, David Platt's dilemma was overshadowed by Paul Gascoigne's long-awaited return to action in Week Four against Genoa in Rome. The England midfielder appeared as svelte as at any time in his career and confirmed that his skills had not been removed along with his cruciate ligaments by the surgeon's knife. Alas, just before half-time, his comeback was cut short by a fairly innocuous challenge from Genoa's wafer-thin playmaker, Mario Bortolazzi.

Fears that Gazza's injured knee had been further damaged were soon relieved by Lazio's club doctor, whose diagnosis revealed merely a 'dead leg'. The game concluded with a 1-1 scoreline. Fortunately for Lazio and England, Gascoigne's Serie A debut did not end in tragedy. However, severe storms in the port city of Genoa caused the postponement of Sampdoria's fixture against Milan and sadly claimed two lives.

In Europe, all six of the Italian sides progressed to the second round of their respective competitions. Milan overpowered Olimpia Ljubljana from Slovenia in the Champions' Cup and Parma saw off the challenge of the Hungarians, Ujpest Dosza, in the Cup Winners' Cup, while Juventus, Roma, Napoli and Torino comfortably advanced into round two of the UEFA Cup.

By the end of the opening month, Milan's predicted domination had yet to emerge. The Champions, however, won all their matches in September, presenting the likes of Inter and Juventus with a taste of what they would be up against in the weeks ahead. Serie A's leading clubs would need to be at their best in order to overthrow the current kings of Italian football.

Top left: Sampdoria-Lazio – a showpiece opener to the season.

Above left: Another injury scare for Gazza.

Above: David Platt scores for Juventus against Genoa.

RESULTS

Week 1 (6 September 1992)

Atalanta	2-1	Parma
Cagliari	0-0	Juventus
Fiorentina	1-1	Genoa
Milan	1-0	Foggia
Napoli	0-0	Brescia
Roma	0-1	Pescara
Sampdoria	3-3	Lazio
Torino	4-1	Ancona
Udinese	2-1	Inter

Week 2 (13 September 1992)

Ancona	2-3	Sampdoria
Brescia	0-0	Torino
Foggia	2-4	Napoli
Genoa	0-0	Roma
Inter	3-1	Cagliari
Juventus	4-1	Atalanta
Lazio	2-2	Fiorentina
Parma	3-1	Udinese
Pescara	4-5	Milan

Week 3 (20 September 1992)

Brescia	1-0	Pescara
Cagliari	1-1	Lazio
Fiorentina	7-1	Ancona
Genoa	2-2	Juventus
Milan	2-0	Atalanta
Napoli	1-2	Inter
Roma	3-1	Foggia
Torino	3-0	Parma
Udinese	1-2	Sampdoria

Week 4 (24 September 1992)

Ancona	1-1	Napoli
Atalanta	2-1	Cagliari
Foggia	1-0	Udinese
Inter	2-2	Fiorentina
Juventus	1-1	Roma
Lazio	1-1	Genoa
Parma	2-0	Brescia
Pescara	2-2	Torino
Sampdoria	P-P	Milan

ottobre

The month began with a record-breaking Sunday. Forty-eight goals, 32 of which were scored in four fixtures, shattered the long-standing record of 42 goals for an 18-team Serie A. Milan's away fixture against Fiorentina won the pick of the day's matches, as Van Basten and company romped to an astonishing 7-3 victory.

RESULTS

Week 5 (4 October 1992)

Brescia	4-1	Foggia
Cagliari	1-0	Roma
Fiorentina	3-7	Milan
Genoa	4-4	Ancona
Inter	1-0	Atalanta
Lazio	5-2	Parma
Napoli	2-3	Juventus
Torino	2-2	Sampdoria
Udinese	5-2	Pescara

Week 6 (18 October 1992)

Atalanta	0-0	Torino
Foggia	2-2	Genoa
Juventus	0-0	Brescia
Milan	5-3	Lazio
Parma	3-0	Ancona
Pescara	0-2	Fiorentina
Roma	4-1	Inter
Sampdoria	2-0	Cagliari
Udinese	2-0	Napoli

Week 7 (25 October 1992)

Ancona	3-0	Foggia
Brescia	0-2	Cagliari
Fiorentina	4-0	Sampdoria
Genoa	4-3	Pescara
Inter	3-1	Juventus
Lazio	3-0	Atalanta
Napoli	2-1	Roma
Parma	0-2	Milan
Torino	1-0	Udinese

Napoli's San Paolo Stadium provided the setting for the visit of Juventus and another spectacular encounter. Juventus, 'La Signora', finally exhibited a display worthy of 'her' illustrious name and triumphed in a five goal bonanza. Strikes from Roberto Baggio, his first of the season, the German Andy Moeller and Gianluca Vialli handed Juve a three goal advantage. Nevertheless, Napoli's hurt pride ensured a grandstand finale. Two goals, one from Daniel Fonseca and the other from their pocket-sized genius, Gianfranco Zola, late in the game had Juve's players living on their nerves during the closing minutes, but they held out long enough to win 3-2.

Sadly, the Neapolitan fans' behaviour cast a shadow over a bright afternoon and the darker side of the sport surfaced. Juve's stylish Brazilian, Julio Cesar, suffered a broken shin bone following an apparently harmless collision with a Napoli forward. As the sweeper was carried off for treatment, missiles of all kinds were hurled from the stands and one almost caused the paramedics to drop his colossal frame onto the tarmac surrounding the pitch. In some quarters, the combination of black skin and a Juventus shirt is regarded as tantamount to committing a crime.

Lazio, with Paul Gascoigne very much in evidence, inflicted a 5-2 defeat on the Italian Cup holders, Parma. Beppe Signori celebrated his first hat-trick in Serie A and Diego Fuser scored two more as Parma went down to their worst defeat in two seasons.

The league programme then paused for a week to accommodate the Italian national side who were on World Cup duty – a welcome breather for all. Two late strikes, one from Roberto Baggio and the other from Milan's Stefano Eranio, earned the *Azzurri* a disappointing draw against the Swiss in Cagliari.

However, the fireworks exploded again the following weekend. Milan against Lazio proved to be one of Italy's most absorbing contests of recent years. The match produced a further eight goals (who ever said Italian football was boring?). Almost inevitably, the Champions found the target five times, but Lazio's enterprising game enchanted the Milanese public – not to mention the three million British viewers glued to their television sets.

In Rome, Lazio's city rivals fully exploited Inter's uncertain start to their campaign with four memorable goals, although Matthias Sammer, the former East German, scored a consolation goal for Inter. Napoli's crisis deepened and yet another defeat, at Udinese, raised doubts about the future of their likeable Roman coach, Claudio Ranieri. Their next match at home to Roma, labelled *Il Derby del Sud* (the Derby of the South), became a tense and desperate battle for Napoli.

Two goals from the South American striking partnership of Fonseca and the Brazilian Antonio Careca, one each side of the half-time break, handed Ranieri the lifeline he needed.

Milan maintained their winning streak by overcoming Parma and stretched their unbeaten league run to 41 matches. Meanwhile, at the San Siro, Inter and Juventus contested the *Derby d'Italia* (Derby of Italy). This is traditionally the biggest fixture in Serie A and neither side relishes a defeat at the hands of the old enemy. Inter demolished Juve by three goals to one, all four goals coming from overseas players. Ruben Sosa, Igor Shalimov and Matthias Sammer eased the home side ahead, before Andy Moeller salvaged some pride for Juve. World Cup hero, Inter's Salvatore Schillaci, nicknamed Toto, took further delight in defeating the club that had made him an international superstar and a household name. The timid Sicilian is a man of few words – and, for that matter, a man of few goals since his World Cup fairy tale – but he could not conceal his disappointment at the way in which he had been discarded by the club he had supported from childhood. 'Juventus bought Vialli to replace me, but they continue to have problems,' Toto remarked. 'I would have loved to score against my former team – there is no room for sentiment in football. If there was, I would never have left.'

Nor did there seem to be room for sentiment in his marriage to Rita – she left him! The couple had been growing apart since Italia '90 and Rita inflicted the final blow when she wrote a letter to one of the country's leading daily newspapers describing the reason for their separation. The pitiful letter made the front page! Toto was left bewildered by his wife's perfidious act, but chose not to comment. A man of few words …

Back to the real action. Napoli's season was turning into a disaster after only two months. A 2-0 defeat at home to Paris Saint Germain in the first leg of the UEFA Cup put further pressure on coach Ranieri. Torino were also beaten at home in the same competition by Dynamo Moscow. In Turin, the fans' derision was unceremoniously aimed at the club President, Gian Mauro Borsano. The close season sale of crowd favourite Gianluigi Lentini to Milan had sparked riots in the city streets. Borsano added fuel to the raging fire by raising ticket prices and further depleted his first-team squad by selling three other star names. The city's magnificent Delle Alpi Stadium, which holds more than 70,000 spectators, filled a mere quarter of its capacity once the fans began to boycott home fixtures. In spite of their troubles, Torino climbed to second place in Serie A.

The other four Italian clubs playing in Europe were well positioned to go through the next round of their respective competitions. Milan virtually assured themselves of a place in the European Champions' League with a 1-0 win in Bratislava and although Parma drew at their Ennio Tardini Stadium against Boavista, they did enough to suggest a victory in Portugal was well within their reach. In the UEFA Cup, a goal from David Platt settled a tight encounter for Juventus against Panathinaikos and Roma earned a sizeable advantage over Grasshopper in the Olympic Stadium to take to Switzerland in the second leg.

With seven weeks of the season gone, Milan had once again clearly become the team to beat in Serie A. Six wins out of six matches and 12 goals scored in their last three games highlighted the extent of their superiority over other championship hopefuls. Inter and Juventus continued to show the inconsistency that had marred their recent campaigns.

GIUSEPPE SIGNORI

(b: 17/02/68 Villa di Semio, Bergamo) The left-sided striker surpassed all expectation in only his second season in Serie A since joining Lazio from Foggia in the summer of 1992. Signori scores the lion's share of his goals with his potent left foot and has developed into one of Europe's leading strikers. Arrigo Sacchi capped the livewire forward on Italy's summer tour of the United States in 1992, where he scored against the Republic of Ireland on his full debut.

LEAGUE TABLE

AT THE END OF WEEK 7

		P	Pts
1	Milan	6	12
2	Torino	7	10
3	Fiorentina	7	9
4	Inter	7	9
5	Lazio	7	8
6	Juventus	7	8
7	Genoa	7	8
8	Sampdoria	6	8
9	Brescia	7	7
10	Roma	7	6
11	Udinese	7	6
12	Napoli	7	6
13	Cagliari	7	6
14	Parma	7	6
15	Atalanta	7	5
16	Ancona	7	4
17	Pescara	7	3
18	Foggia	7	3

Top left: Genoa goalkeeper Stefano Tacconi.
Top middle: Jean-Pierre Papin celebrates after scoring for Milan against Lazio.
Top right: Juve's Julio Cesar is stretchered off at Naples.

novembre

ROBERTO BAGGIO

(b: 18/02/67

Caldogno, Vicenza)

The national team

coach, Arrigo Sacchi,

refers to Baggio as the 'best player in the world' and few would argue with this description of the Juventus playmaker when he's at the peak of his game. Baggio has taken time to adjust to life in Turin, but he is now showing the form that prompted Juve to pay the £8,000,000 that, in 1990, made him the most expensive player in soccer history.

LEAGUE TABLE

AT THE END OF WEEK 11

		P	Pts
1	Milan	10	18
2	Inter	11	15
3	Juventus	11	14
4	Sampdoria	10	13
5	Torino	11	13
6	Fiorentina	11	12
7	Cagliari	11	12
8	Parma	11	12
9	Atalanta	11	11
10	Lazio	11	10
11	Brescia	11	10
12	Genoa	11	10
13	Roma	11	9
14	Udinese	11	9
15	Foggia	11	9
16	Napoli	11	8
17	Ancona	11	6
18	Pescara	11	5

November was an important month for Italy's leading lights. First against second kicked off the month. At the San Siro, Milan were hoping to maintain their 100 per cent record against Torino, but for all the *Rossoneri*'s efforts, Torino's defenders held out for a goalless draw. Milan saved their goalscoring powers for the return leg of their European Cup tie against Slovan Bratislava three days later with an emphatic 4-0 victory. Inter travelled to lowly Pescara and disposed of the bottom club, winning 4-1. Despite the encouraging result, Inter's sagacious coach, Osvaldo Bagnoli, was dissatisfied with his players, who had managed to secure the two points only in the last 15 minutes of an even match, scoring three times. A thigh injury to Toto Schillaci, which would sideline the striker until the new year, further dampened Bagnoli's spirits. 'If ever a result failed to tell the true story, that was one,' Bagnoli claimed. 'It just goes to show that anything can happen in football.'

Anything can happen during a Derby match, when tensions tend to mount to fever pitch. Genoa staged the first cross-city Derby of the season. Sampdoria have had the upper hand in the recent past, but Genoa, Italy's oldest club and in their centenary year, were seeking a springboard from which to leap into life. They didn't find one. Samp effortlessly eased past their rivals, which prompted even the usually sedate Des Walker to abandon his inhibitions and join in the joyous celebrations after the 4-1 victory.

Lazio, without the services of Serie A's top scorer, Giuseppe Signori, obtained a point at Udinese after a goalless draw. Signori's absence in Week Eight was significant; Lazio had always scored with the waspish striker in their line-up. Italy's leading Southern clubs, Roma and Napoli, lost again, to Brescia and Atalanta respectively. Roma gained consolation from their qualification to the third round of the UEFA Cup at the expense of the Swiss, Grasshoppers, but Napoli could manage only a goalless draw in Paris and were eliminated, as were Torino by means of Dynamo Moscow. Parma earned a commendable 2-0 victory over Boavista to reach the quarter final of the Cup Winners' Cup.

Juventus warmed up for their eagerly anticipated confrontations with Torino and Milan later in the month with two successive 5-1 victories, against Ancona and Udinese. Roberto Baggio had finally got into gear and scored six of the ten goals. Juve also progressed to the third round of the UEFA Cup on the strength of David Platt's first leg goal in Greece.

Milan needed to conquer Napoli at the San Paolo Stadium before facing Inter in the Milan Derby the following week and Juventus seven days later. A defeat for Napoli would spell the end of the road for coach Ranieri, who had done so much to restore the club's image after Maradona's departure Marco Van Basten was in devastating form and buried Napoli's beleaguered defence under an avalanche of goals. The Dutchman rifled four past the former international goalkeeper, Giovanni Galli, and Stefano Eranio added

another to complete a miserable day for Diego Maradona's old club. Gianfranco Zola's token effort six minutes from full-time could not save Ranieri's job.

At least he was not alone in joining the unemployed. Genoa's Bruno Giorgi resigned as a result of his team's poor start to the season and was replaced by the former coach of Juventus, Gigi Maifredi. The club's supporters, having just suffered the humiliation of losing their Derby match, were further embarrassed when Cagliari departed from the Luigi Ferraris Stadium with the two points. Angry scenes followed as more than a hundred Genoa fans protested by blocking the players' exit from the stadium. Stefano Tacconi, the charismatic former Juventus goalkeeper, was made the scapegoat for the club's woeful performance and he required a police escort from the ground.

To replace Ranieri, Napoli recalled Ottavio Bianchi, the man who had led them to an unprecedented league title in 1987. During his first week in charge, a scattering of home fans took out their early season frustration on the players. Wielding baseball bats, thugs stormed the training ground in nearby Soccavo, attacking those they felt were chiefly responsible for Napoli's decline. Bianchi had experienced the special Neapolitan ambience during his previous reign, but he could never have envisaged such alarming disquiet.

Italy's World Cup qualifier against Scotland in Glasgow presented Serie A with another week's respite. In a scoreless match, Italy was disappointed once again and the bruising battle left Juve's principal hope for

success, Roberto Baggio, nursing a broken rib. Baggio's injury was devastating for Juventus, who were forced to confront rivals Torino and Milan without their virtuoso captain.

Both the Milan and Turin Derbies were staged in Week Ten. At the San Siro, Gianluigi Lentini finally began to justify his exorbitant price tag, opening the scoring with an outstanding strike. De Agostini's speculative drive 15 minutes from full-time provided Inter with a point. At the Delle Alpi Stadium in Turin, an own goal by Torino's Giorgio Venturin in the final minute handed Juventus a precious 2-1 victory. The midfielder was so upset after the match that he threw on a track suit and left the stadium immediately.

In the second edition of the European Champions' League, Marco Van Basten netted all four goals for Milan as they humbled the Swedes from Gothenburg. Both Juventus and Roma came away from their UEFA Cup third round first leg ties, against the Czechs Sigma Olomouc and Galatasaray of Istanbul respectively, with convincing wins.

Buoyed by their success, Juventus went into their match against Milan with renewed optimism. The Champions, through Marco Simone, opened the scoring early in the second half and later found an unlikely hero in Sebastiano Rossi. The six foot six goalkeeper came on for the injured Antonioli and saved a Gianluca Vialli penalty with only minutes of the contest remaining. Milan were now the clear favourites for the *Scudetto*.

Week 11 also included the Rome Derby. Paul Gascoigne became the hero of Rome – well, Lazio's side of it – after scoring an 87th minute equalizer. Gazza was back!

After three months, the top of Serie A had a familiar look about it. Milan had dropped just two points and increased their lead over their nearest challengers, having played one game fewer. Pescara and Ancona were already showing signs of resignation to an immediate return to Serie B.

Week 8 (1 November 1992)

Atalanta	3-2	Napoli
Cagliari	2-1	Fiorentina
Foggia	1-0	Parma
Juventus	5-1	Ancona
Milan	0-0	Torino
Pescara	1-4	Inter
Roma	2-3	Brescia
Sampdoria	4-1	Genoa
Udinese	0-0	Lazio

Week 9 (8 November 1992)

Ancona	5-1	Brescia
Atalanta	2-1	Foggia
Fiorentina	2-1	Roma
Genoa	2-3	Cagliari
Inter	0-0	Sampdoria
Juventus	5-1	Udinese
Lazio	1-2	Torino
Napoli	1-5	Milan
Parma	1-0	Pescara

Week 10 (22 November 1992)

Brescia	1-1	Fiorentina
Cagliari	0-1	Parma
Foggia	2-1	Lazio
Milan	1-1	Inter
Pescara	2-0	Atalanta
Roma	2-1	Ancona
Sampdoria	3-1	Napoli
Torino	1-2	Juventus
Udinese	3-0	Genoa

Week 11 (29 November 1992)

Ancona	0-1	Cagliari
Atalanta	2-0	Udinese
Foggia	1-0	Pescara
Genoa	2-1	Torino
Inter	2-1	Brescia
Juventus	0-1	Milan
Lazio	1-1	Roma
Napoli	4-1	Fiorentina
Parma	1-0	Sampdoria

Top left: Local police in action at Genoa.

Top middle: Celebrations for Juventus in the Turin Derby.

Top right: Napoli coach Ottavio Bianchi.

dicembre

Milan's defeat of Juventus in Week 11 had reduced 'La Signora' to a shadow of 'her' former glorious self. Their hopes for the league championship were ripped apart. Losing to the Rossoneri was difficult enough to digest without the prospect of playing their bitter rivals Fiorentina a week later – a fixture that is, without doubt, the grudge match of Italian football. Florence, for all its culture, reserves the most hostile of receptions for visiting football teams, particularly Juventus. Fiorentina's fans have never forgiven Juve for 'stealing' the league title from them – on the last day of the season – in 1982. This was compounded by their defeat to Juventus in the 1990 UEFA Cup final. Fiorentina's resentment intensified when their most prized possession, Roberto Baggio, left for Turin one month later, provoking violent unrest among home fans. The hatred was apparent during World Cup year, when the Italian national team prepared for the tournament in Coverciano, merely a stone's throw from the famous Duomo and Ponte Vecchio. On the Azzurri's arrival, the players selected from Juventus were ignominiously stoned and spat upon.

The Fiorentina fans were more subdued for this month's drama, but the Juventus players seemed to be stricken with stage fright. An early goal from the Dane, Brian Laudrup, was followed by an own goal from the teenage defender, Luigi Sartor, making his Serie A debut. The match ended 2-0, but it could quite easily have turned into Juve's worst defeat in decades. After knee surgury, David Platt joined Julio Cesar on the club's injured list. The cartilage operation would sideline the England midfielder for two months.

December was a gloomy month for another of Italy's most prestigious sides, Inter. While Milan's draw with struggling Udinese came as something of a surprise, the 3-0 defeat of their city rivals at Ancona was almost impossible to forecast. Ancona, enjoying their first

season in Serie A, were dealt a double blow when their owner and President were incarcerated following fraud allegations. In spite of Ancona's crisis, Inter were simply overwhelmed by the Dorici's spirited display. In addition, their dashing goalkeeper, Walter Zenga, was sent off for a professional foul on 'The Condor', Massimo Agostini. The red card earned him a one-match ban, thus ruling him out of their next clash against Lazio in Rome.

Gascoigne and company prepared for Inter's visit with a controversial 3-2 win in Pescara. Paul Gascoigne scored the first of the game's five goals after a majestic run, but it wasn't until the final minute that the game exploded. Pescara's fans, who had been growing increasingly impatient with the referee's erratic decisions, launched various objects at the official's accomplice, the linesman. With the score level, at 2-2, the linesman's missile-induced injury brought a three-minute halt to the activity.

When play resumed, a headed goal from Lazio's central defender, Luca Luzardi, caused uproar among the Pescara fans. This was reminiscent of Geoff Hurst's infamous goal in the 1966 World Cup final; it was unclear whether the ball had crossed the goal line after it had cannoned off the underside of the crossbar. Neither a Russian linesman nor a flag-waver of any description was called for on this occasion, as the referee took it upon himself to award a goal. The Pescara fans had only themselves to blame: had they refrained from rebelling, the referee would not have added the extra time. Still, the Pescara club President, Pietro Scibilia, was convinced there was a conspiracy against the club.

'We're finding it difficult to win games as it is, without our opponents being given a helping hand,' he said. 'They're driving us down to Serie B!'

LEAGUE TABLE

AT THE END OF WEEK 13

		P	Pts
1	Milan	13	23
2	Fiorentina	13	15
3	Torino	13	15
4	Inter	13	15
5	Sampdoria	13	14
6	Juventus	13	14
7	Lazio	13	14
8	Cagliari	13	14
9	Atalanta	13	14
10	Parma	13	13
11	Genoa	13	13
12	Roma	13	12
13	Udinese	13	12
14	Brescia	13	12
15	Foggia	13	12
16	Napoli	13	8
17	Ancona	13	8
18	Pescara	13	6

MARCO VAN BASTEN

(b: 31/10/64 Utrecht, Holland) The goalscorer supreme, Van Basten has surpassed Diego Maradona's total of 81 goals to become Serie A's most prolific overseas scorer since the embargo on foreign players was lifted in 1980. The Dutchman appears to find the target at will and his displays during his six years in Milan have earned him the title of European Footballer of the Year on three occasions. Surgery on his injured ankle wrecked what promised to be Van Basten's best ever season in Italy.

As Pescara slipped deeper into relegation trouble, another provincial team, Atalanta, began their ascent of the league table with an away victory against Sampdoria. Maurizio Ganz, the previous season's Serie B top scorer when he was with Brescia, gained sweet revenge against the side that had rejected him four years earlier by scoring two exceptional goals.

Milan, Juventus and Roma were involved in European competition before Week 13. Milan brushed aside the attentions of PSV Eindhoven with a 2-1 victory and Juventus alleviated their anxieties in the league with a comprehensive 5-0 destruction of Sigma Olomouc. Roma, who took their 3-1 first leg lead to Turkey, also qualified for the quarter final of the UEFA Cup, despite losing 3-2 against Galatasaray.

Week 13 provided the last of the action before the Christmas break and it proved unlucky for Juventus and Inter, as well as for Milan's Marco Van Basten. Already fighting to retain their Serie A status, Foggia reminded Juventus that money does not guarantee success with a performance worthy of a championship winning side, culminating in a victory.

Inter were outplayed for the second consecutive week at Lazio. Diego Fuser, the Dutchman, Aron Winter and Giuseppe Signori each found a way past Inter's valiant

reserve goalkeeper, Beniamino Abate, during their 3-1 triumph. Signori had now scored 13 times in his 12 league matches to squeeze past Marco Van Basten at the top of the Serie A scorers' charts.

At the San Siro, Van Basten limped off with a damaged ankle before the end of their 2-0 win against Ancona. Surgery took place almost immediately in Belgium, after which Dr. Rene Marti announced Van Basten would be out of action for at least three months. The shock news from Milan filtered through to Serie A's chasing pack, presenting Inter and Juventus with the glad tidings they believed had forsaken them on the eve of the festive season.

Napoli's players could also have benefited from some much-needed Christmas cheer. Ottavio Bianchi's appointment had failed to alter the pattern of the *Azzurri*'s poor results.

'It's the hardest job I have ever taken on,' he revealed. 'There's so much work to be done.'

Bianchi describes himself as 'small, ugly and nasty', but for all his vanity, his coaching ability remains beyond question.

One week before Christmas, Italy travelled to Malta for another World Cup qualifying match. Milan's Franco Baresi was sent off for the *Azzurri* in a dispirited 2-1 win. Four days later Sampdoria played Milan in the fixture re-scheduled from September. Goals from Marco Simone and Ruud Gullit secured the two points for Milan; Ivano Bonetti replied for Sampdoria.

The opening four months set the pattern for the remainder of the season. Milan's dominance reduced the Serie A championship to a battle for second place. More than half the league's clubs were in contention for a European spot, while the rest were faced with the fight to survive in the toughest league in world football.

RESULTS

Week 12 (6 December 1992)

Ancona	3-0	Inter
Brescia	2-2	Genoa
Cagliari	1-0	Napoli
Fiorentina	2-0	Juventus
Milan	1-1	Udinese
Pescara	2-3	Lazio
Roma	1-0	Parma
Sampdoria	2-3	Atalanta
Torino	1-1	Foggia

Week 13 (13 December 1992)

Atalanta	1-1	Brescia
Foggia	2-1	Juventus
Genoa	2-1	Napoli
Lazio	3-1	Inter
Milan	2-0	Ancona
Parma	1-1	Fiorentina
Pescara	2-2	Sampdoria
Torino	0-0	Roma
Udinese	2-1	Cagliari

Rearranged from Week 4 (23 December 1992)

Sampdoria	1-2	Milan

Top left: Gianluca Vialli and Stefano Pioli tangle during Fiorentina-Juventus. Above: Walter Zenga gets his marching orders.

gennaio

1993 kicked off with a bombshell. Fiorentina had hit the headlines for their open and entertaining brand of football, but were now heading for troubled times. The club, whose 13 matches had generated more than 50 goals, had inexplicably lost faith in their capable and respected coach, Gigi Radice. Radice did not meet with the approval of Vittorio Cecchi Gori, son of the club's owner, film producer Mario Cecchi Gori. Although Radice had guided his team to second place in Serie A, he became the third coaching casualty of the 92/93 season.

Fiorentina's 1-0 defeat at home to Atalanta – only their fourth all season – became one too many for the man who delivered Torino's last *Scudetto* in 1976. In the post-match press conference, Vice President Vittorio Cecchi Gori voiced his dissatisfaction and indicated, in not so many words, that Signor Radice would be dismissed. The coach was surrounded by sympathetic reporters as he left the changing room area and following a short, intense assembly, he was applauded as he left the Artemio Franchi Stadium. His dismissal was broadcast later that evening. The next day, television pundit, Aldo Agroppi, the former Torino midfielder and Italian international, reassumed the post he had forfeited in 1986. The fact that Agroppi had used his power in the media regularly to reproach his fellow professionals put his own coaching ability under intense scrutiny.

The three-week break had certainly benefited Inter. In Week 14, Osvaldo Bagnoli's side overpowered Genoa with four well-executed goals. Midfielder Antonio Manicone started his first Serie A match in Inter's blue and black jersey after relocating from Udinese in November. Manicone's impact was significant, not least for adding much needed equilibrium to Bagnoli's erratic side. His inclusion in the team granted coach Bagnoli the midfield anchor man he craved. The move

prompted the German Matthias Sammer to return to his homeland after four disappointing months. Another overseas player, the 'Cobra', Darko Pancev, from Macedonia, had already lost his venom and was to spend the majority of his Sundays sitting on the bench.

Milan continued their advance to the *Scudetto,* breaking another record in the process. Their 1-0 victory against Roma was the club's eighth consecutive win on the road. Although Franco Baresi received his marching orders as early as the fifth minute, the expulsion did not prevent Milan from maintaining their eight point lead at the top of Serie A.

Week 15 saw both Milan giants victorious and also staged another Derby match. The Adriatic Derby was labelled the 'Derby of Desperation' by the Italian media in the light of Pescara's and Ancona's apparently impossible task in escaping the drop to Serie B. Pescara, the home side, edged the seven goal contest to collect two welcome points.

Roma's season could also be described as desperate. The club plunged to 16th place after their 3-1 defeat at Atalanta and, once again, their coach was in danger of losing his job. The Serb, Vujadin Boskov, had left the tranquillity of the city of Genoa, after spending six years with Sampdoria, only to inherit a team plagued by torment and controversy.

Aldo Agroppi took his Fiorentina side to Udine, close to the Austrian border. Not even the outspoken Tuscan could believe what ensued.

Barely nine seconds had passed when Udinese opened the scoring! Fiorentina old boy, Marco Branca, bagged the Serie A record and went on to score a hat-trick against his former club, making Agroppi's first match in charge unforgettable.

RESULTS

Week 14 (3 January 1993)

Ancona	0-3	Lazio
Brescia	2-1	Udinese
Cagliari	0-0	Torino
Fiorentina	0-1	Atalanta
Inter	4-0	Genoa
Juventus	2-2	Parma
Napoli	2-0	Pescara
Roma	0-1	Milan
Sampdoria	3-3	Foggia

Week 15 (10 January 1993)

Atalanta	3-1	Roma
Foggia	1-3	Inter
Lazio	2-0	Brescia
Milan	1-0	Cagliari
Parma	1-0	Genoa
Pescara	4-3	Ancona
Sampdoria	1-1	Juventus
Torino	0-1	Napoli
Udinese	4-0	Fiorentina

Week 16 (17 January 1993)

Ancona	1-0	Udinese
Brescia	0-1	Milan
Cagliari	1-1	Foggia
Fiorentina	0-0	Torino
Genoa	1-0	Atalanta
Inter	2-1	Parma
Juventus	2-1	Pescara
Napoli	3-1	Lazio
Roma	0-0	Sampdoria

It would have been interesting to hear Agroppi's summary of the day's events had he been sitting in the comfort of a Milan television studio.

'Everything that could go wrong, did go wrong,' is what he did say.

By the end of the month Agroppi was still searching for his first victory.

Napoli began a revival with two impressive victories against Torino and Lazio, while Roma collected four points from three games to ease coach Boskov's anxiety. Inter consolidated their position behind Milan with a third and fourth successive triumph against Parma and Torino respectively. Roberto Baggio returned from injury for Juventus, scoring five times in as many games.

With the battle for the *Scudetto* a non-event, the focus of attention fell on Milan's daunting unbeaten league run which stood at 52 matches by the time the Champions visited Foggia on 31 January. The compact Pino Zaccheria Stadium was sold out for the confrontation of Serie A's two 'Red Devils'. Foggia had the demons on their side in the first half and after 36 minutes, Pierpaolo Bresciani, once on Milan's books, scored from close range. In the second half, Foggia had a gilt-edged opportunity to extend their lead from the

penalty spot after Costacurta had brought down Mandelli. With their regular penalty taker, Oberdan Biagioni, strangely sitting on the substitutes' bench, the unenviable task of converting Foggia's seventh spot kick out of seven for the season fell to 21-year-old Luigi Di Biagio. The six foot six inch frame of Milan's goalkeeper, Sebastiano Rossi, appeared to fill the entire goal as the young midfielder strode up to shoot. Rossi stretched out his lengthy arms and parried the ball. Within ten minutes Milan were ahead. The goals, from Jean-Pierre Papin and Frank Rijkaard, would have forced most teams into submission. Foggia retaliated with a late onslaught. A corner from the left was dropped by Rossi and the Captain, Andrea Seno, equalized with ten minutes of the match remaining. The 2-2 draw revealed a slight chink in Milan's armour, but that was all. Fabio Capello's side were still eight points clear of Inter in second place.

The Italian Cup had reached the quarter final stage and interest was raised by the line-up, which represented the cream of Italian football. Juventus hosted the visit of the Cup holders, Parma, in a repeat of the previous year's final. Gianluca Vialli, who had been suffering a despairing loss of form in the league, scored twice in a 2-1 first leg victory. An error by Lazio's goalkeeper, Valerio Fiori, enabled Torino to salvage a draw in Rome. Paul Gascoigne was in fine fettle, but Lazio's inert defending erased his positive exertion. Torino were now favourites to win the 2nd leg in February and reach the semi final. Two Derbies followed. Napoli and Roma fought out a goalless *Derby del Sud* and at the San Siro, Milan and Inter produced another stalemate.

At the stage of the season when mental strength and nerve become as important as physical fitness, Milan began to feel the pressure in retaining their historic unbeaten run. Fabio Capello's side could falter only by pressing the self-destruct button.

Top left: From pundit to coach, Aldo Agroppi returns to the Fiorentina bench. Above: Lazio's Luzardi and Juve's Vialli during their 1-1 draw.

febbraio

One week after Milan's scare in Foggia, the Champions trampled over Pescara before travelling to Bergamo to face the club with the best home record in Italy's premier division, Atalanta. The provincial club were occupying joint third spot in Serie A with Lazio on the eve of the showdown in Week 20 and were in high spirits following their 2-1 win over Juventus the previous week. The prospect of confronting Fabio Capello's all-star cast did not unduly concern their coach, Marcello Lippi.

'Out of 1,000 meetings against Milan, we would probably lose 999 times,' he said. 'Who knows if this might be that one match we win?'

Without the influential Dutchmen, Marco Van Basten, Ruud Gullit and Frank Rijkaard, who were all injured, Milan were relying on their Italian internationals to break Atalanta's resistance and deliver their first home defeat in eight months. An insipid cat-and-mouse affair ensued. The match did come alive in the final 20 minutes, with the score at 0-0, when Milan conceded a penalty kick. Roberto Rambaudi was entrusted with the responsibility of shattering Milan's 53 match unbeaten league run, but the winger's hesitant effort was comfortably saved by Sebastiano Rossi. In the post-match press conference Rambaudi cleverly played down his error.

'Perhaps it was just as well I didn't score,' he said. 'I would have become too famous.'

In contrast, Rossi, who, prior to this season, hadn't been noted for his penalty saving expertise, revelled in his newly found glory. His third stop in three months fuelled a late Milan assault on Atalanta's goal. In the final four minutes, Jean-Pierre Papin gave Milan the lead with a header, but, before the Frenchman had finished celebrating his ninth league goal of the season, Maurizio Ganz broke Milan's offside trap and brought the scores level. Both clubs had to settle for a point and took comfort in the news that second placed Inter had been held to a goalless draw at the San Siro by Napoli. The *Neroazzurri* drew three successive games in the month of February.

Napoli and, indeed, Roma had enjoyed a calmer period after morale-boosting results. Napoli did not concede a goal in their three February matches against Foggia, Inter and Ancona. Roma, in particular, enjoyed an impressive return to form. In Week 19, two goals from the striker Andrea Carnevale, and one from the German international Thomas Haessler secured a comfortable win against Genoa. After drawing in Foggia, Roma then conquered Juventus in the Olympic Stadium. Roberto Baggio gave Juve an early advantage, but his positive display failed to halt Roma's second half recovery. The 'Prince', Giuseppe Giannini, scored the first goal for the home side with a strike from close range and Thomas Haessler sealed the victory 20 minutes from full time. Juve's sixth defeat of the season aroused speculation that the most successful coach in Italian football, Giovanni Trapattoni, would soon be seeking employment elsewhere.

'I realize if my name wasn't Trapattoni, I wouldn't be given so many chances to get things right,' he said boldly.

RESULTS

Week 19 (7 February 1993)

Atalanta	2-1	Juventus
Cagliari	0-0	Inter
Fiorentina	0-2	Lazio
Milan	4-0	Pescara
Napoli	2-0	Foggia
Roma	3-0	Genoa
Sampdoria	3-1	Ancona
Torino	1-0	Brescia
Udinese	1-0	Parma

Week 20 (14 February 1993)

Ancona	2-1	Fiorentina
Atalanta	1-1	Milan
Foggia	0-0	Roma
Inter	0-0	Napoli
Juventus	1-0	Genoa
Lazio	1-2	Cagliari
Parma	2-2	Torino
Pescara	2-0	Brescia
Sampdoria	2-0	Udinese

Week 21 (28 February 1993)

Brescia	0-1	Parma
Cagliari	2-1	Atalanta
Fiorentina	2-2	Inter
Genoa	2-3	Lazio
Milan	4-0	Sampdoria
Napoli	0-0	Ancona
Roma	2-1	Juventus
Torino	3-1	Pescara
Udinese	3-2	Foggia

While Trap pondered his future, his former pupil and goalkeeper, Dino Zoff, received deserved praise for keeping Lazio in the hunt for a UEFA Cup place. The league's top marksman, Beppe Signori, had a quiet month, but continued to lead the goalscorers' charts. His 19th goal of the season arrived from the penalty spot in Genoa in Week 21. Lazio were two goals down before Riedle added to Signori's strike to achieve a sprightly 3-2 win.

Paul Gascoigne learned more about the sometimes harsh reality of Italian football that afternoon. A fairly innocent skirmish with Mario Bortolazzi, the man who had abruptly ended Gazza's debut in September, resulted in a red card for the English playmaker. Genoa's third consecutive defeat proved the undoing of their coach, Gigi Maifredi.

Genoa ended the month occupying one of the relegation places and, by then, the patience of the club's owner, Aldo Spinelli, was exhausted. The youth team trainer and former Genoa player, Claudio Maselli, became the port city team's third coach of the 92/93 season. The troubled home fans took exception to their team's wretched campaign and the police had to be summoned to quell their violent reaction at the end of Genoa's fixture against Lazio. Once again, the armed services escorted the players from the Luigi Ferraris Stadium.

Time was also running out for Arrigo Sacchi, the national team boss. Italy were still unbeaten under the former Milan coach, but their alarming inconsistency had brought the critics out in force. The moment of truth had arrived. Sacchi took his 17-man squad to Oporto to face Portugal in what was said to be the most difficult match in their World Cup qualifying group. Two quick goals from Juventus team-mates Roberto Baggio and Pierluigi Casiraghi soon contradicted his doubters. Although the Portuguese pulled back a goal in the second half, a third player from Juve's ranks, Dino Baggio, placed the result beyond doubt with an outstanding delivery from long range. The final score was 3-1.

Juve's internationals reproduced the same positive form in the Italian Cup, but their main source of inspiration came from a German. A vicious 30-yard volley from Andy Moeller wiped out Parma's earlier advantage to propel 'La Signora' into a semi-final showdown with neighbours Torino. Revenge was sweet. Torino booked their ticket with a 3-2 victory over Lazio after the 2-2 draw from the first leg in Rome. In the Eternal City, Roma won the battle for southern supremacy. Goals from Mihajlovic and Carnevale saw off Napoli's determined challenge, while in the tie of the round, Milan crushed Inter 3-0.

The overall picture changed little in the shortest month of the year. Milan's draw in Bergamo did cause a few hearts to flutter, but the inconsistency of the clubs below the Champions allowed Fabio Capello's side to increase their lead at the top.

		P	Pts
1	Milan	21	37
2	Inter	21	27
3	Lazio	21	25
4	Torino	21	24
5	Atalanta	21	24
6	Juventus	21	23
7	Cagliari	21	23
8	Sampdoria	21	23
9	Roma	21	21
10	Parma	21	21
11	Napoli	21	19
12	Udinese	21	19
13	Fiorentina	21	18
14	Foggia	21	18
15	Brescia	21	16
16	Genoa	21	16
17	Ancona	21	13
18	Pescara	21	11

LEAGUE TABLE
AT THE END OF WEEK 21

Far left: Atalanta goalkeeper Ferron gives some advice.
Middle left: Milan's Simone and Atalanta's Porrini.
Above left: Fonseca and Ferri battle for the ball in Inter-Napoli's 0-0 draw.
Bottom right: Giovanni Trapattoni contemplates his future at Juventus.

marzo

'Il Milan Atterra,' read the headline in the Milan-based sports daily, *La Gazzetta Dello Sport*, the day after Parma had finally brought the Champions' 58-match unbeaten run in Serie A to an end. 'Milan brought down to earth', or words to that effect – a welcome sight to the masses of fans who had waited for soccer's Harlem Globetrotters to fall from the heavens.

The end of Milan's unbeaten league run came just 11 days after Roma had dramatically inflicted their first defeat in 11 months in the first leg of the Italian Cup semi final. Fabio Capello's men continued to command admiration, respect and a certain sympathy. Injuries to key players added to fatigue from midweek cup exploits, eventually took their toll. For the match against Parma in Week 24, the three Dutchmen, Van Basten, Gullit and Rijkaard, were again ruled out through injury. So, too, were Italian internationals Gianluigi Lentini and Roberto Donadoni, while the club's lucky charm, the influential Demetrio Albertini, was sidelined due to suspension. Albertini had never been on the losing side for Milan. The Champions lacked their customary spark and Parma took full advantage. As the referee's whistle brought the game to a close, rapturous applause rang out from San Siro's vast stands. 75,000 fans united to show their appreciation to players who had given them so much pleasure over the course of two years. A defeat rarely commands such a warm and devoted reception.

'We had to lose a league game sooner or later,' said the diplomatic Capello after the match.

'Capello's fired!' came the tongue-in-cheek retort from the club President, Silvio Berlusconi.

Faustino Asprilla's stroke of genius from a free kick not only left goalkeeper Sebastiano Rossi motionless, but brought the entire sporting nation to a standstill.

'Attenzione!' yelled the radio announcer. 'Il Parma in vantaggio … GOL DI ASPRILLA …'

Of course, Milan had gone behind before. This time, there was no way back. Ironically, the Rossoneri's 22-month unbeaten run in Serie A began with a goalless draw at home to the Italian Cup holders.

Milan's defeat did little to enliven Giovanni Trapattoni's sombre mood. Juventus appeared on the way back after an encouraging 4-3 win against a revitalized Napoli in Week 22. However, Juve's performances away to Brescia and then to Inter in Turin, which both culminated in 2-0 defeats, disgraced Trapattoni to the extent that he publicly questioned the heart of his leading players.

'I'm thoroughly ashamed of this team,' Trap lamented. 'Some of my players are not worthy of the Juventus jersey.'

Paul Gascoigne was back on the goal trail in March. He scored one of Lazio's two in a draw with Milan and headed a first half equalizer against Atalanta in a fixture that also ended in a 2-2 draw. Gascoigne was on England duty at the end of the month and so missed Lazio's 4-0 destruction of Udinese. The fixture brought together Serie A's leading scorers, Signori and Udinese's Argentinian striker, Abel Balbo. Signori added another two goals to bring his total to 22, three more than Balbo.

With barely more than two months of the season left to play and with Milan practically assured of their 13th league title, the battle for a place in Europe and the fight for survival drew the media's attention. Any one of ten clubs could still conceivably attain a UEFA Cup place, while at the tail end of Serie A, poor Pescara seemed the only team with little or no aspiration to

LEAGUE TABLE
AT THE END OF WEEK 25
		P	Pts
1	Milan	25	41
2	Inter	25	33
3	Lazio	25	29
4	Torino	25	28
5	Sampdoria	25	28
6	Parma	25	28
7	Juventus	25	27
8	Atalanta	25	27
9	Roma	25	26
10	Cagliari	25	26
11	Napoli	25	24
12	Fiorentina	25	22
13	Udinese	25	22
14	Foggia	25	22
15	Genoa	25	21
16	Brescia	25	21
17	Ancona	25	15
18	Pescara	25	12

FAUSTINO ASPRILLA

(b: 10/11/69 Tulua Valle, Colombia) The Colombian caught the eye during the South American Olympic qualifying tournament in 1992 and Parma outbid Fiorentina in the auction that followed. His ability, added to his breathtaking pace, rapidly earned him the respect of the country's toughest defenders. His goals are often spectacular, as are the somersaults which accompany his celebrations. Asprilla will be remembered as the man who scored the goal which ended Milan's historic unbeaten run.

stay in the top flight. Their Neapolitan coach, Giovanni Galeone, was sacked after their 2-0 defeat at home to Genoa in Week 24, bringing the season's total of dismissals to four. His assistant, Vincenzo Zucchini, was promoted with a view to restoring some pride in the city.

In Week 25, Fiorentina were ordered to play their home fixture against Cagliari on neutral ground and behind closed doors following crowd disturbances earlier in the season. The eerie atmosphere in Verona's Bentegodi Stadium seemed to have a heartening effect on Agroppi's side as they defeated the Sardinians 2-1. However, the threat of relegation lingered.

Torino scraped through against Juventus to reach their first final in the *Coppa Italia* for five years. Torino advanced on the away goals rule despite the fact that the two clubs share the Delle Alpi Stadium. Both legs ended in parity. The first produced a 1-1 scoreline with Torino as the home side. In the second, Carlos Aguilera scored the decisive second goal in a 2-2 draw. Torino had finally disposed of their contentious president, Gian Mauro Borsano, following months of speculation. Torino's fans were convinced Borsano constantly neglected club affairs in order to pursue his political career. Roberto Goveani, the youngest Serie A President, took over the club's major shareholding, thus rejuvenating an apparently spent force.

In the second Italian Cup semi-final, Roberto Muzzi, Italy's leading Under 21 international striker, and the Argentinian, Claudio Caniggia, scored the two goals which ended Milan's hopes of a unique treble. Roma were defeated by one goal in the second leg in Milan, but progressed to meet Torino in the final by virtue of their 2-0 first leg victory. After saving Papin's penalty kick in the 87th minute, Roma's goalkeeper, Giovanni Cervone, was the hero of the hour in Milan. Unfortunately, he allowed his emotions to get the better of him as he walked off at the end of the match accusing the officials of bias. Cervone was brandished a red card in the players tunnel, as was his understudy, Giuseppe Zinetti. Both goalkeepers recieved suspensions that would rule them out of the final.

Milan found European competition an easier proposition. The four times Champions' Cup winners preserved their 100 per cent record with two victories over Porto. Parma were through to the semi-finals of the Cup Winners' Cup, where they would meet Atletico Madrid, and Juventus brushed aside another Portuguese outfit, Benfica, to play Paris Saint Germain in the semi-final of the UEFA Cup. Roma's fine run was dented by their defeat at the hands of Borussia Dortmund in the same competition. The disappointment was deepened by news of the arrest of Giuseppe Ciarrapico, the club President. The 'Mineral Water King' was linked with the wave of corruption which had been sweeping across the country.

On the international front, Italy resumed their quest to qualify for the 1994 World Cup Finals with an effortless 6-1 win against Malta. The extraordinary reception that greeted the *Azzurri* in Palermo highlighted the enthusiasm generated by Italy's win in Portugal the previous month.

Inter, unbeaten in Serie A since the turn of the year, had Schillaci back from his four-month convalescence. Also, in Ruben Sosa, they possessed a striker with a restored appetite for the game. The Uruguayan had found the target 10 times in 1993. With nine matches left to play, Milan's lead was reduced to eight points.

RESULTS

Week 22 (7 March 1993)

Ancona	0-0	Genoa
Atalanta	1-1	Inter
Foggia	0-0	Brescia
Juventus	4-3	Napoli
Milan	2-0	Fiorentina
Parma	2-1	Lazio
Pescara	2-2	Udinese
Roma	1-1	Cagliari
Sampdoria	0-1	Torino

Week 23 (14 March 1993)

Ancona	1-1	Parma
Brescia	2-0	Juventus
Cagliari	0-2	Sampdoria
Fiorentina	2-0	Pescara
Genoa	0-0	Foggia
Inter	1-1	Roma
Lazio	2-2	Milan
Napoli	3-0	Udinese
Torino	1-1	Atalanta

Week 24 (21 March 1993)

Atalanta	2-2	Lazio
Cagliari	3-2	Brescia
Foggia	1-0	Ancona
Juventus	0-2	Inter
Milan	0-1	Parma
Pescara	1-2	Genoa
Roma	1-1	Napoli
Sampdoria	2-0	Fiorentina
Udinese	1-0	Torino

Week 25 (28 March 1993)

Ancona	0-1	Juventus
Brescia	0-2	Roma
Fiorentina	2-1	Cagliari
Genoa	0-0	Sampdoria
Inter	2-0	Pescara
Lazio	4-0	Udinese
Napoli	1-0	Atalanta
Parma	4-0	Foggia
Torino	1-1	Milan

Top left: Inter joy at Atalanta.

Above: Franco Baresi and Beppe Signori during Lazio-Milan.

aprile

RUBEN SOSA

(b: 25/4/66 Montevideo, Uruguay) The robust Uruguayan international striker received a new lease of life in 1993, producing his finest displays in Serie A since his arrival from the Spanish club Real Saragozza in 1988. Sosa joined Inter at the start of the season after spending four years in Rome with Lazio. His pace and lethal left foot have terrorized the world's finest defenders.

Milan's dominion began to crumble. In week 26, three fixtures were played on the Saturday in view of the upcoming European semi-finals. At the San Siro, Napoli threatened to avenge their 5-1 slaughter from November with a courageous and vehement performance at the San Siro. Roberto Policano and Antonio Careca scored to give Napoli a 2-0 lead at half time. Gianluigi Lentini was beginning to find his expensive feet and came to his team-mates' rescue with two exquisite strikes in the second half. The draw confirmed that Milan were not the invincible force from the first half of the 92/93 season.

Juventus continued to struggle for form and were fortunate to leave Udine with a point after Abel Balbo's legitimate goal was ruled offside by the referee. Parma prepared for their trip to Madrid to play Atletico with a comfortable 2-0 win against Pescara.

The following day, Inter exposed the vulnerability of Sampdoria's defence in a 3-1 victory to gain one more precious point on Milan. Toto Schillaci, who hadn't found the target in six months, rediscovered his goal touch and scored twice. Nicola Berti added a third before the Serb, Vladimir Jugovic, grabbed a consolation for Des Walker's side. The stage was set for the Milan Derby in Week 27. A victory for Inter would supply an exhilarating, if unexpected climax to the Serie A championship. The confrontation attracted the routine media hype as the Inter players tried desperately to deny that the coveted *Scudetto* was within their reach.

'It's not impossible, just difficult,' declared Toto Schillaci. His view summed up the general feeling at the club's training ground in Appiano Gentile, a short distance from the city of Milan. A defeat for the Champions would still leave them with a commanding five point lead.

In the UEFA Cup, Juventus again displayed the determination coach Trapattoni desired. In the first leg in Turin, Roberto Baggio's double strike overturned a 1-0 deficit against Paris Saint Germain. In the Cup Winners' Cup, Parma earned an invaluable 2-1 victory against Atletico Madrid. The 23-year-old Colombian, Faustino Asprilla, was the hero of the night, scoring both goals. Meanwhile, Milan warmed up for their Derby match with a victory against Gothenburg in the European Champions' League, thanks to a late goal from Daniele Massaro.

The Milan Derby was hardly a classic, but the tactical battle was enough to keep the connoisseurs entranced as Inter beckoned Milan into their territory in order to pounce on the counter attack. The first half was almost at an end when the moment most of Italy had been anticipating arrived. The Italian international, Nicola Berti, powerfully forced the ball past Sebastiano Rossi in the Milan goal. Inter were ahead at the half time interval. The second half marked a relentless Milan charge on Walter Zenga's goal and seven minutes from full time Ruud Gullit rifled an angled shot past the helpless Zenga to level the score. In spite of the 1-1 draw, the country's optimists still believed that the 92/93 championship race was not yet a foregone conclusion.

Juventus and Torino contested their Derby match for the fourth time in five months. Antonio Conte, a 23-year-old midfielder from Lecce, scored the two goals which secured a 2-1 win for Juventus. Carlos Aguilera, whose goal eliminated Juve from the Italian Cup, once again found the target, but this time he failed to inspire Torino to victory.

The national team was then in action in another World Cup qualifier. Italy met Estonia in Trieste's new Nereo Rocco Stadium and comfortably defeated the small

Lazio action – (left) Corino against Torino's Aguilera, and (above) Gazza surrounded in the Rome Derby.

republic 2-0. Roberto Baggio scored the first and Lazio's Giuseppe Signori added the second towards the end of the contest with a spectacular strike.

Juventus carried their restored confidence to Milan in Week 28. The match was staged on a Saturday because of the impending midweek European second leg ties. Marco Simone touched Milan ahead in only the sixth minute. Juventus retaliated with gusto and, within fifteen minutes, Andy Moeller struck twice to put Juve ahead. Roberto Baggio sealed a memorable win in the second half with one of the goals of the season. Later that evening, Parma lost for the first time in two months away to Sampdoria in Genoa. Inter triumphed 3-1 in Brescia the next day, which whittled two more points from Milan's margin at the top of Serie A. In the season's second instalment of the Rome Derby, Paul Gascoigne failed to inspire Lazio to victory and the keenly contested fixture ended level for the sixth successive time.

In Europe, Milan defeated PSV Eindhoven, Marco Simone grabbing both the goals in their 2-0 win. The *Rossoneri* progressed to the European Cup final to be held in Munich with an unprecedented 100 per cent record. Juventus overcame Paris Saint Germain in the UEFA Cup, Roberto Baggio slaying French hopes with a late goal. This put them through to the two-legged final 3-1 on aggregate. They would meet Borussia

Dortmund, the conquerors of Roma from the quarter final stage. In the Cup Winners' Cup, Parma survived Atletico Madrid's vigorous attempt to reverse their 2-1 deficit from the first leg in Spain and advanced to their first European final. Parma qualified on the away goals rule despite their 1-0 defeat and did so without the services of Faustino Asprilla. The striker had returned to his native Colombia to visit his dying mother only to return to Parma with a gashed calf. Conflicting reports on the injury puzzled the Italian authorities. At first, it was suggested the injury was caused by a broken bottle that had been dropped by his wife. Other reports point to an incident where it is claimed an inebriated Asprilla kicked in the headlights of a bus! The injury threatened to keep him out of the Wembley final.

In Week 29, Inter managed to gain a further point on Milan, following a convincing 3-0 win against Ancona. After a goalless draw in Udine, the belated return of Marco Van Basten to Milan's ranks brightened an otherwise dull afternoon for the weary Champions. Juve's 3-0 victory over Fiorentina signalled a premature end to Aldo Agroppi's term as Fiorentina's coach. The side from Florence were just one point away from the relegation zone having won only two games with Agroppi at the helm. The arrogant former TV pundit had rediscovered the hardships of Serie A management. Lazio's 2-1 win over Pescara in Rome condemned the promoted side back to Serie B after one season in the top flight. Parma climbed to joint third beside Lazio and Juventus, having disposed of a Roma side surrounded, once again, by controversy. Their Argentinian international striker, Claudio Caniggia, received a 13-month suspension for failing a dope test after the club's home fixture with Napoli on 21 March. Caniggia admitted using cocaine for his personal use, but not for enhancing his performance.

The eventful month granted football fans the climax they deserved with five weeks left on the Serie A calendar. Inter, undefeated in 16 league matches, had gradually eaten away Milan's 11 point lead to just four. By contrast, the Champions hadn't won in seven games. The race was on.

RESULTS

Week 26 (3 April 1993)

Milan	2-2	Napoli
Pescara	0-2	Parma
Udinese	0-0	Juventus

(4 April 1993)

Brescia	1-1	Ancona
Cagliari	3-0	Genoa
Foggia	1-0	Atalanta
Roma	1-1	Fiorentina
Sampdoria	1-3	Inter
Torino	1-1	Lazio

Week 27 (10 April 1993)

Ancona	1-1	Roma
Atalanta	2-1	Pescara
Fiorentina	2-2	Brescia
Genoa	1-0	Udinese
Inter	1-1	Milan
Juventus	2-1	Torino
Lazio	1-1	Foggia
Napoli	1-1	Sampdoria
Parma	3-1	Cagliari

Week 28 (17 April 1993)

Milan	1-3	Juventus
Sampdoria	2-1	Parma

(18 April 1993)

Brescia	1-3	Inter
Cagliari	3-0	Ancona
Fiorentina	1-1	Napoli
Pescara	2-4	Foggia
Roma	0-0	Lazio
Torino	1-1	Genoa
Udinese	1-2	Atalanta

Week 29 (25 April 1993)

Atalanta	1-2	Sampdoria
Foggia	0-0	Torino
Genoa	1-1	Brescia
Inter	3-0	Ancona
Juventus	3-0	Fiorentina
Lazio	2-1	Pescara
Napoli	1-0	Cagliari
Parma	3-1	Roma
Udinese	0-0	Milan

maggio

During the month of May, the Italians were dreaming of a clean sweep in the three European competitions. While Milan put their Champions' Cup final on hold in order to concentrate on making sure of the *Scudetto*, Inter were clinging to their faint hopes of the ultimate domestic prize. The *Neroazzurri* had to win all their remaining five fixtures in order to catch the Champions.

In the interim, the Italian national team travelled to Berne for their last World Cup qualifier in the 92/93 season. After a promising start, the *Azzurri* were stunned by the harsh dismissal of Juve's Dino Baggio a minute before half time. The Swiss took full advantage, scoring the only goal of the game early in the second half, as Italy suffered their first defeat during Arrigo Sacchi's term as coach.

Play in Serie A resumed a week later. Inter secured a comfortable 2-0 victory against a Lazio side without the services of Paul Gascoigne, who was on England duty, but Milan had little difficulty in disposing of Ancona. Marco Van Basten made his return to the starting line-up, following his ankle injury, and scored his first goal in five months in the 3-1 triumph. The most engrossing match in Week 30 took place in the Olympic Stadium, where, in a remarkable contest, Roma were defeated 5-4 by Torino in a curtain raiser for the final of the *Coppa Italia*.

If the capital city produced the day's highest total of goals, the port city of Genoa produced the most bizarre incident of the entire season. During the half-time interval of Sampdoria's 1-1 draw against Pescara, thousands of bees gathered around one of the goalposts and delayed the start of the second half by almost an hour. Apparently, the invasion was caused by a potent shot from Pescara's Massimiliano Allegri, which disturbed the bees' nest inside the goal!

The race for the championship still had a few laps to run and, in Week 31, Milan seemed once again to be tied to their starting blocks. The *Rossoneri* delivered another languid display at the San Siro, against Roma on this occasion. The match ended goalless. Inter were disappointed to have picked up only one point in Genoa after Ruben Sosa countered Christian Panucci's earlier effort in their 1-1 draw. Meanwhile, Paul Gascoigne reported for club duty at Lazio following his excursion with England. Gazza was still recovering from an operation on an injured cheekbone, suffered against the Dutch at Wembley, when he was surprisingly given the all-clear to play against relegated Ancona at the Olympic Stadium. It isn't often you see Gascoigne hide his cheek as he turned out wearing a protective mask made of carbon fibre. He inspired Lazio to a 5-0 win, producing his most complete performance since his arrival in Italy. Beppe Signori added two more goals to bring his season's total to 26, shattering Giorgio Chinaglia's 19-year-old club record in the process. Lazio went on to qualify for European competition for the first time in 16 years. Another 5-0 scoreline came out of Turin, where Cagliari, who were in the hunt for a UEFA Cup place, inflicted Torino's worst home defeat for more than 30 years. At the bottom of Serie A, four clubs were still fighting for their lives. With only two matches left of the season, Fiorentina, Genoa, Brescia and Udinese were locked in battle to avoid the drop.

In Week 33, Milan virtually assured themselves of the *Scudetto*. Their fixture away to Cagliari was brought forward to Friday, granting them two extra days' preparation for the European Champions' Cup final. Coach Fabio Capello rested numerous players, but his side managed to leave Cagliari's San't Elia stadium with a point. After their draw at Genoa the previous week, Inter could ill afford to lose further ground on their city rivals when they met Foggia at the San Siro.

LEAGUE TABLE

AT THE END OF WEEK 33

		P	Pts
1	Milan	33	49
2	Inter	33	44
3	Parma	33	40
4	Lazio	33	38
5	Juventus	33	37
6	Sampdoria	33	36
7	Cagliari	33	35
8	Torino	33	35
9	Atalanta	33	34
10	Roma	33	32
11	Foggia	33	32
12	Napoli	33	31
13	Genoa	33	30
14	Udinese	33	29
15	Fiorentina	33	28
16	Brescia	33	28
17	Ancona	33	19
18	Pescara	33	17

FRANCO BARESI

(b: 8/5/60 Travagliato, Brescia) Baresi has made over 300 Serie A appearances for Milan. He won his first Scudetto as an 18-year-old in 1979 and skippered the Rossoneri to two further league titles, in addition to two succesive European Cup triumphs. Milan's defeat to Marseille denied Baresi a hat-trick of European Cup wins, but he secured his fourth Scudetto four days later.

In the first half, Sosa opened the scoring and then missed a twice-taken penalty. The referee, Signor Brignoccoli, penalized Inter's forwards for encroachment and ordered the first kick, which Sosa had converted, to be retaken. Inter felt this decision was unjust but were staggered in the second half by another aberration from the eccentric referee. Towards the end of the contest, Inter's experienced defender, Luigi De Agostini, was mysteriously punished with a red card for a foul committed by the young substitute, Paolo Tramezzani. After the match, Brignoccoli claimed he acted on the advice of the linesman, who was 50 yards away from the incident! To make matters worse, Brian Roy levelled the score three minutes before full-time with his left elbow. Milan required only one point from their next match at home to Brescia to clinch the league title.

First, there was the small matter of the European Champions' Cup final to be decided. Juventus in the UEFA Cup and Parma in the Cup Winners' Cup had already captured two of the three European trophies by the time Milan departed for Germany on their quest to complete a hat trick of Italian victories. Munich's Olimpiastadion provided the setting as Milan attempted to win the most coveted club competition for the fifth time. Marseille, who had vanquished their domestic league in five consecutive years, provided the opposition. Milan dominated the first half, but missed three golden opportunities to take the lead. The Frenchmen needed just the one chance, which their international defender, Basile Boli, converted a minute before the half time whistle. For all Milan's efforts in the second half, Marseille strongly defended their lead to take a European trophy back to France for the first time.

Milan compensated for losing the European Cup Final by claiming the league title just four days later. 85,000 fans packed the San Siro for Milan's meeting with Brescia. Both teams played for a point, although Demetrio Albertini threatened to re-write the script when he scored one of the best goals of the season in the final ten minutes of the match. Milan's defenders 'sportingly' allowed Brescia an instant equalizer and the match ended level. Meanwhile, in Parma, Inter lost a league game for the first time in 1993 and the *Rossoneri* were crowned Serie A Champions for the 13th time. With only one week left on Serie A's calendar, many issues were still unresolved. Cagliari, Torino and Sampdoria were each looking to clinch the final UEFA Cup place. At the bottom, four clubs were still fighting to avoid joining Ancona and Pescara in Serie B.

RESULTS

Week 30 (9 May 1993)

Ancona	1-3	Milan
Brescia	2-0	Atalanta
Cagliari	1-1	Udinese
Fiorentina	1-1	Parma
Inter	2-0	Lazio
Juventus	4-2	Foggia
Napoli	2-2	Genoa
Roma	4-5	Torino
Sampdoria	1-1	Pescara

Week 31 (16 May 1993)

Atalanta	2-1	Fiorentina
Foggia	1-0	Sampdoria
Genoa	1-1	Inter
Lazio	5-0	Ancona
Milan	0-0	Roma
Parma	2-1	Juventus
Pescara	3-0	Napoli
Torino	0-5	Cagliari
Udinese	2-2	Brescia

Week 32 (23 May 1993)

Ancona	5-3	Pescara
Brescia	2-0	Lazio
Cagliari	1-1	Milan
Fiorentina	2-2	Udinese
Genoa	1-1	Parma
Inter	1-1	Foggia
Juventus	1-1	Sampdoria
Napoli	1-1	Torino
Roma	2-2	Atalanta

Week 33 (30 May 1993)

Atalanta	1-2	Genoa
Foggia	1-1	Cagliari
Lazio	4-3	Napoli
Milan	1-1	Brescia
Parma	2-0	Inter
Pescara	5-1	Juventus
Sampdoria	2-2	Roma
Torino	1-1	Fiorentina
Udinese	2-0	Ancona

European glory for (top left) Parma's Alessandro Melli in the Cup Winners' Cup, and (above) Juventus in the UEFA Cup.

giugno

Week 34 (6 June 1993)

Ancona	0-2	Atalanta
Brescia	3-1	Sampdoria
Cagliari	4-0	Pescara
Fiorentina	6-2	Foggia
Genoa	2-2	Milan
Inter	3-0	Torino
Juventus	4-1	Lazio
Napoli	1-1	Parma
Roma	1-1	Udinese

GABRIEL BATISTUTA

(b: 10/1/69 Reconquista di Santa Fe, Argentina) The Argentinian international rose to prominence during the 1991 South American Championships (Copa America) and immediately joined Fiorentina from Boca Juniors for £3 million. 'Bati-Gol' became an instant hit with the Florentine fans, but despite scoring 16 goals in his second season, he failed to steer the *Viola* from their disastrous relegation to Serie B.

With the *Scudetto* already won, the battles against relegation and for UEFA Cup places caught the public's attention. While Milan celebrated their 13th league title at Genoa, one of the sides hoping to survive the drop, six other matches still had a bearing on the final positions of the 92/93 season. The media hype centred predominantly around Florence, whose football club were on the verge of going down to Serie B for the first time in more than 50 years. Only two points separated the four clubs hoping to escape the two remaining relegation places.

A win for Fiorentina at home to Foggia would not necessarily guarantee them a place in Serie A for the next season. Luciano Chiarugi's team had to rely on favourable results from Brescia, Genoa and from Roma, where Udinese were hoping to collect their first away win of the season in order to stay up. Goal difference is not taken into account when major issues in Italian football are being decided, so when teams are level on points, a complicated system comes into effect. The Italians call the practice adopted at this stage *la classifica avulsa*.

The season's results of the direct confrontations between the four teams fighting for survival are used to determine which clubs stay up and which go into a play-off. At the last count, 81 different permutations were recorded; only eight favoured Fiorentina.

Brescia were in confident mood prior to their fixture against Sampdoria. The club President, Luigi Corioni, was certain his side would make at least a play-off.

'I don't expect Genoa to beat Milan,' he said. 'And as for Udinese, they haven't won away from home all season. In addition, they have never beaten Roma in the Olympic Stadium. If they win, then surely there's something wrong!'

By half time, Fiorentina led Foggia 4-0, while Brescia and Udinese were drawing their respective games. With Genoa beating Milan 1-0, Brescia were heading for the second division and Fiorentina and Udinese would feature in the play-off. Fiorentina's fans were in high spirits as their team added two more goals against Foggia in the second half. Meanwhile, Brescia went 2-1 ahead against Sampdoria and, at the Luigi Ferraris Stadium, Milan had overturned their 1-0 deficit against Genoa. At that stage, Fiorentina were safe, while Udinese, who had fallen behind to a Thomas Haessler penalty, were edging ever closer to Serie B. However, with ten minutes left of the 92/93 season, three goals from three different grounds turned the relegation issue upside down. A Florin Raducioiu penalty increased Brescia's lead against Sampdoria, Genoa equalized at home to Milan through Andrea Fortunato and the ex-Roma midfielder, Stefano Desideri, levelled the score for Udinese in Rome. Suddenly, Fiorentina were down. Foggia managed two late goals to give the scoreline an air of respectability as a deathly quiet came over the Artemio Franchi Stadium. The Florentine fans could not believe their club would be playing teams such as little Fidelis Andria and Lucchese after enjoying half a century of combat against Juventus, Milan et al. Genoa celebrated their survival, leaving Brescia and Udinese to contest the play-off.

Sampdoria's defeat in Brescia terminated their hopes of a place in the UEFA Cup and the same applied to Torino after their 3-0 drubbing by the runners-up for the *Scudetto*, Inter. Their defeats paved the way for Cagliari to squeeze into the top six, almost unnoticed, to secure a place in European competition for the first time in 23 years. As well as Inter, the Sardinians joined Juventus and Lazio in the UEFA Cup. The two clubs were drawn together on the last day of the season and Juve won the match 4-1. Giuseppe Signori failed to add to his season's tally of 26 goals, but he had already

LEAGUE TABLE
FINAL POSITIONS

		P	Pts
1	Milan	34	50
2	Inter	34	46
3	Parma	34	41
4	Juventus	34	39
5	Lazio	34	38
6	Cagliari	34	37
7	Sampdoria	34	36
8	Atalanta	34	36
9	Torino	34	35
10	Roma	34	33
11	Napoli	34	32
12	Foggia	34	32
13	Genoa	34	31
14	Udinese	34	30
15	Brescia	34	30
16	Fiorentina	34	30
17	Ancone	34	19
18	Pescara	34	17

reached the highest total in Serie A since 1961, when Sergio Brighenti netted 27 times for Sampdoria. Although Signori didn't score, Roberto Baggio capped an exceptional 92/93 season by converting two penalties to claim the runner-up spot in the goalscorers' charts, alongside Udinese's Abel Balbo, with 21 goals. Remarkably, Baggio had scored 35 goals in all competition, including international matches.

The Italians still had another place available in Europe, which would be assigned to the winners of the *Coppa Italia*. Italy's two 'cursed' clubs, Torino and Roma, were set to meet in the two-legged final and the winners would join Parma in the Cup Winners' Cup. Torino had failed to beat Roma in three previous Italian Cup finals.

Both the relegation play-off and the Italian Cup final were played on the Saturday. First, Udinese and Brescia met on neutral ground in Bologna. Udinese had failed to win a match against the 'Swallows' in their last six league meetings, but started the game in fine form, with Abel Balbo scoring after only 13 minutes. Sergio Domini, Brescia's Captain, brought the score level midway through the first half, only for Alessandro Orlando and playmaker Francesco Dell'Anno to add two more goals in the second half and preserve Udinese's Serie A status.

Later that evening, Torino staged the first leg of the Italian Cup final. Roma, who were without their two first choice goalkeepers, Cervone and Zinetti, were compelled to field the inexperienced Patrizio Fimiani. The nervy young goalkeeper was beaten three times, which handed Torino a sizeable advantage to take to Rome the following week.

Despite the 3-0 defeat, Roma's fans turned out in force for the return leg and they were almost rewarded with a dramatic aggregate victory. Roma won 5-2 in a match that included three penalties, but it was Torino who captured their first major trophy in 17 years – on the strength of the away goals rule.

The 1992/93 season, which seemed to be over by the midway point due to Milan's dominance, was given an injection of life by the resurgence of Inter, Lazio's attractive, attacking game and Parma's continued success. Perhaps the season will be remembered for the 858 goals scored in the 306 matches, the highest total in Serie A for 34 years. Milan scored their fair share and certainly secured their 13th league title during the first half of the season – their performances in the second half alone would have only just earned them a place in the UEFA Cup. Still, their earlier memorable exploits must be acknowledged. The right team won the *Scudetto* and not for the first time.

CAPOCANNONIERI
TOP SCORERS

26	Signori	Lazio
21	R Baggio	Juventus
	Balbo	Udinese
20	Sosa	Inter
16	Fonseca	Napoli
	Batistuta	Fiorentina
15	Mancini	Sampdoria
14	Ganz	Atalanta
13	Van Basten	Milan
	Papin	Milan
	Raducioiu	Brescia

Top left: Torino lift their first major trophy for seventeen years after beating Parma on the away goals rule in the *Coppa Italia* final.

Above: Ruud Gullit only appeared fifteen times for Milan in his last season with the club, but his contribution was immense. Gullit scored seven goals, each one vital, but none more so than his equalizer against Inter in the second Milan Derby.

ATALANTA

Of all Serie A's teams, this club from the reserved northern city of Bergamo, situated approximately 30 miles from Milan, bears the most ambiguous name. Atalanta is neither a suburb of Bergamo nor a landmark. In 1907, the founder members of the club resisted the obvious temptation of calling their new team after their city. So, what or who is Atalanta? A character from ancient Greek mythology is the answer; left to die at birth and suckled by a she-bear, Atalanta grew up to become the fastest woman on earth. However, the team's early progress failed to match the legend and Atalanta, the football team, moved at a torpid pace during their first 30 years.

ATALANTA

The club celebrated their first promotion to Serie A in 1937. However, Atalanta struggled during their opening season in the top flight and were immediately relegated. 1940 marked the start of a prosperous new era for the provincial side, as they took part in all but one of the next 26 Serie A campaigns. In 1948, Atalanta finished the league season in fifth place, their highest ever placing, and also produced their first Italian internationals. The goalkeeper, Giuseppe Casari, and a midfielder by the name of Giacomo Mari were selected for the 1948 Olympic Games staged in London and made their debuts in Italy's 9-0 destruction of the United States. No other Atalanta players were selected for international duty until the next Olympics four years later. During the Games held in Finland, two defenders, Battista Rota and Giancarlo Cade, represented the national team trained by the legendary Giuseppe Meazza. Angelo Longoni may have felt aggrieved that he wasn't chosen to wear Italy's blue jersey more than once after scoring both goals for the *Azzurri* in their 2-1 win against Austria in 1956.

Atalanta have seldom spawned players of international class without being constrained to sell them to bigger clubs. For example, two of the aforementioned internationals, Casari and Mari, furthered their careers with the more prestigious sides, Juventus and Napoli. Two more, Antonio Cabrini, who arrived from Cremonese, and the late Gaetano Scirea, entered Italian folklore after leaving for Juventus. The free-scoring Adriano Bassetto is one exception. With only three caps, he flew Atalanta's flag on the international stage more times than any other *Bergamasco*, after his arrival from Sampdoria. Bassetto scored more than 150 Serie A goals in his career, 56 while in Bergamo.

In 1958, Atalanta were demoted to Serie B, but immediately jumped back up as Champions. The club settled for mid-table security during their first two seasons back in Serie A, but were on the verge of the most successful period in their history. In 1962, Atalanta ended the season occupying sixth place and, in midfielders Pierluigi Ronzon and Humberto Maschio, provided two more players for the national

side. The following year, the *Bergamaschi* reached their first major final – in the Italian Cup. The team that Atalanta fielded against Torino included the talented winger, Angelo Domenghini, who, in Atalanta's colours, went on to win his first international cap before transferring to Inter and then Cagliari. By the end of his career, Domenghini had made 33 appearances for Italy. After a distinguished performance, Atalanta lifted the *Coppa Italia*, with Domenghini instrumental in the team's 3-1 victory. The achievement was marred by the almost unbelievable, sudden dismissal of coach Tabanelli just 24 hours after the victory. Atalanta's officials had not expected the team to capture a major trophy and had already lined up Carlo Alberto Quario as his replacement long before the Italian Cup conquest. Quario failed to steer Atalanta past the first hurdle in the European Cup Winners' Cup six months later. Their tie with the eventual winners, Sporting Lisbon, ended level on aggregate, so a third match decided the outcome. The Portuguese squeezed through in Barcelona, but needed extra time to complete their 3-1 win.

Atalanta struggled to sustain their position among Italy's elite and battled against relegation for the next four years. In 1966, the appearance of the club's goalkeeper, Pierluigi Pizzaballa, in Italy's national team colours supplied one of only a few bright spots in an otherwise inauspicious period in the club's history. The *Bergamaschi* also discovered the finishing skills of Giuseppe Savoldi, who was to became the world's first £1 million player when he was sold by Bologna to Napoli in the mid-1970s. Atalanta finally succumbed to the inevitable in 1969 and were relegated. During the 1970s, Atalanta kept switching between the top two divisions until, in 1981, they went down to Serie C for the first time. They quickly re-established themselves in the second division a year later and in 1984, reached the top flight again. During the summer preceding the *Campionato*, Atalanta recruited the talented Swede Glenn Stromberg from the Portuguese giants Benfica. Stromberg's importance to the team grew after the departure of their playmaker Roberto Donadoni to Milan, who was sold for a then club

Club Name:
Atalanta Bergamasca Calcio
Founded: **1907**
Address:
Via Scotti 26, 24100 Bergamo
Ground:
Stadio Comunale (Capacity: 33,100)
Club Colours:
Blue and Black Striped Shirts, Black Shorts, Black Socks (Away Colours: White Shirts, White Shorts, White Socks)
Major Honours:
Italian Cup Winners (1963)

Left: Maurizio Ganz experiences that after-goal feeling.
Above: The Atalanta faithful.

GIUSEPPE SAVOLDI

(b: 21/1/47 Gorlago, Bergamo)
The prolific striker carved a name for himself when he became the world's first £1 million player in 1975, joining Napoli from Bologna. However, Savoldi began his Serie A career with Atalanta in the late 1960s and made six appearances for the national team at Under-21 level while in Bergamo. He scored 168 Serie A goals with three different clubs, placing him in the top ten on Italy's all-time scorers' chart.

GLENN STROMBERG

(b: 5/1/60 Bramaregaarden, Sweden)
After eight years, the Swede left a remarkable impression on the citizens of Bergamo. He began his career with Gothenburg, helping them to a UEFA Cup conquest in 1982, before moving on to Benfica in Portugal. Stromberg signed for Atalanta in 1984 and became one of the club's longest-serving players. He made more than 200 league appearances in the club's colours before retiring at the age of 32.

record of £4 million in 1986. The year also saw the arrival of England's Trevor Francis who joined from Sampdoria for one last season in Italy before returning to his homeland.

The following year, Atalanta experienced a strange mix of fortunes. They were relegated to Serie B, but enjoyed a glorious run in the Italian Cup. They reached the final and although well beaten by Napoli, still qualified for the European Cup Winners' Cup competition. Napoli, inspired by Diego Maradona, also won their first *Scudetto,* and so took part in the Champions' Cup, which paved the way for the club from Bergamo to play in European competition for the second time. Despite the club's demotion, Stromberg did not desert his adopted city and led the second division side, coached by Emiliano Mondonico, to the semi-final. In contrast to their experience in 1963, when they were eliminated in the first round, Atalanta threatened to become the first team from the second division to seize a European trophy.

The *Bergamaschi* eliminated the Welsh side, Merthyr Tydfil, OFI from Greece and Sporting Lisbon, the side that had knocked them out of Europe 25 years earlier, before they finally met their match in the Belgian side Mechelen. As in 1963, Atalanta lost to the eventual winners of the competition. They compensated for their disappointment with promotion to Serie A and qualified for Europe again in 1989, this time in the UEFA Cup.

Atalanta were strengthened by the acquisition of the Argentinian, Claudio Caniggia, who arrived from another Italian club, Verona. Unfortunately, Mondonico's men lost in the first round of the UEFA Cup to Spartak Moscow, but finished high enough in the league to participate in the same competition the following year. Mondonico departed for Torino and was replaced by Pierluigi Frosio, who arrived from Monza despite the northern club's relegation to Serie C the previous season. Frosio was sacked within six months, even though he had led them to the quarter finals of the UEFA Cup. Atalanta's precarious league

position compelled the club President, Cesare Bortolotti, to summon a man with more experience, hence the appointment of the former Fiorentina coach, Bruno Giorgi. Atalanta were drawn against Inter in the UEFA Cup quarter final and performed admirably in both legs, but they went out of the competition, beaten 2-0 on aggregate. That season, the UEFA Cup was dominated by Italian clubs and the final was contested by Inter and Roma, with the team from Milan victorious by 2-1 on aggregate. Giorgi concentrated on dragging his team away from the relegation zone and managed to lead them to a comfortable mid-table position. Sadly, Cesare Bortolotti passed away that summer and his father, Achille, resumed his position as club President.

At the start of the 91/92 season, Atalanta's fans expected more from their heroes, but they waited five weeks before the club's first league victory – against local rivals Cremonese. Atalanta won only six of their next 20 league matches and were also eliminated in the third round of the Italian Cup by Juventus. By this time, Antonio Percassi had taken over the club presidency. Percassi is the only current Serie A President with a football pedigree, having left the game in his early twenties to establish his clothing business.

The club might have been forgiven for thinking that it was not their year, when their Comunale Stadium became the setting for an incident never before witnessed in a Serie A fixture. On 23 February 1992, Atalanta were leading Cremonese 1-0 with one minute of the match remaining. Cremonese were fighting for their Serie A lives and pushed everyone forward for a corner, including their goalkeeper, in a last ditch attempt to salvage a point. As the ball was flighted into Atalanta's penalty area, it eluded everybody except the Cremonese goalkeeper, Michelangelo Rampulla, who promptly nodded it into an empty net for the equalizer. A goalkeeper had never previously scored from open play in Serie A. Atalanta finished the season in 11th place and received a further blow when their most influential player, Glenn Stromberg, announced his retirement from the game.

As he was only 32, Stromberg's decision came as something of a surprise and try as he might, the new club President, Antonio Percassi, failed to change Stromberg's mind. Percassi described the mild-mannered Swede as the symbol of both the club and the city – 'a human image of Bergamo'. Stromberg was a role model for the citizens of Bergamo, particularly its children, and regularly visited schools in an attempt to deter potential young offenders from transgressing the law. After eight years in Bergamo, the Swede was regarded as a fully fledged Italian by his colleagues, who were stunned by his retirement. Stromberg's influence during his time with Atalanta was summed up by President Percassi, who said, 'Stromberg's virtue makes him the most important overseas player ever to have arrived in Italy'.

Bruno Giorgi also left, for Genoa, before the 92/93 season and Marcello Lippi, the Tuscan with a striking resemblance to Paul Newman, took over the reins. The sale of Claudio Caniggia to Roma allowed them to invest £3 million in Serie B's top scorer, Maurizio Ganz of Brescia. Then, one week before the opening day of the Serie A championship, Percassi recruited the experienced Brazilian, Ricardo Alemao, from Napoli. Before the season got underway, President Percassi offered to reimburse fans 10 per cent of the cost of season tickets should his club reach the targeted 35 points by June. Atalanta enjoyed a record-breaking first half of the season, reaching the midway point in third

place. Fine displays by Maurizio Ganz and their defender, Sergio Porrini, led to international recognition. In February 1992, Ganz was selected for the Italian squad which defeated Portugal 3-1 in a World Cup qualifier, but made his way only to the substitutes' bench. The following month, however, against Malta, Porrini became the first Atalanta player to wear Italy's jersey since Pierluigi Pizzaballa kept goal for the *Azzurri* in 1966. The *Bergamaschi* were on course for a European place, but triumphed only four times in their last 15 games and ultimately squandered the opportunity. Their disappointment was compounded, initially by the news of the death of former President, Achille Bortolotti, and also by exceeding 35 points, which obliged Percassi to uphold his promise to the fans and refund thousands of pounds from season ticket sales – without having anything to show for it.

Atalanta are arguably the most resilient of all Serie A's smaller clubs. They lack the resources to challenge for the *Scudetto*, but have taken part in 38 out of the 62 Serie A Championships – more than any other provincial side. The *Bergamaschi* begin each Serie A season hoping to survive in the top flight, yet they often prove to be more than a match for bigger and richer clubs. Glenn Stromberg's decision to stay in Bergamo, at the expense of moving to a more prestigious side, is a measure of the fine quality of life Bergamo and its football club offer.

Above: Atalanta's 1963 Italian Cup-winning side – bizarrely, coach Tabanelli was dismissed 24 hours later.

CAGLIARI

Cagliari is situated on the island of Sardinia. Its single league title success is as isolated as the club is itself from the Italian mainland. A man of great skill and total loyalty was needed to motivate this small club to reach the very top of Italian football. Luigi Riva's name is inextricably linked with Cagliari, more so even than Gianni Rivera with Milan or Giancarlo Antognoni with Fiorentina. The big clubs have, at least, seen a few players of similar quality and influence come through their doors but for Cagliari, Riva remains the symbol of the short time their team was the envy of every other side in Serie A.

CAGLIARI

Founded in 1920 as Cagliari Football Club, the side struggled along in Serie B or, even less impressively, in small regional leagues, throughout the first 30 years of its existence. It was only in the 1950s that the side began to make any sort of an impact at all on the national football scene. In 1954, they finished joint second in the Serie B and only lost out on a place in Serie A due to a play-off defeat at the hands of Pro Patria. The island side could not maintain even this relatively low level of play, though, and collapsed into Serie C in 1960.

However, one inspirational figure saw to it that Cagliari not only reached the top division but also that they went so far as to take the Serie A title – a feat which had escaped many richer and better supported clubs. The 19-year-old Luigi Riva caught the eye of the Bologna coach and renowned talent-spotter at the time, Fulvio Bernardini. Cagliari proved quicker to act and the youngster from Lombardy was snapped up to help push the side from Serie B, where they stood in 1963, into the first division.

It was no sooner said than done for Riva and his Cagliari side as he contributed eight goals to the side's historic promotion to Serie A. They announced their arrival in high style when they took a sixth place finish in their first season in the top flight. Although the following season was somewhat disappointing, Riva was clearly developing into a left-winger with a great eye for goal, as his 11 Serie A goals proved. However, new coach Manlio Scopigno decided to switch *Rombo di Tuono* (Roll of Thunder), as Riva was nicknamed, to the centre of the attack for the 1966-67 campaign. Critics felt that it was foolish to turn the best left-winger in Italy into just another centre forward. A total of 18 goals in 23 games went some way to proving them wrong but injury in an international match showed the added risks that a player took by playing in the front line.

By now Riva was attracting big interest from other clubs. Earlier in the 1960s, Inter had tried to bring the player to Milan and now it was Juventus's turn to try

to lure *Tuttosinistro*, another nickname Riva earned because of his preference for shooting with his left foot, away from the island.

'It wasn't easy to say no to Juve, at that time, but it has to be said that we had six internationals in the side compared to their two. It would have been a change for the worse,' is how Riva explains his commitment to Cagliari and his reasons for resisting lucrative offers to leave the club.

It was now becoming clear that Riva and the rest of the team were actually title-challengers. Enrico Albertosi, the goalkeeper signed from title rivals Fiorentina, was a rival for Dino Zoff in the national team. Pierluigi Cera, a defensive midfielder, was also called up to the Italian national team. The 1968-69 season saw Cagliari finishing runners-up in the Italian Cup and battling with Fiorentina in the Serie A until the Tuscan side eventually pulled away to take the title.

For a couple of seasons, meetings between the two teams went a long way towards deciding the outcome of the Serie A. Goalkeeper Albertosi must have held many regrets for leaving the newly-crowned champions of Italy, but he would soon have his revenge.

Having lost the talented Roberto Boninsegna to Inter, Cagliari risked weakening their side but in came Sergio Gori and Angelo Domenghini from the Milan club to see to it that this was not the case. The 1969-70 season proved to be the most memorable in the history of the club and one unlikely ever to be repeated. With an impressive 21-goal haul from Riva and a home record which saw them never lose a game, Cagliari took the title by four points from Inter, leaving their rivals Fiorentina trailing in fifth spot.

This was also the first season that Cagliari ventured into Europe thanks to the second place they had taken in 1969. They defeated Aris of Greece before succumbing to the East German side Carl Zeiss Jena in the UEFA Cup second round. The following season they made their way into Europe's most prestigious

Club Name:
Cagliari Calcio
Address:
Viale Bonaria 66, 09125 Cagliari
Founded: **1920**
Ground:
Stadio Comunale 'Sant'Elia'
(Capacity: 43,177)
Club Colours:
Red and Blue Halved Shirts, Blue
Shorts, Blue Socks with Red Trim
(Away Colours: White Shirts, White
Shorts, White Socks)
Major Honours:
League Champions (1969-70)

Left: Cagliari's Stadio Comunale Sant'Elia.
Above: Enzo Francescoli one on one with
Gianluigi Lentini.

CAGLIARI

ENRICO ALBERTOSI

(b: 2/2/39 Pontremoli)
Despite the competition
of none other than Dino
Zoff, Albertosi picked up
34 caps for Italy while with Fiorentina and
Cagliari. This placed him behind only Zoff, Zenga
and Gianpiero Combi in the all-time list of most
capped Italian goalkeepers. After ten seasons
with the Florence club, he left the side the
season before they won Serie A but picked up
the title with Cagliari in 1970 and Milan in 1979
at the age of 40.

NENÉ

(b: 1/2/42 Santos, Brazil)
Full name Claudio
Olindo De Carvalho,
this tall Brazilian star and
sometime replacement
for Pelé spent 12 years with Cagliari and played
311 Serie A matches for the team. Originally
signed by Juventus in 1963, he was discarded
after just one season despite scoring 11 goals in
28 games for the Turin club. He went on to
become an essential part in Cagliari's
championship winning side.

competition, the European Cup, and eliminated French champions Saint Etienne before losing out to Atletico Madrid.

The side's league fortunes began to dip as they became involved in European matches and as injury after injury began to dog Riva's last years with the side. In 1972, they managed a good fourth place finish but the signs of imminent decline were growing. The following year, Juventus once again tried to sign the 29-year-old Riva, despite his growing history of injuries, and made a staggering offer of 1,000,000,000 lire plus no fewer than seven players. At today's prices, this could be reckoned to be worth about £16 million, which makes even the transfer of Gianluigi Lentini seem cheap by comparison.

Still, Riva refused to move on and stayed with the club until a final injury, suffered while playing in Milan on 1 February 1976, put an end to his career and an end to Cagliari's most glorious days. The side finished the season at the bottom of Serie A and dropped into Serie B where they remained until 1979, when they returned to the first division.

It proved to be a short stay as the side slipped back down a division in 1983. In the meantime, however, they managed a good sixth place Serie A placing in 1981 with a side that included some useful talent in the shape of ex-Juventus player Alberto Marchetti and faithful forward Luigi Piras. Despite the acquisition of the Peruvian star Uribe and the consistent Giovanni Vavassori, Serie B, and worse, awaited the island team.

Even on its arrival in Serie B the team was struggling and 1987 saw Cagliari topple into Serie C1, the third division. They actually spent two successive seasons at this low level before they won promotion twice in successive seasons to return them to the Serie A in 1990. The team turned to Uruguayan talent to keep them competitive at this level and drafted in the experienced Enzo Francescoli in the summer of 1990 along with his countrymen José Herrera and Daniel Fonseca. They formed the backbone of this new

Cagliari side along with young Italian stars like Gianluca Festa and Aldo Firicano in defence, and Massimiliano Cappioli in the midfield. The safe goalkeeping of Mario Ielpo, who was courted by several major clubs, added further security at the back.

Although the side barely avoided relegation in its first two seasons, certain individuals stood out enough to be lured onto the mainland by bigger clubs. Coach Claudio Ranieri went to Napoli in 1991 where he suffered very mixed fortunes – he was followed to the same club a year later by the young Uruguayan Fonseca. This might have sent some clubs slumping into Serie B but Cagliari showed good sense in bringing veteran Carlo Mazzone to the club in 1991, after a short and disappointing spell under Massimo Giacomini, and signing the young Brazilian, Luis Oliveira, the following year to replace Fonseca. In addition, Serie A veterans Gianfranco Matteoli and Vittorio Pusceddu helped turn the 1992-93 Cagliari team into winners of a place in the UEFA Cup for the following season.

Despite their recent upturn in fortunes, Cagliari have never looked like matching the international recognition they achieved in the late 1960s and early 1970s. Their championship-winning side contained no fewer than six internationals including regulars like midfielder turned sweeper, Pierluigi Cera, and right-winger Angelo Domenghini, as well as Luigi Riva. Recently, young defender Matteo Villa's call-up to the Under-21 side has been the only national recognition of note for a side so far out of the limelight that its players have to perform wonders even to gain the attention of the national team manager. It would take another talent of similar stature (with the sort of loyalty so uncommon nowadays) to get anywhere near Luigi Riva's club record of 42 international caps – which would have certainly been more had it not been for injury.

With a small but loyal band of supporters, Cagliari always prove a tough prospect for any Serie A opponents when playing in their own Stadio 'Sant'Elia'

CAGLIARI

LUIGI RIVA

(b: 7/11/44 Leggiuno)
A left winger cum striker with a deadly left-foot shot, Riva did more for Cagliari than any other player in their history. His physical strength and eye for goal made him an almost impossible opponent for most defenders. His 35 international goals in just 42 appearances are an Italian record and testify to the quality of the player.

ENZO FRANCESCOLI

(b: 12/11/61 Montevideo, Uruguay)
Something of a footballing nomad, Francescoli played in Argentina and France before being signed from Marseille by Cagliari. A talented, if somewhat unpredictable midfielder, he proved a great success on the island and helped his countrymen Herrera and Fonseca to settle into playing in a foreign country for the first time.

(named after an area of the city which is in turn named after the patron saint of lepers!). For obvious geographical reasons, they can usually be assured that the number of away supporters coming to the ground will be less than it might be for other fixtures and the added element of a flight across the water makes this the most inconveniently placed away match in the Serie A. Any successes that the side has enjoyed have usually been heavily dependent on good home form and the participation of an intelligent, tactically aware coach. Manlio Scopigno, mastermind of the 1970 championship win, was nicknamed 'The Philosopher' because of his intense analysis of the game and recent occupants of the Cagliari bench like Claudio Ranieri and Carlo Mazzone have also shown great ability in the art of producing surprisingly good results with seemingly limited playing talent. This may always be the fate of the Cagliari coach.

Being the only team of note on the island of Sardinia leaves Cagliari without any natural local rivals. Perhaps, like most provincial sides, they raise their game most for the arrival of Juventus, Italy's most successful side. If you can beat Juventus in front of your home fans, they are likely to forgive you almost anything. Also, throughout the period when Cagliari enjoyed their greatest successes, Fiorentina emerged as one of the biggest obstacles in their way and meetings between the two sides were close and combative affairs.

Overall, Cagliari's isolation and difficulty in attracting top players mean that it is difficult for them to achieve great success. However, with the help of the stubborn loyalty of Luigi Riva and his accurate eye for goal and thunderous shot, Cagliari stand among the elite few who have won the Italian championship. This, in itself, is an immense achievement and one which gives Cagliari, the only island side to have taken the Serie A title, a special place in the hearts of the followers of Italian football.

Above: Cagliari's mighty 1969-70 championship-winning side had an unbeaten home record.

CREMONESE

The residents of Cremona, a small town near Milan in the Lombardy region, do not envy the riches of their neighbours. On the contrary, the Cremonese are quite happy with the small rewards that come their way, none more so than when it concerns promotion to the noble kingdom of Serie A. The club's resources are often stretched and with a small ground, which barely attracts gates over 10,000, they struggle to turn over enough revenue to sustain the little success they achieve.

Cremonese pride themselves on their youth policy, which has unearthed at least three major talents during the last 20 years. The World Cup winner, Antonio Cabrini, began his career in Cremona (his hometown), and Gianluca Vialli also developed from Cremonese's youth ranks before earning fame and fortune with Sampdoria. The club provided Sampdoria with another of its jewels, Attilo Lombardo, in 1989. More recently, three Cremonese players strongly influenced Italy's 1992 European Championship conquest at Under-21 level. Defenders, Giuseppe Favalli and Mauro Bonomi, and the cultured midfielder, Dario Marcolin, were sold to Lazio almost immediately for a combined fee of £10 million.

Formed in March 1903, Cremonese U.S. were one of the first Italian clubs; they also took part in Serie A's inaugural season in 1929. The *Grigiorossi*, as they are nicknamed because of their grey and red club colours, finished bottom and were relegated from a division they would not experience again for more than 50 years. During this era, Cremonese made its one and only contribution to the national team. The former Milan winger, Mariano Tansini, made two appearances for Italy in 1926, against the Republic of Ireland and Switzerland. The club's perpetual trips through the lower divisions began in the late 1930s in rather ill-fated circumstances. In 1937, a play-off match against Foggia determined the *Grigiorossi*'s future as a Serie B club. The first encounter failed to produce a winner, so a second match, which Foggia won 1-0, decided the outcome. Cremonese spent the next 20 years up and down Serie B and C before entering unknown territory in the form of the then semi-professional fourth division in 1967. In 30 years, Cremonese's identity altered distinctly from that of a Serie A club to one fighting to escape from the anonymity of the lower divisions.

Their decline persisted through to the beginning of the 1980s, a decade in which they constantly flirted with Serie A. Cremonese took part in no less than three promotion play-offs, winning just one – against Reggina – on penalties in 1989. However, things were beginning to change for the better and they spent the next four years fluctuating between the top two divisions, going up twice only to go back down to Serie B on each occasion after one season. It has always been difficult for a club of Cremonese's stature to recruit high-quality players, particularly foreigners. The giant Pole Wladyslaw Zmuda, Anders Limpar from Sweden and Ruben Pereira of Uruguay each failed to prevent the club from being relegated to Serie B. Ruben Pereira became the club's record signing when he joined from the Uruguayan side Danubio. However, Cremonese could afford to pay only half his £3 million transfer fee – the other half was provided by Juventus. In Italy, such an arrangement is called *comproprietà*, which makes the player joint-property between two clubs. The idea is for a big club, in this case Juventus, to 'park' their investment with a provincial side, thus enabling them to monitor his progress. If the player is successful, then Juventus would sign him outright and would then pay the outstanding amount to Cremonese. Unfortunately, the Uruguayan failed to adjust to life in Serie A and both Cremonese and Juventus lost their investments.

Club Name:

Cremonese Unione Sportiva

Address:

Via Persico 19, 26100 Cremona

Founded: **1903**

Ground:

Giovanni Zini (Capacity: 18,000)

Club Colours:

Grey and Red Striped Shirts, Red Shorts, Red Socks (Away Colours: White Shirts, White Shorts, White Socks)

Major Honours:

Anglo-Italian Cup Winners (1993)

Left: Cremonese captain Corrado Verdelli holds aloft the 1993 Anglo-Italian Cup. Below: Midfielder Riccardo Maspero.

ANTONIO CABRINI

(b: 8/10/57 Cremona)
The stylish left-back made his league debut for Cremonese at the age of 16 in a Serie C fixture. Cabrini joined Atalanta in 1975, but signed for Juventus after one season in Bergamo. He won every major honour in European Club competition during 13 memorable seasons in Turin and made 73 appearances for the Italian national side, including the 1982 World Cup final. Cabrini ended his career with Bologna in 1992.

GUSTAVO DEZOTTI

(b: 14/2/64 Monte Buey, Argentina)
The striker, nicknamed 'The Gazelle', joined Lazio from the Argentinian side, Newell's Old Boys, in 1988. After one disappointing season in Rome, Dezotti was transferred to Cremonese, where he has scored more than 40 goals in four happy years. He took part in the 1990 World Cup finals for the Argentinian national side, only to be sent off in the final against the winners, West Germany.

For all Cremonese's failings on the foreign transfer market, the Argentinian international, Gustavo Dezotti, has savoured his time in Cremona. Around the globe Dezotti will be remembered as a villain for being sent off in the 1990 World Cup final against West Germany, but in his adopted city he is undeniably a hero. Dezotti played a part in the club's fine conquest of the 1993 Anglo-Italian Cup against Derby County. Wembley Stadium staged the final of the revived tournament, which had been dormant for almost 20 years, and the *Grigiorossi* comfortably defeated Derby County 3-1 to lift their first major trophy. It was an historic achievement for Cremonese. Only Milan, winners of the 1963 European Champions' Cup final, and Sampdoria, runners-up in the same competition in 1992, had previously played in a final at the 'venue of legends'. The Vice-President, Signor Miglioli, was so thrilled with the victory that he refused to let go of the trophy from the moment the team left the stadium.

'Tonight, I'm taking this cup to bed with me – as well as my wife,' said the joyous Miglioli.

His thoughts on that day were also with the club President, Domenico Luzzara, his close friend for more than 20 years, who was back in Cremona following heart problems.

Domenico Luzzara has been a part of Cremonese for more than 30 years and has taken his club back to the forefront of Italian football after 50 years of oblivion. All Cremonese's achievements are obtained through sheer endeavour and sacrifice; relegation to Serie B is never looked upon as a disaster, but just another standard setback. For Cremonese, when it comes to Serie A, it is the taking part that matters, not the winning.

The Italian first division is a relatively young competition with less than 100 years of history. The first Italian championship was held in 1898 and won by Genoa. However, there have been several changes, restructurings and unifications employed since the early days, in order to reach the current successful formula.

Initially, the championship was just a matter of a few clubs from Turin, Milan and Genoa playing over, at most, a couple of months. The very first championship was played in just one day in Turin but the following year this altered. A set of preliminary matches was introduced, the winner of which would go on to play the reigning champions in a one-off final. This was usually played in, and won by, Genoa. In 1905 the format of the competition changed once more as teams were divided into three regional groups, from Piedmont, Lombardy and Liguria. The winners of these groups would play off on a league basis to ascertain the champions.

This process of regional subdivisions continued until 1927 although the number of groups and the regions that they represented varied considerably. The only major exception to this was the 1908 championship which was disputed by just four sides in a single league. The reason for this, however, was clearly the ban on the inclusion of sides containing foreign players. This led to Milan, Genoa and

the story of serie A

Torino taking no part in that year's championship, leaving the way open to all-Italian Pro Vercelli. Even so, the next season, with the banned sides re-admitted and the Veneto region represented for the first time, Pro Vercelli still took the title.

Other important alterations to the pre-war championship came in 1911, with the addition of sides from Emilia Romagna, and again in 1913, with the first participation of sides from central and southern Italy. By the time the Italian championship of 1915 had been suspended due to World War I, there were no fewer than three separate divisions, northern, central and southern, which were in turn divided into a further nine groups. Although this did allow most of the major teams of the day to participate in the tournament it did little to promote national unity, as sides from different divisions could only meet if they happened to reach the national championship final.

This system of regional divisions persisted after the war had ended, with the country split into northern and southern divisions, subdivided according to region. The champions of each division would then play off in a grand final which, not surprisingly, was never won by the southern champions. In the end, it took the Fascist régime to unite the country in footballing terms by providing its first taste of a truly national championship.

In 1927, although still divided into two sections, the championship no longer took into account geographical reasons for creating the sections. Group A, for example, contained Genoa and Napoli, while Group B saw Torino and Livorno in competition. It was a small step from this system to the *Campionato a Girone Unico*, the Single League Championship, which was created in 1929 at the behest of the Fascist president of the Italian Football Federation, Leandro Arpinati. It marked the end of the regionalization of Italian football and the future success of Serie A was quickly assured by the best teams touring the entire country.

This first single league contained 18 teams although the original plan was to include only the top eight sides from the top two divisions of the previous campaign. However, Napoli and Lazio had finished in joint eighth place and, after three play-offs failed to decide the matter, both sought to be admitted. In addition, Triestina, who had taken ninth place in their division, requested admission to the first division. As a result, the league contained 18 rather than just 16 sides.

Since then, only minor changes have affected the championship. In 1934, the league was trimmed to 16 sides. This situation remained until the end of World War II. The 1945-46 championship was a throwback to the old regional divisions with northern and southern leagues before 1946-47 saw the return of a slightly cumbersome 20-side single league Serie A. This was extended to 21 for the 1947-48 campaign and was reduced to 20 sides the following season and 18 sides in 1952. In 1967 a further two sides were cut out and a 16-team format was favoured as the most competitive for the sides involved without placing excessive physical demands on the players.

The most recent change came in 1988, when once again the league expanded to include 18 sides with four relegation spots. This allowed for fewer teams to be involved in meaningless games at the end of the season, since most would be battling for UEFA Cup spots or to avoid relegation. This has proved a successful format and has guaranteed the popularity of Italy's premier league with the Serie A sides and their supporters.

FOGGIA

Foggia Calcio bear the same colours as their illustrious counterparts, Milan, hence their nickname the 'Red Devils', but the resemblance ends there. The *Rossoneri* from the North have enjoyed more success than any other Italian side apart from Juventus, while Foggia, an unfashionable outfit from the south-east of the country, have failed to win any major trophy in their history. Foggia's Serie A experience is confined to the last 30 years and their appearances in Italy's premier division have only just reached double figures. However, for a club with limited Serie A pedigree, they have come a long way. In the 1950s, the club was still languishing in the semi-professional leagues. By the 1990s, Foggia had developed into a proficient outfit, upstaging many of its more distinguished opponents.

Football reached Foggia in 1909, sixteen years after the foundation of Italy's oldest club, Genoa, but the city waited until 1920 before forming its own club. Sporting Club Foggia initially took part in the regional championship, *Campionato Pugliese*, and were soon promoted to the national league. In 1933, having already merged with a local side, Velo, and assumed the title of U.S. Foggia some time earlier, the club eventually managed to climb out from the minor league and into Serie B. Their stay proved transitory and they were to spend much of the next decade in Italy's third division.

Foggia were unfortunate not to have regained their Serie B status just after World War II; in 1948, they won their division only for the Football Federation to suspend promotion in order to reduce the number of teams in the top divisions. Then, three years later, the *Rossoneri* missed promotion again following a play-off defeat at the hands of lo Stabia, now called Juve Stabia, a team from the Neapolitan seaside town of Castellamare. The effects were damaging. After finishing third from bottom in 1952, Foggia went out of the league and into the semi-professional ranks, IV Serie.

In 1957, the year the non-league championship changed from IV Serie to Campionato Interregionale, Foggia merged with G.S. Incedit, another team from the same division, and played under their new banner, U.S. Foggia Incedit. The city's new club won promotion in consecutive seasons to reach Serie B following an absence of 24 years. The Red Devils were approaching a fruitful era in their history. Foggia achieved their first ever promotion to Serie A within two years, in 1964, having missed by a whisker the previous season.

They quickly established a reputation for being difficult to beat at their Pino Zaccheria Stadium and also claimed prestigious victories, notably against Juventus and the European Champions, Inter, who went on to capture the *Scudetto* and the European Champions' Cup again that season. Foggia ended the campaign in a

creditable ninth place and two of their players were graced with international caps. On 1 May 1965, their left-back, Romano Micelli, and centre forward, Cosimo Nocera, represented the national side in a friendly match against Wales staged in Florence. Italy, under the guidance of coach Edmondo Fabbri, defeated the Welsh 4-1. Two of the goals were scored by Milan's Giovanni Lodetti, one from the Sampdoria winger, Paolo Barison, and the fourth, in the last minute of the contest, came from Foggia's very own Cosimo Nocera, who had come on as a half-time substitute. Despite their promising displays, Micelli and Nocera, were never called up to play for Italy again.

Foggia struggled in their second season in Serie A and although the *Rossoneri* were still strong at home, their deplorable away form almost cost them their place in the top flight. Ultimately, just two points separated them from relegated Sampdoria in 16th place, the very same position Foggia occupied when they went down a year later. In 1968, the club returned to a version of its old title, U.S. Foggia, removing Incedit, and was promoted to Serie A for the second time at the start of the new decade. The 1970s were characterized by Foggia's constant movement up and down the top two divisions, until they were eventually relegated to Serie C in 1979. Foggia found it difficult to adjust to playing in a division they hadn't experienced for almost 20 years and it wasn't until 1989 that they clawed their way out and up into Serie B.

Foggia recalled the Czech-born Zdenek Zeman as coach, having dismissed him three years earlier. Zeman had settled in Palermo, Sicily, as a 21-year-old, where he also progressed to become youth team coach in 1981. The composed Czech had the perfect grounding for a successful career, which he thoroughly exploited. His

Club Name:

Foggia Calcio

Address:

Via Torelli 4, 71100 Foggia

Founded: **1920**

Stadium:

Stadio Pino Zaccheria (Capacity: 25,000)

Club Colours:

Red and Black Striped Shirts, Black Shorts, Black Socks (Away Colours: White Shirts, White Shorts, White Socks)

Left: Andrea Seno in action for Foggia in a pre-season training match.
Below: A young Giuseppe Signori in his Foggia days.

ANDREA SENO

(b: 1/2/66 Burano, Venice)

The hard-working midfielder and club captain was still playing semi-professional football with little Pievigina in 1987 and has adjusted well to life in Serie A. He was signed from third division Como in 1992, having failed to make the grade with Padova and his hometown team, Venezia, at the start of his professional career.

FRANCESCO BAIANO

(b: 24/2/68 Naples)

The striker was born a short distance from Napoli's training ground, but failed to break into the first team of his hometown side. In 1990, after continual loan spells around the country, he was eventually sold to Foggia, where he formed a lethal striking partnership with Beppe Signori. The Italian international moved to Milan for £4.5 million in 1992 and, in true Baiano tradition, was instantly sent on loan to Fiorentina.

uncle, Cestmir Vycpalek had already spent much of his adult life in Italy, as both a player and coach. Vycpalek left his homeland at the end of World War II and joined Juventus and, in the early 1970s, coached Juve to two successive league titles.

During Zeman's second year back in Foggia, he was presented with a squad of talented players by the club's Neapolitan President, Pasquale Casillo. Zeman's considerable skills flourished in Foggia and, in 1991, he steered the *Rossoneri* to Serie A as Champions, after an awe-inspiring campaign during which they scored 67 goals – 48 from the striking trio, Giuseppe Signori, Roberto Rambaudi and Serie B's joint top scorer (with 22), Francesco Baiano. Foggia looked to Eastern Europe for the three permitted foreigners in Serie A and signed the Romanian full-back, Dan Petrescu, and the two Igors – Shalimov and Kolyvanov – from Russia, for a total of less than £2 million. Two of the imports proved to be inspired signings, but Kolyvanov failed to win a place in the team's explosive attack and sat out the majority of the season.

The club's Pino Zaccheria Stadium, the venue of many open and often spectacular contests, was still being renovated at the start of the 91/92 season, so Zeman took his players to nearby Bari for their opening home match. Foggia had already come away from the San Siro with a commendable draw against mighty Inter on the first day of the season, prior to their fixture with Juventus. At the San Nicola Stadium, 50,000 spectators turned out for the visit of Italy's best supported club, producing record gate receipts of £700,000 – more than double the sum Foggia could ever expect from a match at their own compact stadium. A Toto Schillaci goal separated the two sides, but Foggia more than deserved a point from the contest, which ended 1-0.

Foggia's fearsome forwards wreaked havoc on Serie A's notorious defenders for most of the season and in Francesco Baiano, they boasted a new international striker. The club suddenly emerged as genuine contenders for a top five finish and a place in Europe. Their hopes failed to materialize, but they managed to

equal their best Serie A placing of ninth. More importantly, they captured Italian hearts with their exuberant and adventurous style of play.

Only the bottom side, Ascoli, conceded more goals than Foggia, but by the same token, only the Champions, Milan, scored more. The two Red Devils met on the last day of the season in Foggia and the match produced an astounding ten goals. From a 2-1 deficit at half time, Milan came back with seven goals in a 40-minute spell, which left the watching former Milan boss, Arrigo Sacchi, almost lost for words. The national team coach left after Milan's sixth with two words that said it all, '*Mamma mia!*'.

The following year, President Casillo's lack of rapport with the club's fans grew decidedly worse. They were shocked by the news that Casillo had sold every one of his prized assets for a combined total of £25 million and replaced them by bringing in 17 players from the lower divisions, mainly from Serie C, to the collective value of a mere £8 million. The fans' derision increased when Casillo suspended the sale of season tickets for the entire campaign. Matchday tickets cost more, so a season ticket is essential for those who follow their team at every home game. Needless to say, many stayed away during the opening weeks, but returned once they acknowledged Zeman had assembled another entertaining side. The Czech is noted for sending scouts to explore the lower divisions for unknown talent each and every week. He did make an exception in recruiting Oberdan Biagioni from second division Cosenza, but, at a club record £2 million, found that even a lesser-known Italian player does not come cheap. At the start of the 92/93 season, few predicted anything but relegation for Foggia. Following a turbulent opening two months, Zeman steered his ship back on course, preaching the football that has made him one of Italy's most respected coaches. His 'miracle' in south-east Italy suggests that a capable coach may sometimes be of greater importance to a team than a squad comprised exclusively of international players. Serie A is not just a haven for the rich and famous, as Foggia have clearly demonstrated.

SIGOR SHALIMOV
(b: 2/1/69 Moscow, Russia)

The £8 million Inter paid Foggia for the Russian in 1992 set a transfer record for an Eastern European. Shalimov made his debut for Spartak Moscow aged 17 and went on to make close to 100 league appearances for the Russian side, winning a league title in 1989. He moved to Foggia two years later and made a stunning impact during his one season in south-east Italy.

OBERDAN BIAGIONI
(b: 17/10/69 Rome)

At £2 million, Biagioni is Foggia's record signing. The talented and confident forward played a significant part in the club's fight against relegation in 1993 – not least due to his ability to score from the penalty spot, scoring five out of five. The Roman once rejected by Lazio was rated one of Serie B's outstanding performers in the 91/92 season while at Cosenza.

Opposite: Igor Kolyvanov squeezes past Frank Rijkaard in a 1992 Milan-Foggia clash.

GENOA

With over 100 years of footballing history, Genoa are the oldest club in Italy and one of the most successful. Their victories, however, took place almost exclusively in the distant past, their last league title being in 1924. They have never managed to recapture the level of dominance that they had attained in football by the turn of the century. Their famous red and blue strips (hence their nickname the *Rossoblu*) were symbols of the city of Genoa until Sampdoria were formed by merging two local clubs after World War II and began to divide the city in terms of footballing loyalties.

GENOA

The story of the *Grifone*, the Griffin, so called because of the mythical beast featured on the club's badge, began long ago, on 7 September 1893, five years before the first Italian championship was played. The Genoa Cricket and Athletic Club, a name clearly giving away their English origins, quickly began to devote more and more time to football and, by 1897, voted to allow Italians into the club. This proved to be a wise decision as the side was strengthened by the best local talent and in 1898 they were able to take on the Football Club Torinese in the first recorded game between sides from different cities. A crowd of just 154 turned up to watch the game which the team from Turin won 1-0, and so the story of Italian competitive football began.

Having swiftly established themselves as one of the most eminent footballing forces of the day, Genoa could not miss out on the first ever Italian championship which took place on 8 May 1898 in Turin. After eliminating the Società Ginnastica Torino, Genoa went on to beat Internazionale Torino in the final, 2-1 after extra time. The side included many British players and indeed the goalkeeper Dr. James Spensley carried on to play in all of Genoa's first six title wins.

An idea of just how important Genoa were in these first championships can be gained merely by looking at how they took six of the first seven league titles contested. This was a feat which assured them a place at the very top of Italian football and went a long way towards guaranteeing them a tally of league title wins which only three giant clubs, Juventus, Inter and Milan, would ever better.

Although the side failed to win the title between 1905 and 1914, they were rarely far off the top teams of the day and it came as no surprise when they managed to add their seventh league title in 1915. As war broke out, Genoa were top of the northern part of the league and were awarded the title by the Italian Football Federation without having to play off against either Lazio or Internazionale Napoli who were placed at the top of the central and southern groups respectively.

It was also during the years prior to World War I that the first well-documented *Derby della Lanterna* took place between Genoa and local rivals, Andrea Doria. It took no fewer than three matches to separate the sides, with Genoa finally winning through to the final championship group on the strength of a single goal from the midfielder, Senft. This was the cue for chaos both on and off the pitch. The Genoese daily of the time, *Il Caffaro*, reported that 'It would be desirable for players to ignore the comments from the crowd during the game.'

Even after World War I, Genoa remained firmly the top team from the port city. They added another two championships in 1923 and 1924 with a side that still contained several elements of the 1915 championship winning side. Most notable among these were Italian internationals like full-back Renzo De Vecchi, midfielder Ettore Leale and the gifted inside-forward Aristodemo Santamaria. They had also added superstars of the day like goalkeeper Giovanni De Prà who would keep goal on 19 occasions for his country and midfield star Ottavio Barbieri. Indeed, nine of the regular first team players in that side would go on to play for their country which was hardly surprising considering the fact that the 1923 side went through the whole season undefeated.

Club Name:

Genoa 1893

Address:

Via Roma 7/3, 16121 Genova

Founded: **1893**

Ground:

Stadio 'Luigi Ferraris' (Capacity: 43,868)

Club Colours:

Red and Blue Halved Shirts, Blue Shorts, Blue Socks with Red Trim

(Away Colours: White Shirts with a Red and Blue Hoop, White Shorts, White Socks with Red and Blue Trim)

Major Honours:

League Champions (1898, 1899, 1900, 1902, 1903, 1904, 1914-15, 1922-23, 1923-24), Italian Cup Winners (1936-37)

Left: Czech striker Tomas Skuhravy.

Below: The unmistakeable Stadio Luigi Ferraris.

GENOA

RENZO DE VECCHI

(b: 3/2/1894 Milan – d: 1967)

Three times a championship winner with Genoa, De Vecchi was certainly the outstanding full-back of his generation, earning him a national team call-up at the age of just 16. Nicknamed Figlio di Dio, 'Son of God', by the Genoa fans, he became a respected sports journalist after his retirement from the game.

TOMAS SKUHRAVY

(b: 7/9/65 Ceske Budejovice, Czechoslovakia)

Standing over 6 feet 4 inches tall but still impressively nimble, Skuhravy joined Genoa in 1990 from Sparta Prague and his goals alongside Carlos Aguilera made him a favourite with the fans. However, comments about wishing to rejoin his old manager, Bagnoli, at Inter, soured his relationship with the Genoa faithful during the 1992-93 season.

These were, sadly, to be the last moments of true glory in Genoa's history. They could not keep up with the likes of Bologna, Juventus, Inter and Torino who dominated the years leading up to World War II. In 1929, they were, like Inter, forced to change their name as it was not considered to be sufficiently Italian-sounding. Until 1945, therefore, the club was known as Genova 1893. For the first time in their history, the side slipped down into Serie B in 1934 and, although they made a speedy recovery to Serie A the following season, a trend had been set that would dog Genoa throughout their post-war history. An isolated Italian Cup win in 1937 over Roma and some consistent league finishes seemed to augur well for the club as war approached. However, come 1946, the side was obviously no longer the force that it once was and in future would have to compete fiercely with the newly created Sampdoria for the affections of the Genoese people.

Genoa soon became an 'elevator' club, as sides who cannot establish themselves as Serie A regulars are known, shuttling up and down between Serie A and Serie B and never being in a position to challenge for the league title. When they suffered their third post-war relegation in 1965 it was to take them a further eight seasons to return to Serie A. In 1970, they suffered the worst humiliation in the club's history, finishing bottom of the Serie B with just six wins to their credit and plummeting into Italy's third division, the Serie C. Although this nightmare lasted only one season, it took the club a long time to return to anywhere near the top of the Italian game.

The 1970s and 1980s proved to be yet another period of instability for the club as they could not establish a regular position in the Serie A. It was not until 1989, when the side won promotion from the Serie B for the seventh time in its history that it seemed that they might be able to compete with the very best outfits in Italy. With young talent like battling midfielders Stefano Eranio and Gennaro Ruotolo, along with the undoubted talents of striker Davide Fontolan, the side stormed to the top of the second division.

Although the side struggled in their first season back in Serie A, there were obvious signs of ambition in their summer signings campaign of 1990. Veteran coach Osvaldo Bagnoli was brought in to replace the erratic, if sometimes inspirational, 'Professor' Scoglio. The giant Czech striker, Tomas Skuhravy, who had so impressed at Italia '90, joined the diminutive Uruguayan, Carlos Aguilera, to form one of the most unlikely, and successful, strike forces in the club's history. Mario Bortolazzi was brought in from Atalanta to complete a line-up which looked like being the most competitive Genoa side for many years.

The 1990-91 season saw Genoa's best post-war league finish as they rose to take fourth place behind championship winning Sampdoria, thereby guaranteeing the side their first outing in European competition. Along the way, Genoa scored notable home wins over Inter and Juventus with the Aguilera-Skuhravy double act scoring no fewer than 30 Serie A goals.

Their first year of European competition proved to be an eventful one in which they managed to defeat Liverpool 4-1 on aggregate in the quarter-finals. This was due, in some part, to a blistering Branco free-kick in the 88th minute of the first leg in Genoa, affording the side a comfortable 2-0 lead to take to Anfield. Genoa's European dream finally ended with a narrow 4-3 defeat on aggregate against Ajax, failing to set up an all-Italian final with Torino.

However, all was not well at the club as rumours grew that Bagnoli was bound for Inter and supporters' favourites Stefano Eranio and Carlos Aguilera were bound for Milan and Torino respectively. The volatile but colourful supporters from the Curva Nord were not slow to show their displeasure. Banners like *Spinelli vattene!* ('Spinelli get out!', in reference to the club's president Aldo Spinelli) were accompanied by more sarcastic lines such as *'Tacconi torna a Sanremo'*, ('Tacconi go back to Sanremo', encouraging the ex-international goalkeeper to return to the city where he had helped to host Italy's major song contest.)

GENOA

Coaches came and went – first Bruno Giorgi, then the flamboyant flop Gigi Maifredi and finally youth team coach Claudio Maselli. Matters came to a head when the side threw away a two goal lead at home to Lazio, eventually losing 3-2. Fans invaded the pitch and the police had to intervene to allow the final three minutes of the game to be played. This marked the end of Maifredi and the start of a fight to remain in Serie A which was only guaranteed on the last day of the season.

Despite their fluctuating fortunes, Genoa have contributed well to the Italian national team, especially during the 1920s. Renzo De Vecchi, who gained 31 caps while at the club, still holds the record for international appearances. In 1924, he was joined by three of his club-mates, Giovanni De Prà, Ottavio Barbieri and Luigi Burlando in the national team. This proved to be a peak in the side's international fortunes as they slid into the second division and only a few players, like Fosco Becattini and Paolo Barison, won caps with the club throughout the post-war period. Only recently have Stefano Eranio and Gennaro Ruotolo figured in the plans of the *Azzurri*.

Although Genoa have struggled gallantly for success since their earliest years, the rivalry between themselves and Sampdoria remains one of the strongest throughout Italy. With Genoa's history of league titles and other successes, their supporters consider Sampdoria to be a sort of 'poor relative', even though in recent years the *Doriani* have had considerably more to cheer about. Despite the fact that Genoa have shown only small bursts of form, most notably under Osvaldo Bagnoli's sensible coaching, they remain the most popular side in the city of Genoa itself. Recently the number of Sampdoria followers has undoubtedly increased, but there is still a certain tradition for those from the city to support the side bearing its English name. Sampdoria are a brash modern team, in the eyes of Genoa followers, compared to the history and tradition of the *Grifone*. Genoa boast a number of famous followers, including musicians Fabrizio De Andrè and Francesco Baccini, who recently penned a song dedicated to the club. Gianni Brera, one of Italy's top sports writers until his death in 1992, was also a known sympathizer to the club to the extent that he wrote a two volume history about them.

With such a rich history, it remains difficult for Genoa to come to terms with their present situation and to accept the struggles that beset a club trying to avoid relegation. However, with the loyal support of their fans and a notable tradition of producing a number of exciting young talents, for example Christian Panucci and Roberto Arco, there may still be reason to hope that the Griffin will fly high once more.

Above: Dr. James Spensley and the 1904 Genoa squad, all set for yet another championship win.

STEFANO ERANIO

(b: 29/12/66 Genoa) After making his debut for Genoa at just 18 years of age, Eranio spent nine seasons with the club before his controversial move to Milan. A strong but skilful midfielder, he also plays as full-back, receiving his first cap for the Italian national team after showing some very impressive form during the club's good run in the UEFA Cup in 1992.

GENNARO RUOTOLO

(b: 20/3/67 S. Maria a Vico) Signed from Arezzo in 1988, Ruotolo immediately slotted into the Genoa midfield and gave them an extra touch of class. A player who gives his all in every game, he also earned an international call-up and was one of the few stars to remain with the club during the troubled summer of 1992.

INTER

Although Juventus have been by far the most successful club in Italian domestic competition they were, for a long time, upstaged by Inter on the world stage. As European competitions began in the 1950s and 1960s, it was Inter, more often than Juventus, that represented Italy. Inter have often seemed to be the only option to total Juventus domination of the championship and their meetings, in *Il Derby d'Italia* (The Derby of Italy) have often decided the whereabouts of the championship. The *Nerazzurri* (blue and blacks) have achieved some of the most outstanding moments in Italian football both at home (58 points in a 34 match season in 1989) and abroad (back to back European and World Club Cup wins in the 1960s). Along with Juventus they are the only Italian side never to have been relegated from the Serie A.

The side was born, as often happened, out of another team – in this case, Milan. It took the club only two years to achieve their first success. When the Italian Football Federation refused to change the date of their final following a Pro Vercelli complaint, Vercelli sent their youth team in protest. Not surprisingly, Inter disposed of them 10-3, thereby breaking the dominance of the provincial side.

This championship win in 1910 started a sequence of Inter taking the title at the start of every decade until 1950. In 1920 they were crowned Champions once again. They defeated Livorno 3-2 with a side that boasted one of the finest players of the time in Luigi Cevenini who played 29 times in the Italian midfield.

One of the most important moments in Inter's history came in September, 1927 when the young Giuseppe Meazza made his debut for the club against U.S. Milanese. Meazza would go on to affirm himself as the greatest player in Inter's history and, indeed, probably in the history of Italian football. In 1928, another important change took place as the club took on the name Ambrosiana as opposed to Internazionale. The reason for this was that the Fascist dictatorship had no great love of external influence on the country and a name like 'Internazionale' was not considered to be Italian enough!

Even with the new name there was no break in the title-winning sequence. Inter won the championship in 1930 – the first to be played in a single league format – finishing two points ahead of Genoa. Meazza finished top of the goalscoring chart with an impressive 31 strikes.

Eventually the sequence of ten years between titles was broken in 1938 although Inter did win again in 1940. With a Coppa Italia win sandwiched in between, this was the most successful pre-war spell in Inter's history. Part of that team was the thoughtful winger, Annibale Frossi, who won just five caps for Italy but struck eight goals for them. He was certainly unlucky not to win more caps.

Inter did not emerge from the war at their strongest. Meazza returned to Inter to finish his career and played his last game against Bologna in 1947 at 36 years of age and the side required stern rebuilding work. In 1948 they finished a disappointing 12th, equalling their worst ever Serie A performance which had come in 1942. However, by the following season they were back in contention for the league title.

By the time the new decade came around, the old WM formation was being swept away by the new *verrou* or *catenaccio* system based on tight defence. One of the first to adopt this system successfully in Italy was Alfredo Foni with Inter in the early 1950s. His side won back to back titles in 1953 and 1954 with a stern defence based around the uncompromising Attilio Giovannini with Giorgio 'Kamikaze' Ghezzi in goal.

However, Inter were soon swept away by Milan and Juventus, who dominated the late 1950s, and it was not until the arrival of oil giant, Angelo Moratti, at the presidency of the club that things began to turn around. One of the first things that Moratti did was to appoint the Argentinian Helenio Herrera as coach and this proved to be an inspired choice.

Herrera arrived in 1960 and suddenly threw the position of coach into the spotlight. Until his arrival, with few exceptions, it had been the players who made the headlines. He placed the coach in a new light where it seemed that the personal charisma and character of the man in charge were responsible for the quality of his side's performances.

Initially, things did not go particularly well as Herrera's side finished behind Juventus and Milan in 1961. Following a pitch invasion in their match with Juventus that year, Inter believed that they should have been awarded a 2-0 victory as is normally the case in Italy in such circumstances. When a replay was ordered (and Juventus had the title sewn up) Inter sent their youth team to Turin in protest and were promptly thrashed 9-1. Omar Sivori grabbed six goals while the name on the score-sheet for Inter was that of Alessandro Mazzola.

Club Name:

Internazionale Football Club

Address:

Piazza Duse, 1, 20122 Milano

Founded: **1908**

Ground:

Stadio Comunale 'Giuseppe Meazza' (Capacity: 75,510)

Club Colours:

Black and Blue Striped Shirts, Black Shorts, Black Socks with Blue Trim (Away Colours: White Shirts, Black Shorts, Black Socks with Blue Trim)

Major Honours:

League Champions (1910, 1920, 1929-30, 1937-38, 1939-40, 1952-53, 1953-54, 1962-63, 1964-65, 1965-66, 1970-71, 1979-80, 1988-89), Italian Cup Winners (1939, 1978, 1982), European Cup Winners (1964, 1965), UEFA Cup Winners (1990-91), World Club Cup Winners (1964, 1965)

Left: Lothar Matthaus in Inter's blue and black.

Above: Inter coach Osvaldo Bagnoli.

GIUSEPPE MEAZZA

(b: 23/8/10 Milan – d: 22/8/79) Rated by many as the greatest Italian player ever, Meazza picked up two World Cup Winners medals in the 1930s. Initially a centre-forward but switched into the midfield by Italian national team coach Vittorio Pozzo, he was famed for his skill and coolness in front of goal. He scored 197 goals for Inter as well as 36 goals in 53 international appearances making him second only to Luigi Riva in terms of international goals.

GIACINTO FACCHETTI

(b: 18/6/42 Treviglio) One of the first attacking left-backs in

the game and captain of Italy on no fewer than 70 occasions. At over six feet tall, he retained incredible ball control and an eye for goal that was second to none among Italian defenders. Four championships, two European Cups and two World Club Cups testify to his success. Playing over 90 matches made him the most capped Italian international ever until the arrival of Dino Zoff.

ALESSANDRO MAZZOLA

(b: 8/11/42 Turin) A midfielder of frail appearance who started out as a striker, Mazzola was the heart of Helenio

Herrera's successful Inter team. He was gifted with great vision and goal-scoring ability and one of his strikes against Vasas Budapest in the 1966 European Cup even sent the opposition supporters wild. He was to grab 117 goals and make over 400 appearances for the club.

Opposite page: In 1964 and 1965 Inter won back to back European Cups.

The following season, however, the fruits of Herrera's work began to show. Having cast aside Argentine goalscorer Antonio Angelillo (accused of having an affair with a divorced singer), Herrera decided to build his team around the left-footed winger cum midfielder Mario Corso, ex-Barcelona star Luis Suarez, the tall left-back Giacinto Facchetti and that fragile -looking youngster, Sandro Mazzola.

By 1962, Inter had moved up to second place and in 1963 they took the title leaving Juventus and Milan trailing behind them. By now the defence had been perfected with Armando Picchi sitting in behind Aristide Guarneri and Tarcisio Burgnich and Facchetti guarding the flanks. Their league victory was secured by four points and sent them into the European Cup for the first time in their history.

While they progressed in Europe, Inter were also fighting one of the tightest league campaigns ever with Bologna in 1964. In the end, the title came down to a play-off in Rome between the two sides as the Italian league is never decided on goal-difference. Although Inter went into the match as favourites, they lost out 2-0 and failed to retain their title. Inter made their way, however, to the European Cup final in Vienna that year against the legendary Real Madrid. Sandro Mazzola struck twice as Inter won their first European Cup. This victory was made all the more sweet by the fact that it equalled the feat performed by Milan the season before. Soon after they took on Independiente and won, thereby becoming the first Italian team to win the World Club Cup.

In 1965, Inter pulled off an historic treble as they took the Serie A title, the European Cup, defeating Benfica in the final, and the World Club Cup, beating Independiente once again. They had achieved their aim of taking control of the domestic scene as well as making their mark on the world stage.

The last great victory for Herrera's side came in 1966 as they once again took the Italian title making it three in four years and making Inter only the second side to

wear the gold star on their shirts indicating ten title victories. Having added classy winger, Angelo Domenghini, to the side, Inter had improved their attack while retaining an immensely strong defence. They slipped up in Europe in 1967 when they went all the way to the final only to lose a one goal lead to Glasgow Celtic. It appeared that Helenio Herrera's magic was beginning to fade as his side were passed on the last day of the league season by Juventus. Indeed, it was soon time for Herrera to pack his bags and head off to Roma.

It was still the basis of Herrera's team that took Inter to their 11th title in 1971. One new star in their constellation was Roberto 'Bonimba' Boninsegna, signed from Cagliari. Still, the age of most of the players in the side meant that this was never likely to be the start of another glorious period for the side and so Inter had to wait another nine years before they returned to the top.

Between championships they took another *Coppa Italia* and began to rebuild their side after the retirement of the stars of the 1960s. Their title win of 1980 was made all the more enjoyable by the fact that Milan were relegated to the Serie B in the same season. The team was not one of the greatest ever to grace the Italian scene but in Gabriele Oriali they had one of the game's most tenacious midfielders and a partner of no little class in Evaristo Beccalossi. Up front, the inimitable Alessandro Altobelli struck 15 goals to help his side on their way.

A further nine year gap between titles produced another new group of players. Under the guidance of Giovanni Trapattoni, who had recently left Juventus, this 'record-breaking Inter' took the title with a record points total of 58 from 34 matches leaving Napoli 11 points adrift. The German duo of Matthaus and Brehme helped Inter to the top. A generous helping of Italian internationals in the shape of Walter Zenga, Giuseppe Bergomi, Riccardo Ferri, Nicola Berti and top goalscorer Aldo Serena also contributed to keeping the side so far ahead of their rivals.

Inter's most recent triumph came in the UEFA Cup in 1991. A memorable turnaround against Aston Villa in the second round, now with the German trio of Matthaus, Klinsmann and Brehme, set Inter up for an eventual final showdown with fellow Serie A stars Roma. It was to be Trapattoni's farewell to the club as he was lured back to Juventus and there followed a disastrous season when Corrado Orrico tried to convert Inter to a zonal defensive system. It took the arrival of Osvaldo Bagnoli and the departure of the all-too-powerful German trio to return Inter to the top of Italian football.

Since the arrival of Arrigo Sacchi as national team coach, Inter players have rarely featured in the national team with the exception of Alessandro Bianchi. In the World Cup of 1990, the likes of Zenga, Bergomi, Ferri and Aldo Serena all featured heavily in Italy's plans. However, by far the biggest contingent of Inter players came to the national team on the back of their 1960s triumphs and in 1966 against the USSR, Italy fielded no fewer than nine Inter players. Indeed, Mazzola,

Facchetti, Burgnich and Domenghini all had lengthy careers in Italy's colours with Facchetti captaining the side on no fewer than 70 occasions. Other Inter players to have played a significant part in the story of the Italian side were Giuseppe Meazza and Alessandro Altobelli both of whom collected more than 50 caps for their country and still stand among the *Azzurri*'s top goalscorers.

One of the major influences on the Inter side was, undoubtedly, Helenio Herrera. To have won so much in such a short spell of time is testimony to the coach's mastery of the game but also to the group of players at his command. For a short time, Inter were also influenced in terms of style and success by Herrera's natural heir, Giovanni Trapattoni, but with his return to Juventus, the Inter style evolved once more under Osvaldo Bagnoli.

The other major feature in both Inter's past and present has been their rivalry with Milan and Juventus. *'Superiori da sempre, mai stati in B!'* (Always superior, we've never been in Serie B!) proclaim banners at the Milan Derby, although history shows an advantage in favour of Milan. With eight major European titles and five World Club Cups between them, no city Derby can boast such an enormous array of silverware. In recent years the Inter camp has been incredibly keen to steal some of the limelight back from Milan. The other major rivalry, that with Juventus, has hardly faded although it is no longer the case that their meetings decide the whereabouts of the Serie A title. However, there is still a certain tradition and history which retains a special atmosphere at all meetings between the two clubs. Although Juventus hold the upper hand on the domestic scene, Inter have won some notable victories more than often enough to keep the Zebras on their toes and make their mark at the very top of Italian football.

LUIS SUAREZ

(b: 2/5/35 La Coruna, Spain) After eight years with Barcelona, some of them spent under the guidance of Helenio Herrera, Suarez joined Inter in 1961. His elegance and efficiency in the midfield were essential to his side and he was called 'the architect' by none other than Alfredo Di Stefano. He returned to Inter on two occasions as coach, most recently in the 1991-92 season.

LOTHAR MATTHAUS

(b: 21/3/61 Erlangen, Germany) When Inter looked to sign German players to rival Milan's Dutch stars, Matthaus was the first player they brought to the club. A stocky midfield general, he was the typical modern footballer with the ideal combination of power and skill that made him a tough opponent for anyone. He was the driving force in Inter's record-breaking championship of 1989 and helped take them to their 1991 UEFA Cup win.

WALTER ZENGA

(b: 28/4/60 Milan) One of the most extravagant and outspoken characters in the Italian game, but also a top class goalkeeper. Zenga has been Inter's first choice goalkeeper since 1983 and was also a regular international. He was voted best goalkeeper in the world following the Italia '90 World Cup, although many will never forget his failed attempt to stop Claudio Caniggia scoring an equalizer in the World Cup semi-final.

JUVENTUS

If there were an aristocracy in world football, then Juventus Football Club would definitely be part of it. With their Latin name (it means 'youth') and their tradition of an almost English style of fair play, they have always been the nearest thing to an upper-class team in Italian football. Success and the guidance of the FIAT owners, the Agnelli family, have had as much to do with this tradition as anything else.

'*La Vecchia Signora*' ('The Old Lady'), as the club is known, is by far the most successful on the domestic scene with 22 titles making them the only side in Italy to have two gold stars on their strips.

JUVENTUS

The side was born in 1897 in the most exclusive school in Turin, the Massimo d'Azeglio, along with members of U.S. Torinese. Before choosing the name of the side, other names were discussed such as Vis et Labor, Massimo d'Azeglio, Iris and even Viafort. In the end they chose 'Sport Club Juventus'. The original strips were pink with black bow-ties and the famous black and white shirts, (the Notts County colours), were only adopted in 1903 through the links between Turin and the Nottingham textile industry.

The original Juventus side had strong English and Swiss influences. The team also soon became the pacesetters in the Italian game when it came to standards of professionalism, fitness and tactics. It only took them until 1905 to win their first title. However, they were to wait a further 20 years for their next league title although work had begun to build a side that would profoundly affect the development of football in Italy.

One of the first signs of how serious Juventus were about getting to the top of Italian football came in 1923 when they caused the game's first transfer scandal. They signed Pro Vercelli's full-back, Virginio 'Viri' Rosetta, with the promise of a fixed wage for playing football. Initially, amateur football rebelled against this and Juventus were penalised for all the games in which Rosetta played during the 1923-24 season. However, when the official deal was made with Pro Vercelli and a transfer fee of 50,000 lire agreed upon, the player came to Juve.

The results of Juventus's investment, now that FIAT boss Edoardo Agnelli was in charge, were plain for all to see. In 1926, they added a second title to their trophy cabinet. Of that team, Giampiero Combi in goals, Rosetta in defence and Federico Munerati in attack would all go on to play in the Juventus side that would win five straight titles between 1930 and 1935.

Before that era began, Juventus made further additions to their side. In 1929, they spent 100,000 lire and promised a FIAT 509 to the Argentinian star left-winger Raimondo 'Mumo' Orsi. His fellow

countryman Renato Cesarini was also brought in. Other important additions were Giovanni Ferrari from Alessandria and Umberto Caligaris from Casale. The days of the provincial sides had ended, the time of *stranieri* and sky-high transfer fees had just begun.

In 1931 Juventus won their third title by four points from Roma. It was obvious that Juventus were well ahead of their rivals but, with the foresight of a truly great team, they did not take this situation for granted. Instead they invested once more on the transfer market by signing up another Argentinian in the imposing form of Luisito Monti, a giant centre-half. Luigi Bertolini, a quality midfielder from Alessandria, was signed as well.

Titles followed in 1932, 1933, 1934 and 1935 taking Juventus to the magical five-in-a-row that only city rivals Torino have managed to equal. In the meantime, Juve had added to their ranks Felice Borel, a precocious 18-year-old talent who burst onto the Serie A scene with 29 goals in 28 matches in the 1932-33 season. This strike rate of over a goal a game has never been bettered by any other Serie A top-scorer.

That 1932-33 championship was the peak of Juve's dominance before the war. They left Inter trailing eight points behind them and had an unbelievable goal difference of +60. They were victorious in 16 of their 17 home games. It was this side that provided the backbone for Italy's World Cup win of 1934 with Combi, Monti, Bertolini, Ferrari and Orsi all playing in the final. As well as bolstering the national team, Juventus helped secure the success of the new single league format which had only been adopted in 1929. Suddenly, all of Italy was involved in the championship and all of Italy could view this powerful Juventus line-up. Half of the country loved them, while the other half longed to beat them. It is a situation that has continued to the present day.

Of course, Juventus could not expect to have things their own way forever and soon Bologna and Inter had created strong sides of their own. These sides

Club Name:
Juventus Football Club
Address:
Piazza Crimea 7, 10147 Torino
Founded: **1897**
Ground:
Stadio Delle Alpi (Capacity: 70,012)
Club Colours:
Black and White Striped Shirts, White Shorts, White Socks with Black Trim (Away Colours: Yellow Shirts, Blue Shorts, Yellow Socks)
Major Honours:
League Champions (1904-05, 1925-26, 1930-31, 1931-32, 1932-33, 1933-34, 1934-35, 1949-50, 1951-52, 1957-58, 1959-60, 1960-61, 1966-67, 1971-72, 1972-73, 1974-75, 1976-77, 1977-78, 1980-81, 1981-82, 1983-84, 1985-86), Italian Cup Winners (1938, 1942, 1959, 1960, 1965, 1979, 1983, 1990), European Cup Winners (1984-85), Cup Winners' Cup Winners (1983-84), UEFA Cup Winners (1976-77, 1989-90, 1992-93), World Club Cup Winners (1985)

RAIMONDO ORSI

(b: 2/12/01 Buenos Aires, Argentina – d: 6/4/86) The first famous foreign signing of Italian football and one of the most successful. Although born in Argentina, Orsi was capped 35 times for Italy and picked up the World Cup with them. A forward of fragile appearance, he had incredible dribbling skills and a powerful shot with either foot. He was prepared to drop back into defence to help his side gain possession before joining the counter-attack and this commitment saw him score 77 goals in 177 matches for Juve.

Left: Roberto Baggio in exultant mood.

GIAMPIERO BONIPERTI

(b: 4/7/28 Barengo)
A blonde-haired striker of great style and strength, inextricably linked with the history of Juventus. As a player he amassed 444 matches for the team and scored 178 goals making him the most successful Juventus striker ever. As President, he oversaw the Trapattoni years in which Juventus won every single major European title as well as the World Club Cup.

OMAR SIVORI

(b: 2/10/35 San Nicolas, Argentina)
Controversial and extremely talented attacking midfielder with the nickname El Gran Zurdo ('The Great Left-footer'), Sivori spent eight years in Turin. Over 100 goals for Juventus testify to his quality and in 1959-60 he finished top of the goal-scorers table in Serie A. The following season he picked up the European Player of the Year award, ahead of Luis Suarez. By 1965, his successful spell with Juve came to an end but he still enjoyed three good seasons at Napoli before retiring from the game.

GAETANO SCIREA

(b: 25/5/53 Cernusco sul Naviglio – d: 3/9/89)
Signed from Atalanta at the age of 21, Scirea was quickly shifted from the midfield to the sweeper's position which he made his own both for club and country. An elegant, quiet player, he was a World Cup winner in 1982 and a national team regular for over a decade. In 1988, after his retirement, he was selected as assistant coach to Dino Zoff but died, tragically, in a car crash the following year.

dominated the remaining pre-war years and then the all-conquering Torino side came along. These were quiet years for Juventus as they picked up the *Coppa Italia* in 1937-38 but had to wait another 14 years for their next *Scudetto*.

There can be little doubt that the years of the *'Grande Torino'* team from 1942 to 1949 must have been the hardest of all for Juventus and their followers to swallow. The Superga air crash stopped Torino one short of Juventus's league wins total and, while Juventus went from strength to strength, Torino struggled to recover its position.

Juventus were the first side to benefit from Torino's tragic loss. Some would say that this was the strongest Juventus front-line of all time, featuring as it did Ermes Muccinelli, Rinaldo Martino, the Danes John Hansen and Karl Praest and a man whose fate would be linked to the club for more than 40 years, Giampiero Boniperti. They struck 100 goals in that season and went through their first 17 games without defeat.

Boniperti soon symbolized Juventus and all that they believed their own image to be. After the sometimes extravagant excesses of the South American imports of the 1930s, Boniperti gave solidity, consistency and class to the Juventus side. He helped to define the idea of a player being *da Juventus* (of Juventus). Although there were still to be exceptions, most notably Omar Sivori, the typical Juventus player was supposed to be skilful, strong, stylish and play the game to win but always play within the rules. Shows of temperament, or extravagant flair, were almost frowned upon.

In 1952, Juventus picked up the title again with another Dane, Karl Hansen having taken Martino's place in the side. Only Boniperti remained of the 1950 side, however, when the title came back to Turin in 1958. He had been joined in attack by two new foreigners in the shape of Omar Sivori and John Charles, the Welsh 'gentle giant'. Charles typified the courage and endeavour of the British game while Sivori was something of the Maradona of his day. He had the

ability to do almost anything with a football and in the three title-winning seasons he spent with Juventus (1958, 1960 and 1961) he scored 74 goals in just 90 games.

Although the 1960s started well with the two Sivori-inspired title wins, they were to prove to be one of the worst decades in Juve's history. In 1962, the side ended the season in 12th place – the worst finish in the club's history. In truth, it is a tribute to the high standards that Juventus had set themselves that the 1960s, with three titles and two *Coppa Italia* wins, should be considered a poor period.

By 1972, a new Juventus vintage was about to mature. The classy Roberto Bettega announced his arrival with ten goals in 14 games for the club while Franco Causio, Pietro Anastasi and Fabio Capello had already established themselves. In the midfield, Giuseppe 'Beppe' Furino was the motor of the team. Once again, as they had in the 1930s, Juventus invested in new talent to add to an already powerful squad. A young Dino Zoff was brought in from Napoli along with Jose Altafini the ageing Brazilian striker. Both helped secure the title the following season.

Allowing Lazio to interrupt their dominance briefly, the Bianconeri returned to the top in 1975, now with the central defensive partnership of Gaetano Scirea and Claudio Gentile in harness. They also added Marco Tardelli, Romeo Benetti, Roberto Boninsegna, Antonio Cabrini and Paolo Rossi. They won the title in 1977, 1978, 1981, 1982, 1984 and 1986 – all under the coaching of Giovanni Trapattoni. They also managed, after no fewer than 16 attempts to pick up their first European trophy, the UEFA Cup, in 1977.

The side went from strength to strength as the doors opened first to one foreign player (Liam Brady) then another two (Michel Platini and Zbigniew Boniek). Once again the European Cup eluded them as they were beaten in the disappointing 1983 final by SV Hamburg. However, the following year they were good enough to win the Cup Winners' Cup and completed a

MICHEL PLATINI

(b: 21/6/55 Joeuf, France) The most influential player in Juventus' recent history, he was signed from Saint Etienne in 1982. A midfield genius who could score more often than most strikers, Platini also had the ability to hit passes over 50 yards straight to his team-mates' feet, often, it seemed, without even looking up. He was a European champion with France in 1984 and European Player of the Year for three consecutive years from 1983 to 1985. He took the top scorers title in the Serie A on three separate occasions and won two league titles before retiring from the game in 1987.

glorious treble (they were the first club to win all three European trophies) by beating Liverpool in 1985 at Heysel on a night that will be remembered for anything but football.

By the time Juventus's last title came in 1986, however, the signs of decline were becoming more and more evident. World class players had retired and been replaced by lesser talents. Trapattoni moved on to Inter at the end of the season and in came Maradona and Berlusconi to change the face of Italian football once more.

The Juventus story is one which towers over all other sides in Italy. There are Juve clubs in every major city apart from Florence and support is particularly strong in Sicily, and Puglia in Southern Italy. One of the main reasons for this is that Juventus, particularly in the 1970s, drew the best players from Southern Italy like Franco Causio, and this meant that the large influx of workers from Sicily, Puglia and Calabria into Turin felt something in common with the team. The old Italian footballing proverb, *Tutta l'Italia contro la Juve* (All Italy against Juventus), is therefore only partly true. Since Juventus have won so much, many people wish to see them beaten.

Because of its hugely important role in Italian football, Juventus have always played a key role in making up the Italian national side. The peak of this phenomenon came during the 1978 World Cup when no fewer than nine Juventus players took to the pitch against Hungary, Argentina, Austria and Holland. This matched the feat of 45 years earlier when the same number of players had turned out to play Hungary. No side has supplied as many players to the national team and, between 1972 and 1986, no Italian team played without at least one *juventino* in the side – a period covering an incredible 130 games.

Those who have influenced Juventus Football Club have been many but the true giants in their history are clearly outstanding. FIAT bosses, the Agnelli family, have been linked to the club for over 60 years and were among the first to realize that business could finance a successful football team but also that a successful football team could be very helpful to business. The most successful Juventus coach was ex-Milan star Giovanni Trapattoni, in combination with president Giampiero Boniperti, who helped the club pick up every major trophy available and developed a style of counter-attacking play which was easily recognizable as his own. The recent experiment in 1990-91 with zonal defence under 'Gigi' Maifredi turned out to be a disaster. As one critic remarked, 'It's hard to tell what has more holes in it, the net behind Tacconi (Juve's goalkeeper of the day) or the defence in front of him.' Maifredi lasted just one season before Trapattoni was called back from Inter in 1991. Nowadays, however, Juventus do not rule the roost as they did in the 1970s.

PAOLO ROSSI

(b: 23/9/56 Prato) A quicksilver striker with a knack for being in the right position at the right time, Rossi came to Juventus after successful spells with Vicenza and Perugia. In 1978 he showed his talent in the World Cup in Argentina where he obtained the nickname Pablito which followed him to the 1982 World Cup in Spain where he finished as top scorer. In between times he was banned from the game for his part in the 1980 game-fixing scandal but he returned to win the European Player of the Year Award, two Serie A titles, the Italian Cup and the Cup Winners Cup with Juve.

Above: Giampiero Boniperti and coach Parola during pre-season training for the 1959/60 campaign.

LAZIO

The story of Società Sportiva Lazio is one which contains more disappointment, disaster and disgrace than success. Despite being formed 27 years before the fusion of clubs that created city rivals Roma, the *Biancocelesti* as they are named, because of their white and blue strips, have almost always had to live in the shadow of the *Giallorossi*, the yellow and red of Roma. They have fewer league titles, fewer Italian Cup wins, considerably less European experience and have contributed less to the Italian national side than their famous rivals. Most importantly of all, as far as their loyal fans from the area behind the goal known as the Curva Nord are concerned, the record in Derby matches still shows a fairly wide margin in favour of the club bearing the city's name (45 Roma wins to just 33 for Lazio).

LAZIO

Lazio take their name from the region in which Rome is situated and the early history of the club is indicative of the divide which existed, and to some extent still exists, between the north and south of Italy. While Lazio managed on no fewer than three occasions to reach the championship final (in 1912-13, in 1913-14 and in 1922-23) they were trounced by opponents from the north each time (Pro Vercelli, Casale and Genoa). They always performed very well against sides from their own region but found the gap of quality to be immense when they eventually came up against the giants of the day from Piedmont, Lombardy or Liguria. Lazio were not alone in suffering under the superior ability of such clubs; local rivals Alba (one of the sides that would become part of Roma) also suffered humiliating defeats at the hands of Juventus and Bologna. Indeed, it took 44 years from the first Italian championship in 1898 for the *Scudetto* to make the trip south when Roma picked up the title.

When the championship switched to a single league format in 1929, Lazio were one of only three teams from southern Italy to take part; the others were Roma and Napoli. The wise signing of Silvio Piola from Pro Vercelli helped the side to their best league finish prior to World War II when they managed to take second place just three points away from the powerful Bologna side in 1936-37.

Having come so close to taking the title, Lazio began to fade from contention in the ensuing championships and had to suffer watching Roma become the first side from the capital to take the league title in 1941-42. It was rumoured that Mussolini had taken more than a passing interest in seeing Roma take the championship title, although his children were known to be ardent Lazio supporters.

Following the War, Piola left Lazio but the club remained in Serie A without ever seriously threatening the dominance of Torino, Juventus, Inter and Milan. However, in 1957-58 they picked up their first trophy of note when they beat Fiorentina 1-0 to take the *Coppa Italia*, down to a goal by Prini. It could have

been the launch-pad for future success. Instead it signalled the start of one of the most unpredictable periods in Lazio's history.

In 1961 came their first ever relegation into Serie B. In a miserable championship Lazio won just five games and ended up bottom of the table, seven points adrift of the penultimate club. Throughout the 1960s and early 1970s, Lazio spent three spells in the lower division. It took the signing of another powerful striker, Giorgio Chinaglia, in 1969 to bring to an end this depressing cycle and open up the most successful – and controversial – period in the club's history.

In 1970, the club qualified for European competition for the first time in their history but their involvement in the UEFA Cup did not last long. In a bad-tempered tie with Arsenal, Lazio star Giuseppe Wilson allegedly stood on the feet of his namesake, Bob Wilson, and spat in his face. Many subsequent trips into Europe were to be just as short and unsavoury.

Having been relegated in the very same season they made their first European outing, Lazio needed someone to help push them back into Serie A. Chinaglia snatched 21 goals as Lazio pulled themselves out of Serie B in 1972. The following season, his side managed a very impressive third place finish just two points behind the Champions, Juventus. This was to be followed by their one and only championship victory in 1974. Chinaglia was once again at the heart of this as he struck no fewer than 24 times in 30 games. The key to Lazio's success was an impressive home record which included 12 victories in 15 matches and just one defeat – at the hands of Torino. The team had to be strong to fend off the challenge of dominant Juventus, and Chinaglia's eye-catching attacking partner, Renzo Garlaschelli, along with midfielder Mario Frustalupi were signed from Inter. Rather than being regarded as a victory for southern Italy, most Lazio fans thought of it as 'one up' on Roma who had yet to win the post-war Serie A. Indeed, the title was enjoyed all the more because of Roma's lowly eighth place finish and two 2-1 Derby victories during the league campaign.

Club Name:
Società Sportiva Lazio
Address:
Corso Italia 19/21, 00198 Roma
Founded: **1900**
Ground:
Stadio Olimpico (Capacity: 82,656)
Club Colours:
Light Blue Shirts with White Collars, White Shorts and White Socks (Away Strip: Yellow Shirts, Yellow Shorts and Yellow Socks)
Major Honours:
League Champions 1973-74, Italian Cup Winners 1958

Left: The ranks of the *Laziali* have recently been swelled by Gazza's band of English supporters.
Above: The Stadio Olimpico.

LAZIO

SILVIO PIOLA

(b: 29/9/13 Robbio Lomellina) When it comes to goal-scoring, Piola is without equal in Italian football history. He struck 290 Serie A goals, hitting the target 143 times for Lazio, twice finishing as top scorer in the division. His strength and power made him the perfect foil to the more thoughtful Giuseppe Meazza in the Italian national team. He scored a total of 30 goals in his 34 international matches, the last of which came in 1952 when the 39 year-old Piola captained Italy to a 1-1 draw with England. His six goals scored for Pro Vercelli against Fiorentina in 1933 remain a Serie A record.

GIORGIO CHINAGLIA

(b: 24/1/47 Carrara) Although he was born in Italy, Chinaglia spent his youth in South Wales where his immigrant parents lived. After a disappointing spell with Swansea Town, he decided to try his luck in Italy. Eventually, he was spotted by Lazio and signed for £140,000 in 1969. A temperamental striker of impressive physique, he earned 14 international caps and scored four goals – including one just four minutes into his debut as a substitute against Bulgaria. Nicknamed Il Gobbo – 'The Hunchback' – what Chinaglia lacked in finesse he made up for with commitment. He chose to end his career with the New York Cosmos playing alongside the likes of Pele and Cruyff.

However, the club was to be denied its one chance to take part in the European Cup because of crowd trouble the previous year in a UEFA Cup tie with Ipswich. Once again, a chance for glory had slipped from their grasp and the side began to lose its way as Chinaglia headed off to play for the New York Cosmos in 1976, lured by U.S. dollars and disappointed by his side's fourth from bottom finish just two years after the title had been won. Moreover, talented midfielder, Luciano Re Cecconi, lost his life in a freakish manner while playing a practical joke in 1977. Pretending to be a thief, he was shot dead by a bar-owner who failed to realize it was the Lazio star playing a prank. By the end of the 1970s, the historic Lazio team of 1974 was long gone.

As in the 1960s, Lazio soon suffered relegation problems and were sent into Serie B in 1980, along with Milan, for their part in the game-fixing scandal that rocked Italian football. As well as the club being penalized, many top players were implicated in the scandal and were forced out of the game for periods of up to five years. Among the Lazio stars who suffered this fate were Bruno Giordano, Lionello Manfredonia and Giuseppe Wilson – all of whom had been capped by Italy. Naturally, this meant that, as well as being relegated, Lazio were deprived of some of their best players and thus denied any chance – in the near future at least – of becoming a credible force in Italian football. Indeed, it took them another three seasons to clamber their way back into the top division of Italian football.

By 1983 the time was ripe for a take-over at the top of the club and up stepped Giorgio Chinaglia with a personal fortune which he had amassed playing in the United States. Unfortunately, the Welsh wizard failed to reproduce as club president what he had achieved as a player and his personal dream turned into a nightmare. The club slumped to two dreadful Serie A finishes, one of which cast them back into Serie B once again. By 1985 he had no choice but to sell the club on to top businessman Gian Marco Calleri in the hope that Calleri might improve their fortunes.

It took time and another three seasons out of the top flight for the new régime to have any effect and the 1986-87 season signalled the lowest moment in the club's history. Battling to avoid relegation to Serie C1, the Roman giants only managed to escape this ultimate embarrassment by beating the lowly Campobasso 1-0 in a play-off. To make matters worse, Roma were going through something of a 'purple' patch and spent long spells near the top of Italian football and played important European ties while Lazio fought for their lives in Serie B. Only the narrow escape from total oblivion in Serie C1 seemed to awaken the club to the reality of its dire situation.

From that moment on, the club's fortunes slowly began to improve. They returned to Serie A in 1988 benefiting from the Italian federation's decision to extend the top flight from 16 to 18 teams. Sensible foreign signings like those of Karl-Heinz Reidle, Thomas Doll, Aron Winter and the much-heralded Paul Gascoigne turned the team into a much more 'attacking' outfit, playing entertaining football. Italian stars like sharp-shooting left-footed Giuseppe Signori and the hard-working Diego Fuser have also added to the quality of the team. Moreover, Lazio took a large section of the Italian Under 21 team which won the European Championship when they signed Dario Marcolin, Mauro Bonomi and the impressive left-back Giuseppe Favalli, all from Cremonese. The arrival of banker Sergio Cragnotti in February 1992 also gave the club the sort of financial backing that makes hopes of regularly winning a place in Europe, finishing ahead of Roma and, above all, taking another title seem a little more feasible.

The assured guidance of Dino Zoff, a World Cup winner with Italy and of many major honours with Juventus, has also been an important factor in Lazio's renaissance. As a coach Zoff took Juventus to Italian Cup and UEFA Cup triumph in the same season before he was discarded to make way for disastrous flop Gigi Maifredi. Many felt that the chain-smoking coach had achieved miracles with a mediocre group of players at the Turin club but he was still forced to pack his bags

ACQUISTATE PRODOTTI ITALIA LIA

DIEGO FUSER

(b: 11/11/68 Venaria)
At just 25 years of age
Fuser is already a very
well travelled player
having spent the early
part of his career at
Torino before struggling to get into the team at
Milan. A good season at Fiorentina saw him
finish as the club's top scorer and confirm his
qualities as an energetic midfielder with good
speed and a thunderous shot. He returned to
Milan where he once again failed to fit in and
was glad to move on to Lazio. The move did him
good as a guaranteed first team place gave him
the chance to show off his talents and make his
way into the Italian national team.

and head to Rome. Although Zoff often bore the brunt of the fans' anger for his supposed lack of attacking ambition, he has quickly developed into an accomplished coach, allowing his players to use their attacking imagination while attempting to improve the defensive capabilities of a side which has often given away too many goals. Important, but underrated, players for his side have been midfield anchorman, Aron Winter, and the utility player Roberto Bacci who provide consistency and allow Zoff to shuffle the team around them. Surprisingly, for such a great goalkeeper, Zoff has failed to inspire young Valerio Fiori and this has meant the very experienced Fernando Orsi getting regular appearances in goal.

The improvement in the fortunes of the club has also led to international recognition for some Lazio players, most notably Diego Fuser and Giuseppe Signori. This is a major achievement for the team as well as the individual players since Lazio has rarely contributed very heavily to the Italian national team line-up. The club record for international caps still dates back to the 1930s when Silvio Piola played 30 times for the *Azzurri* while with the club. Nobody since has even come close. The championship winning side of 1974 only catapulted Chinaglia, Re Cecconi and Giuseppe Wilson into the full international scene. However, of the three, only Chinaglia was to win more than a handful of caps.

More recently, centre-forward Bruno Giordano picked up 12 caps during his ten-year stint at the club before going on to help Napoli win their first ever league title. Another long-time Lazio servant, Lionello Manfredonia, also gained international recognition during his time with the club before being forced to retire through poor health.

For Lazio supporters such as the Eagles Supporters and the *Gruppo Rock Sconvolti* who are part of Lazio's most committed followers and also prone to arguments among themselves, recent seasons have given them a little more to shout about. The signing of Paul Gascoigne has seen a sudden spread of Union Jacks among the *Laziali* and has also added fuel to arguments between Roma and Lazio faithful. For one half of the city he is the new Maradona while the other half views him as the greatest waste of money in the history of football. Whatever the truth may be, signings like these have increased Lazio's prestige (both in Italy and abroad) and have helped them to their first league finish ahead of Roma in 14 years. This alone is something for the fans to celebrate after so many dark days.

PAUL GASCOIGNE

(b: 27/5/67 Gateshead,
England) Having played
for Newcastle and
Tottenham Hotspur and
impressed in the 1990
World Cup in Italy,
Lazio moved in for the Geordie talent in 1991.
However, a season of injury and operations put
the transfer on ice and it was not until the
summer of 1992, after strenuous physical tests,
that the player arrived in Rome. He immediately
struck up a rapport with the home fans by
scoring in the Derby against Roma and, despite
the odd moment of off-the-field misbehaviour he
has gone a long way towards proving that he has
found in Italy the maturity needed to succeed.

Above: Lazio line up for a 1934 clash with Milan, Silvio Piola far right.

LECCE

In June, 1993, Lecce were promoted to Serie A for only the third time in their 85-year history. At the corresponding stage the previous year, the inhabitants from the Baroque city in the south-east of the country breathed a sigh of relief when their club escaped relegation to Serie C on the very last day of the season. This unfashionable club, which has long lived in the shadow of their neighbours, Bari, hope to sustain a prolonged run in Italy's premier division.

LECCE

The club was formed on 15 March 1908 and their activities extended to cycling and athletics, hence the name Sporting Club Lecce. Their early years were spent in the regional league, *Campionato Pugliese*, where they played other local teams with colourful titles such as Avanguardia, Veloce, Gladiator, and Juventus (not the famous Old Lady from Turin). On 16 September 1927, Lecce merged with two of these sides, Gladiator and Juventus, to form Lecce Unione Sportiva. They even adopted Juve's famed black and white striped jerseys. This changed a year later to the yellow and red colours the players wear today.

The new club colours appeared to have a propitious effect on the club when they secured their first promotion to Serie B in 1929, after a play-off with Taranto, gaining the title *Campioni del Sud* in the process. Lecce, known as *Salentini* due to the city's position in the Salento region in Southern Apulia, then spent the next 25 years alternating between the second and third divisions. In 1955, Lecce sank to the lowest point in their history, when they found themselves in the semi-professional ranks, IV Serie. They almost managed to crawl out of the division in their second season, but lost to the Sicilian side, Marsala, over two games in what used to be the semi-final of the league competition. Lecce lost 12-3 on aggregate, which included a club record 9-1 defeat in Sicily. In 1958, the club eventually gained promotion to Serie C, where they remained until 1976.

Franco Jurlano, a local surveyor, took over Lecce's presidency following the club's promotion to Serie B and, with his right-hand man Domenico Cataldo, helped Lecce establish their most successful period. After seven years, the pair finally managed to assemble a side worthy of Italy's top division. However, Cremonese pipped Lecce to the last promotion place in 1984, before the *Salentini*, coached by Eugenio Fascetti, moved up to Serie A the following season alongside Pisa and their bitter rivals, Bari. Fascetti later became the master at steering clubs from Serie B into the top flight, accomplishing this feat with Lazio, Torino, and Verona in the space of four years.

Lecce signed the Argentinian duo, Juan Barbas from the Spaniards Real Saragozza and Pedro Pasculli from Argentinos Juniors, but they failed to alter the outcome of the club's unhappy first season in Serie A. Lecce finished in bottom place, but at least drew consolation from Bari's own misfortune as they accompanied Lecce back into the second division. The *Salentini* bounced back almost immediately, defeating Cremonese in a three-way play-off, before losing to Cesena. The side, now led by Carlo Mazzone, achieved its second promotion in 1988.

By this time, the club had a fine blend of youth and experience within its ranks. Lecce's two most promising youngsters, the industrious midfielder Antonio Conte and defender Luigi Garzya played prominent roles in the club's commendable ninth place finish the next season, as did their Argentinian imports, along with Pietro Paolo Virdis, the veteran striker signed from Milan. Lecce were heading for Serie B again in 1990 and only just avoided relegation by obtaining one more point than Udinese in 15th place.

At the start of the 90/91 season Carlo Mazzone moved to pastures new, at Pescara. Consequently, the former Polish international, Zbigniew Boniek, was handed the unenviable task of steering the side away from almost certain relegation – and failed. The drop to Serie B often compels a provincial side to sell their most prized players in order to compensate for the loss of revenue. Antonio Conte and Luigi Garzya were traded in multi-million pound transfers to Juventus and Roma respectively. Lecce suffered

Club Name:

Lecce Unione Sportiva

Address:

Via Ugo Foscolo 89, 73100 Lecce

Founded: **1908**

Ground:

Stadio Via Del Mare (Capacity: 55,000)

Club Colours:

Yellow and Red Striped Shirts, Red Shorts, Yellow Socks (Away Colours: White Shirts, White Shorts, White Socks)

Left: Lecce's Giampaolo Ceramicola rises to the challenge of Serie A promotion.
Below: Coach Bruno Bolchi.

PIETRO PAOLO VIRDIS

(b: 26/6/57 Sassari, Sardinia)

The prolific marksman ended his memorable 18-year career with Lecce, his sixth club. Earlier in his career, Virdis won two league titles with Juventus and another with Milan in 1988. The previous year, the Sardinian topped Serie A's scorers charts with 17 goals. Five years in Milan culminated in a move to south-east Italy where he formed a fearsome partnership with the Argentine, Pedro Pasculli.

ANTONIO CONTE

(b: 31/7/69 Lecce)

Conte came through Lecce's youth ranks and made his league debut in a Serie A fixture in 1986, aged 16 (the result: Lecce-Pisa 1-1). One of Italy's finest midfield prospects went on to make 89 appearances in the club's yellow and red colours and won an international cap at Under 21 level. In November 1991, Conte was sold to Juventus for a club record £3 million.

as a result and were spared the further humiliation of relegation to Serie C on the last day of the 91/92 season. During the campaign, Albertino Bigon, the coach who led Napoli to their second *Scudetto* in 1990, was at first sacked and replaced by Aldo Sensibile and then reinstated in time to save the club from plunging into the third division.

In the summer of 1992, President Jurlano called on the services of Bruno Bolchi to marshall his troops, but his appointment met opposition from a section of home fans: Bolchi was once the coach of rivals Bari. Even though Lecce were heading for their third promotion to Serie A, Bolchi was constantly reproached by the fans. The Milanese coach persevered and by defeating Lucchese on the last day of the season, his players captured joint third spot with Piacenza.

'We were dragged along by our positive results,' said Bolchi. 'We surprised everyone, even ourselves. Eventually, our achievement caused even those who couldn't forget my past with Bari to celebrate.'

So, Lecce returned to Serie A for a third time in their long history, granting their long-suffering fans a further chance to dream of a prosperous future. Southern Italy has waited a long time for another successful side. Lecce could conceivably preserve their standing in Serie A, should their fans fill the club's vast Stadio Via Del Mare, which holds 55,000 spectators. The gate receipts alone from regular capacity crowds would generate the money necessary to mount a serious challenge on Serie A's aristocrats.

Everyone hates to see their sporting heroes of yesteryear in decline, and there can be few more poignant stories in football than those of the great teams from the past now floundering about in the lower reaches of the game.

The most recent additions to this group of sides are Fiorentina, from Florence, relegated in 1993 for the first time in 55 years. With two championship wins and four Italian Cups, they could justifiably claim to be one of the top half dozen teams in the history of Italian football. However, the sacking of Gigi Radice in the 1992-93 Serie A season sent them bombing down the table and even a 6-2 drubbing of Foggia was not enough to save them from their fate on the final day of the season.

There are several other past championship winners who have now sunk to the bottom end of the game. Most notable among these is Bologna, a side which helped to shape the inter-war years of Italian football, taking six titles between 1924 and 1941 and scoring one final league triumph in 1964 after a famous play-off with Inter. The side had never been out of Serie A until their decline resulted in relegation to Serie B in 1982. Although they returned for three seasons in the late 1980s, a miserable 1990-91 campaign put them back into Serie B. Worse followed as they then plummeted towards the bottom of Serie B in 1993 rather than returning to the top flight.

the sleeping giants

The side from Emilia-Romagna are not alone in their plight. Another seven-championship winning side is in an even worse predicament down in the Italian equivalent of the Vauxhall Conference. Pro Vercelli, who took their seven titles in the space of just 11 seasons between 1908 and 1922, are now a mid-table team in the Girone A, Group A, of the Italian fifth division. Once they battled with the likes of Juventus, Milan and Inter at the very highest reaches of the game, whereas now they must struggle against the like of Corsico and Pinerolo in front of meagre crowds. In truth, their fate was never likely to be much different as soon as the law of the lira began to push provincial clubs like Vercelli to the sidelines of Italian football.

Between these two extremes are many sides who have, at one time or another, stood at the top of Italian football. Vicenza, a side which has known considerable success, have struggled in the third division for years before winning promotion back to Serie B in 1993. Throughout the late 1950s, 1960s and early 1970s, the side from the Veneto region were permanent fixtures in the Serie A, managing some more than respectable finishes. After a short spell in Serie B, Lanerossi Vicenza, their full title at the time, shot back into Serie A thanks to the goals of Paolo Rossi, even managing an astonishing second place finish behind Juventus in 1978. However, Rossi moved on and the side nose-dived back into obscurity.

Another side attaining a similar moment of glory were the famous Perugia side of 1979, which actually went the whole season without defeat but still finished their Serie A season as runners-up to Milan. It was a memorable performance but the side could not maintain the same standards and have only recently returned to Serie B. Facing a similar plight one division further down are Alessandria, whose famous grey shirts struck fear into the heart of many sides throughout Italy during the 1920s and early 1930s. The club, which is over 80 years old, returned briefly to Serie A in 1950s before selling the promising youngster, Gianni Rivera, to Milan. After their relegation to Serie B in 1960, the club has never returned to the Serie A.

A division further down sit Casale, who took their one and only title in 1914. Their fate proved to be not dissimilar to that of Pro Vercelli, as they could not compete with the new financial power which arrived in the game in the 1930s. They are now famous, above all, for their oddly-designed strips which are all black apart from a large white star on the front. It will be some time before they shine once more in the first division.

Above: Memories of glories past: the team which won the 1966 *Coppa Italia* for Fiorentina.

MILAN

The famous red and black stripes of Milan have, in recent years, come to dominate Italian football to a far greater extent than any other Italian side. With the financial backing of media magnate, Silvio Berlusconi, Milan have become the embodiment of the modern game in both its good and bad respects. Playing entertaining football where physical strength and ball skills are combined to perfection they have spent immense sums of money to guarantee that they have the best players in the world and, just as importantly, to ensure that everybody else does not.

MILAN

Milan Cricket and Football Club came into being in 1899. The side initially had strong English and Swiss influences in its make-up and this led them to initial success in 1901 as they won their first championship. In 1906 and 1907 they once again took the title and gave themselves a place as one of the strongest sides in the early days of Italian football.

These early successes failed to set up a pattern for Milan as they began to drift out of contention for major honours. It was not until 1951 that the *Rossoneri* (red and blacks) returned to the very top of Italian football. Immediately following World War II, Scandinavian football went through something of a boom in popularity in Italy and Milan showed the importance of these *stranieri* as their much touted Swedish trio of Gunnar Gren, Gunnar Nordahl and Nils Liedholm, abbreviated to Gre-No-Li, helped them lift the title.

Having tasted success once again, Milan were not about to let it go and they turned in another outstanding performance in the 1954-55 season to take the title. Now Juan Alberto Schiaffino had arrived from Uruguay and the side became Italy's first representatives in the European Cup. It was to be the start of a long love-affair with European competition.

In 1957, a third post-war title came along and a youngster named Maldini appeared in the defence. It was Cesare Maldini who would play several seasons for the club and would later see his son, Paolo, follow in his footsteps. The following season they came even closer to realizing their European dream as they made their way to the final only to lose out to Real Madrid. A goal in the second half of extra time from Gento sunk their hopes.

Having met with European failure, Milan returned to domestic success in 1959 making themselves the most successful post-war side of the time, along with Torino. New stars in the side were José Altafini and the Argentinian Grillo. European glory was at last achieved in 1963, having taken the Serie A title once more in

1962. A couple of years previously, a player had been bought from Alessandria who would come to be a symbol for the club for almost 20 years. Gianni Rivera was an integral part of Milan's, and Italy's, first European Cup triumph at the age of just 19. Having gone a goal behind in the Wembley final against Benfica, Milan responded through their foreign striker Altafini, who scored both the goals that gave Milan their European triumph.

Having achieved this important landmark, it seemed that Milan stopped to take stock and found themselves overtaken by Inter, who took two European titles and two World Club Cups in the meantime. As if spurred into action, Milan won the Italian Cup in 1967 and picked up the Cup Winners' Cup and the Serie A title the following season. As if this were not enough, they headed off into the European Cup and won it in 1969 (this time beating Cruyff's Ajax 4-1 in the final) and followed it with triumph in the World Club Cup.

By the 1970s, it seemed that Milan's championship winning days were over as they, and everyone else, made way for Juventus. A couple of Italian Cups and a notable Cup Winners' Cup win over Leeds looked like being the only reward for the *Rossoneri* in the decade until, in 1979, they pulled off another *Scudetto* in Rivera's last year in football. It was Milan's tenth title, making them the third club in Italy to obtain the gold star for their shirts.

Rivera's departure preceded one of the darkest periods in Milan's history in the early 1980s. Their match at home to Lazio in the 1979-80 season was put under the microscope as they were accused of taking part in match rigging. Club president Felice Colombo was arrested on 23 March, 1980, and after lengthy discussions, accusations and trials, it was decided that Milan would be punished with relegation to Serie B. Colombo was banned from the game for life while players Albertosi and Morini also received lengthy suspensions from the game which would effectively end their careers. It was a black mark against the club but one which they worked hard to erase.

Club Name:

Milan Associazione Calcio

Address:

Via Turati 3, 20121 Milano

Founded: **1899**

Ground:

Stadio Comunale 'Giuseppe Meazza'
(Capacity: 76,398)

Club Colours:

Red and Black Striped Shirts, White
Shorts, White Socks (Away Colours:
White Shirts, White Shorts, White Socks)

Major Honours:

League Champions (1901, 1906, 1907,
1950-51, 1954-55, 1956-57, 1958-59, 1961-
62, 1967-68, 1978-79, 1987-88, 1991-92,
1992-93), Italian Cup Winners (1967,
1972, 1973, 1977), European Cup Winners
(1962-63, 1968-69, 1988-89, 1989-90), Cup
Winners' Cup Winners (1968, 1973),
World Club Cup Winners (1969, 1989,
1990)

ALBERTO SCHIAFFINO

(b: 29/7/25 Montevideo, Uruguay) Born in Uruguay of Italian origin, Schiaffino arrived in Italy when he was 29 years old. The historic goal which helped Uruguay beat Brazil in the 1950 World Cup final made him famous around the world and by 1954 he came to Italy. His attacking play helped Milan to three Serie A titles, despite the reputation for being a trouble maker which earned him the nickname Pepe ('Pepper'). After five memorable years at the club he finished his playing days at Roma before returning to Uruguay.

Left: Supporters of the Rossoneri celebrate yet another *Scudetto* in front of Milan Cathedral.

GUNNAR NORDAHL

(b: 19/10/21 Hornfors, Sweden) Weighing in at around 13 stones and six feet tall, the giant Swede was one of the most powerful and prolific centre-forwards in the Italian game. After helping Sweden take the Olympic football title in 1948, Nordahl was snapped up by Milan as much of the rest of that side came to Italy. He finished 5 times as the top scorer in Serie A and his total of 35 goals in 1950 is still a record for an 18 team Serie A. His goal-tally of 210 goals for Milan is likely to remain unsurpassed for several years to come.

NILS LIEDHOLM

(b: 8/10/22 Waldemarkvik, Sweden) Liedholm joined his countryman Nordahl at Milan in 1949 along with another Swede, Gunnar Gren. He proved an outstanding playmaker and tactical asset to the side as well as possessing a powerful long-range shot. He played a part in no fewer than four title wins for the club over his 12 years with them. As a coach he helped Milan take their tenth title in 1979 before moving on to take Roma to the same heights in 1983.

JOSE ALTAFINI

(b: 24/7/38 Piracicaba, Brazil) This swift Brazilian striker arrived in Italy in 1959 and immediately helped Milan take the Serie A title. In his seven years with the club, he played an important part in their European Cup win of 1963. He was sold by Milan to Napoli where he played a further seven years and then went to Juventus where he enjoyed a fine spell despite his 34 years.

Having suffered the double indignity of being relegated for their misdemeanours and watching Inter win the title, Milan were forced to set about winning their way back into the Serie A. To this end, Milan won the Serie B title immediately in one of the toughest competitions of recent years. The quality of the opposition was high as Genoa, Lazio, Sampdoria and Verona were all in the second division at the time. Fifteen goals from forward Roberto Antonelli helped the club make their return. In the end, Milan finished two points clear of Genoa and Cesena who joined them on their happy return to the top level.

However, if the relegation of 1980 had more to do with events off the pitch than on it, the same could not be said for the disastrous season of 1981-82. Milan managed just seven wins in 30 games and suffered no fewer than 13 defeats. They finished one point adrift of Genoa and Cagliari and possible salvation. Undoubtedly this was the worst season ever in the history of the club.

Once again Milan showed their character by rising to the challenge of Serie B and taking the title. They won by a clear eight points from Lazio who had been languishing in the lower division since their relegation with Milan three seasons before. Midfield star Alberigo Evani played a large part in winning promotion along with the goalscoring talents of the Scottish striker Joe Jordan.

Having twice suffered such disappointment, Milan returned to the top with a great desire to remain there. The 1983-84 season proved to be one of re-adjustment to the difficulties of the top flight. However, moves were afoot to try to rebuild Milan and along came Ray Wilkins and Mark Hateley as part of this process. Milan's league performances began to improve as new President Farina, a business tycoon, seemed set to improve the club's fortunes.

Unfortunately for the club, it turned out that Farina had his own best interests, rather than those of the club, at heart. Suddenly he dashed off to Africa leaving the club with large debts and a not particularly impressive mid-table sort of team. The club was lurching towards another dark period unless someone could be found to pay off their debts and then invest heavily in bringing top quality players to the club. It was at this point that television millionaire Silvio Berlusconi took over as president of Milan.

In his first season in overall control of the club, in 1986-87, Berlusconi saw his side make significant progress and even qualify for the UEFA Cup. He placed his faith in the attack-minded coach, Arrigo Sacchi. In the meantime, Berlusconi began to profess his belief in the concept which he called the *panchina lunga* (long bench) which would effectively give the coach two teams from which to choose.

By 1988, the fruits of Sacchi's work were beginning to be seen. Having discarded the English duo of Hateley and Wilkins, in came the Dutchmen Ruud Gullit and Marco Van Basten. Veteran Pietro Virdis finished as the side's top-scorer with just 11 goals. Milan proved strong enough to overhaul Maradona's Napoli and take the Serie A title by three points. In just two seasons, the door had been opened to Berlusconi's dreams of European triumphs.

Although the following domestic campaign was dominated by Inter, Sacchi's side moved into Europe, now strengthened by the arrival of a third Dutch import in the shape of Frank Rijkaard. Milan crushed Real Madrid 5-0 in the San Siro, playing some breathtaking football. This sent a warning to all their rivals and it was only underlined by the 4-0 destruction of Steau Bucharest in the final. They followed their European triumph with the World Club Cup and repeated this formidable double in 1990. However, the league title eluded them once again as they were denied by the quality of Maradona's Napoli team – by now arch-rivals to Berlusconi's Milan.

The 1990-91 season proved to be the end of Arrigo Sacchi's reign at the club as they finished second in the league behind Sampdoria. The final crack came in the

European Cup Quarter-Final with Marseille. After drawing 1-1 at home, Milan were trailing 1-0 in Marseille with a few minutes of the match remaining when a small section of the floodlights failed. The team were pulled off the pitch and a game that looked likely to end in defeat ended in farce and disgrace. The club were banned from Europe for a year and Arrigo Sacchi moved on to take up the position of national team coach.

His replacement was the inexperienced Fabio Capello who many dismissed as merely a puppet for Berlusconi. However, the only undefeated league championship win in the history of the Serie A gave immense credibility to the man. Not content with dominating the proceedings, Milan added to their array of talent with Stefano Eranio from Genoa, Fernando De Napoli from Napoli, the controversial signing of Gianluigi Lentini, and three more foreigners, Jean-Pierre Papin, Dejan Savicevic and Zvonimir Boban.

Club success has pushed current Milan players into the Italian national team in large numbers. They are part of a long tradition within the club of supplying players to the national team – Gianni Rivera and Franco Baresi have both had over 50 caps for their country. Roberto

Donadoni and Paolo Maldini have also had considerable international experience, with the latter more than likely to continue for many years to come.

Early coaches such as Gipo Viani and Nereo Rocco did much to encourage Milan's attractive side of play. Moreover, it is scarcely imaginable that either of the other two giants of Italian football, Juventus and Inter, would have given 501 appearances to such a talented but variable player as Gianni Rivera. This style has continued to the present day where Arrigo Sacchi and Fabio Capello have both encouraged attacking play. Sometimes, they reasoned, the way you play the game can be as important as the results you achieve.

Of course, not everyone in Italy loves Milan and they find their biggest rivals in the other half of Lombardy's power-struggle, Internazionale. Derby games are always tense affairs with Milan holding a slight edge over their neighbours. Another side which has, in recent seasons, emerged as a bitter rival to Milan is Napoli. To some extent this can be seen as part of the more widespread phenomenon of racism towards Napoli fans shown around the grounds of Northern Italy where banners like 'Benvenuti in Italia' (Welcome to Italy) are all too common. However, the roots of the rivalry are actually in the football field. In the late 1980s the title was regularly fought over by Napoli and Milan and each stole titles from the other in the closing games of the season. Moreover, they both contained the two biggest characters in the game at the time in the shape of Diego Maradona and Silvio Berlusconi. It almost seemed at times like a battle between Berlusconi's millions and the Argentinian's outrageous talent. The result, for several seasons, was a draw but with Maradona gone, Berlusconi and his Milan side await their next rivals.

GIOVANNI TRAPATTONI

(b: 17/3/39 Cusano Milanino) Although as a coach his career has been linked to Juventus, Trapattoni played 12 seasons for Milan as an effective and efficient midfielder. In this time he saw his side win 2 league titles as well as two European Cups, the Cup Winners' Cup and the World Club Cup. Capped 17 times by Italy he was, to some extent, fortunate to see injury exclude him from playing in the 1962 World Cup in Chile. As a coach, he also began his career with Milan in the mid-1970s but it was his move to Juventus, and the victories that he won there, that ensured his fame.

GIANNI RIVERA

(b: 18/8/43 Alessandria) In Italy players who come to symbolize a particular club are called Bandiere (Flags), and Gianni Rivera fulfilled this role for Milan. After a short spell with Alessandria he was signed by Milan and picked up his first Serie A title at the age of just 19 in 1962. He represented Milan for over 15 years and his stylish midfield play made him undoubtedly the most skilful Italian player of the day. His 60 international caps could have been even more had not competition with the exceptional Sandro Mazzola sometimes kept him out of the side.

Above: Jubilant *tifosi* chair the Milan team from the pitch after winning the 1961/62 championship.

NAPOLI

Among the largest Italian cities only one, Naples has just one football team. This means that the loyalties of the city are not divided but rather concentrated and intensified by competition with the more economically 'advantaged' sides of the north. With a population of almost three million, it seems incredible that Napoli had to wait over 80 years since their formation for the arrival of their first Serie A title. Indeed, up until that point they had known much more failure than success and were constantly second best even on the occasions when they did mount a serious challenge to the top teams. The *Azzurri* (the blues, just like the Italian national team) have probably the largest away support in Italy since so many Neapolitans have had to move to Northern Italy in search of work. At home, few clubs have such a large following and none have a more passionate set of supporters.

NAPOLI

Naples, as the club were originally known, were formed in 1904 by the English maritime worker, William Poths. The original formation was mostly made up of English, Scots, Danes and Germans living and working in Italy at the time. It was another eight years before the side took part in the Italian championship and by that time it had spawned the rival side Internazionale Napoli. In truth neither side achieved much success when they began to play the sides from their own region. On the occasions when they progressed far enough in competition to meet Lazio, there were always physical games as the two sides fought for the right to be the best in Southern Italy. Roma were not yet on the scene and therefore did not enter into the reckoning.

By 1922, both sides realized the senselessness of carrying on as separate entities since neither was particularly competitive. So they merged to become Internaples and the famous blue shirts were born. In 1926, the club had its most successful season to date as it lost out in the Southern division play-off to Alba of Rome. Later the same year, the name of Napoli was taken on and the club as it is now known was founded.

Things started badly for the club as Italian football moved towards a national competition in the 1926-27 season. Napoli managed just one draw (with Brescia) in the whole season and conceded 61 goals while scoring just seven. Just when it seemed that they were sure to get relegated, the Italian federation stepped in to extend the league from ten to eleven sides and keep Napoli in the first division. Their fate was the same in the following season and, indeed, the season after that.

When the Italian league finally formed one national first division in 1929, Napoli were thus one of only three Southern sides to take part (Lazio and Roma were the others) and they proved the most successful with a fifth place finish. Much of the credit must go to their coach, the ex-Arsenal player Willie Garbutt, one of the most respected coaches of the day. They continued this promising form into the early 1930s with two consecutive third place finishes behind the all-conquering Juventus side of the day but soon after their level of competitiveness began to slip. The side slid further and further towards the danger zone and in 1942 they were relegated for the first time.

It was not to be the last time that the side would fall into the lower division. In fact, there were three more terms in the Serie B before Napoli eventually emerged, never to return, in 1965. These were not kind years to the Neapolitans and 1948 was to prove to be one of the worst in their history. Having had their home pitch banned on no fewer than three instances because of their fans' misbehaviour, Napoli were accused of bribery in their 1-0 away win over Bologna. The accusations were upheld and Napoli were placed in last position and sentenced once more to relegation.

Having fought for two seasons to return to the top under the influential Eraldo Monzeglio, Napoli returned to Serie A in 1950. There then began a serious attempt to rebuild the side and make it competitive at the highest level. Players of the calibre of Italian international striker, Amedeo Amadei, were brought to the club along with Swedish star, Hans Jeppson, and Argentinian maestro, Bruno Pesaola, who was to play 240 times for the club. This side kept Napoli in the top half dozen teams in Italy.

However, by the mid-1950s many of Napoli's players were past their best and this began to show in league performances. The arrival of Luis de Menezes, better known as Vinicio, was not the success that was hoped for and the 1955-56 season saw Napoli on the brink of relegation. In one particularly memorable fixture, the *Azzurri* took on Bologna and gained a 3-0 lead after going into half-time with the score at 0-0. Bologna, however, refused to lie down and pulled back two goals. Then, two minutes into injury time, referee Maurelli pointed to the penalty spot and granted Bologna an equalizer. It was the cue for a pitch invasion which had to be broken up with tear gas and a large police presence. With 140 injured and the stadium badly damaged, Napoli had shown just how passionately they felt about football.

Club Name:

Società Sportiva Calcio Napoli

Address:

Piazza dei Martiri 30, 80121 Napoli

Founded: **1926**

Ground:

Stadio San Paolo (Capacity: 82,126)

Club Colours:

Light Blue Shirts, White Shorts, Light Blue Socks (Away Colours: Red Shirts, White Shorts, Red Socks)

Major Honours:

League Champions (1986-87, 1989-90), Italian Cup Winners (1962, 1976, 1987), UEFA Cup Winners (1988-89)

Left: Diego Maradona's arrival at Napoli galvanized the club into winning its first ever Serie A title in 1987. In the process he became something of a god to Neapolitan fans.

NAPOLI

ANTONIO JULIANO

(b: 1/1/43 Naples) Sixteen seasons with the club, which Juliano recalls as 'the most beautiful years of my life', make him one of Napoli's most loyal servants. A midfield player of quality he was also captain of Napoli in his closing seasons with the club. He became one of the few Napoli players of the 1960s and 1970s to be a regular in the national team. Despite being courted by larger clubs, most notably Inter Milan, he remained loyal to Napoli before ending his career with Bologna after refusing to take a post training the Napoli youth team.

GIUSEPPE BRUSCOLOTTI

(b 30/5/51 Sassano) Few would have thought when this young right-back made his debut for Napoli against Ternana in 1972 that his career would stretch all the way to the club's first championship win in 1987. His 387 Serie A appearances for the club remain a record (only Antonio Juliano has more appearances in all competitions). Despite his excellent defensive qualities he never made the Italian national team but this had much to do with the difficulty of displacing the likes of Claudio Gentile and, later, Giuseppe Bergomi.

In contrast, the 1958 season saw Napoli in the headlines for more sporting reasons. After six games the Neapolitans were top of the league and, although they were to finish the season in fourth place, they twice beat champions Juventus. Indeed, in the home match at their old Vomero stadium, referee Concetto Lo Bello agreed to let thousands of fans sit at the edge of the pitch – just a few feet from the players – such was the interest in this Napoli-Juventus clash. Napoli won the game 4-3 and there was no crowd trouble, a sign of the other side of the team's support.

This good league season failed to inspire Napoli to greater heights and Amadei, who had taken over from Monzeglio as coach in 1956, could do little to keep his team afloat. The side moved to their new 86,000 capacity San Paolo stadium but it did little for their luck and in 1961 they suffered the shame of another trip to Serie B. This time, fortunately, the club returned immediately to the top and picked up the *Coppa Italia*, beating Spal from Ferrara in the final. However, their time at the top was to last but one season before they returned to Serie B for another couple of seasons until, eventually, they came out and have never returned.

Players of the quality of Dino Zoff, Omar Sivori and Jose Altafini (the latter pair both found new leases of life at Napoli after seeming finished with Juventus and Milan respectively) arrived at the club. The side took a good second place in 1968 a long way behind Champions, Milan. Another change at the top of the club in 1969, with the arrival of Corrado Ferlaino as President, proved to be a major turning point for the club since Ferlaino has remained President to this day with just a couple of short breaks along the way.

The side began to change shape under Ferlaino and the coaching of Vinicio. Loyal right-back Giuseppe Bruscolotti came into the team along with Brazilian striker Sergio Clerici and midfield star Antonio Juliano. By 1975 they appeared ready for their first title but in the title clash with Juventus in Turin (around 25,000 Neapolitans made the trip to the game) a 90th minute strike by former Napoli hero Altafini put an end to title

dreams. It seemed that Napoli might never win the *Scudetto* (the 'little shield' used to symbolize the league title).

The *Coppa Italia* arrived again the following season and a few good league finishes followed on from this. It would be fair to say, though, that the biggest moment in Napoli's history came in 1984 when they signed Diego Armando Maradona from Barcelona and finally turned their title dreams into reality. His first season with the club brought only a mediocre eighth place finish but a strong side was being built around him. The Ma-Gi-Ca trio (Maradona, Giordano and Careca) promised plenty of goals for the 1986-87 season and a defence marshalled by Giuseppe Bruscolotti, the young Neapolitan Ciro Ferrara, and Alessandro Renica, was unlikely to give away many goals. The midfield also contained the strong pairing of De Napoli and Bagni who ensured that Maradona saw enough of the ball to make his influence felt. The title was won by three points under stern coach, Ottavio Bianchi, who also helped Napoli take the Italian Cup that same season.

The side remained in the title reckoning for the rest of the 1980s and took the UEFA Cup in 1989. Maradona almost single-handedly ridded the team of coach Bianchi, who was replaced by Albertino Bigon, and another title was taken in 1990. 'Snatched' as this was from Milan, the Napoli fans staged a mock funeral for Milan president Silvio Berlusconi to show how they had killed off his title hopes.

The 'larger than life' Maradona began to have troubles off the pitch, however, as paternity suits were impending and he further delayed his return from holiday in Argentina. The fans were angered by his absence but the moment he returned to the pitch all was forgiven as his magic began to work again. However, even Maradona could not dribble around drugs charges and a ban from the game in 1991 and Napoli were left to make their own way – which they did pretty well thanks to the Sardinian, Gianfranco Zola, who had studied hard under Maradona's

DIEGO ARMANDO MARADONA

(b: 30/10/60 Lanus, Argentina) Undoubtedly the finest footballer of the last twenty years and a hero in Naples despite his ban for drug-taking and his obvious loathing of training. El Principito ('The Little Prince'), with the help of some quality players around him, took Napoli to two championships, the Italian Cup and the UEFA Cup. His outrageous skill and technique helped to put Napoli on the world football map. One of his training methods was to place the ball on or behind the bye-line and curl it into the goal in the space of just a few yards, such was the quality of his ball control. For seven seasons, with 81 Serie A goals to his credit, Maradona was synonymous with Napoli and gave the northern giants much to worry about.

GIANFRANCO ZOLA

(b: 5/7/66 Oliena) One of the few Sardinians to have really made a name for himself in Italian football, Zola only stepped into the limelight after Maradona was forced out of the game. Signed from third division Torres, he was initially Maradona's understudy but when he was given a regular place in the side in 1991-92 he showed that he had learned much from his master. Neat dribbling skills, good vision and swerving free-kicks made him an essential part of Napoli's surprise fourth place finish without their Argentine star and helped earn the diminutive Sardinian midfielder his international call-up as well as the nickname, Mara-Zola.

Above: In 1962 Napoli, back in Serie A after a season of relegation, returned to the top and won the Italian Cup.

guidance. Some poor moves on the transfer market, however, made the 1992-93 season one to forget and the search for a successor to Maradona started in earnest.

Because of their geographic position, Napoli players have always had to work twice as hard to make their way into the national team. Gianfranco Zola is just the most recent example of Napoli stars who would certainly have taken more caps had they played for Inter, Juventus or Milan and been easier for the national team coach to spot. The main contributions have come in recent times from tough midfielders Fernando De Napoli and Salvatore Bagni but even the midfielder Juliano could only manage 18 caps despite his obvious class.

It is partly this situation and the controversial figure of Maradona that have turned Napoli into hate figures for many northern sides – in particular title rivals of the 1980s Milan. Napoli, for their part, still feel the strongest rivalry in *Il Derby del Sud* (The Derby of the South) with Roma as this occasion is still seen as deciding who is the strongest side in southern Italy. Prior to the formation of Roma, it was the matches with Lazio that inspired the same sort of feeling and the trouble, both on and off the pitch, was often hard to control.

Naturally, this history of crowd trouble has given Napoli fans a poor reputation but the truth is that their record is little poorer than many other sides and they often have the extenuating circumstance of extreme provocation. Banners saying things like 'Have you washed before you entered our stadium?' regularly greet fans on away trips to Piedmont, Lombardy and the Veneto so it is perhaps surprising that the regular crowds of 80,000 in the San Paolo do not react more strongly than they do. The supporters of the Curva B, where the Napoli faithful congregate, are one of the most vociferous groups in all Italy and when they get behind their team it is, to use a cliché, like having an extra player on the pitch.

As well as their home support, Napoli have had various other strong influences upon their history. Coaches such as Eraldo Monzeglio and ex-players Bruno Pesaola and Vinicio all met with some success at the club but it was the love-hate relationship between Ottavio Bianchi and Diego Maradona that really brought the club to life. While Bianchi was famous for his gruelling training régime, Maradona often returned from holiday considerably overweight. Their arguments and disagreements were transformed into great displays upon the pitch and made Napoli a force to be reckoned with. If another partnership can do the same for the club, it may be the key to future success.

PARMA

In just seven years, Parma have been transformed from a minor league team into one of Europe's leading lights. Their recent achievements, including their victory in the European Cup Winners' Cup in 1993, did not happen by chance, but resulted from a comprehensive work programme with success as its sole objective. The injection of wealth provided by the city's dairy company Parmalat in 1987 had a significant bearing on Parma's rise to the top of the Italian game and emphasizes the need for a Serie A club to have a sound financial base in order to build a productive campaign.

PARMA

Parma were promoted to Serie A for the first time in 1990. After losing their first match in the top flight at home to Juventus, the club then developed into one of the most difficult sides to beat, as well as one of the most attractive teams in Italy to watch. Parma averaged just eight defeats a season during their first three years in the company of Italy's glamour clubs. The city, noted for its gastronomic delicacies, notably its ham and dairy products, finally had a team worthy of its proud image and thriving economy. The cultural heritage in the city has also attracted admiration, not least because it was the home town of the famous composer Giuseppe Verdi.

On 27 July 1913, Parma's locals formed a football club and commemorated the centenary of Giuseppe Verdi's birth by bestowing the composer's name on the team – Verdi Foot Ball Club was born. The club, nicknamed the *Gialloblu,* bore the yellow and blue colours they still wear today, in the form of chequered shirts.

Their first match was played three months later, on 26 September, against their regional neighbours, Reggiana. The match ended in defeat against the side with whom they would later share an intense rivalry. Verdi's distinguished name evidently failed to inspire the players, who changed the club's name to Parma Foot Ball Club in December that year.

The outbreak of World War I suspended their activity, after which they took part in Emilia Romagna's regional league. In 1922, before the league's structural change, Parma enrolled in Italy's second division, which was at the time, rather confusingly, Italy's equivalent to the third division.

They were promoted three years later, relegated immediately and promoted again in 1929 in time to participate in Serie B's inaugural season. They went back down within three years. During this time, the club changed its name from the English derivative, Parma Foot Ball Club, and assumed the title Parma Associazione Sportiva.

In 1935, Italy's first division became Serie C and there Parma languished until the season preceding World War II. Their stint in Serie B lasted until 1949. Following a play-off staged in Milan against Lo Spezia, the *Gialloblu* found themselves in the familiar domain of Serie C once more. Five years passed before Parma finally assembled a side capable of preserving their Serie B status after clinching promotion as champions in 1954. Under the guiding light of Carlo Alberto Quario, they spent 11 seasons in the division the Italians call *La Serie Cadetta*, the junior division.

In 1965, Parma were again relegated to Serie C and subsequently suffered the most disappointing period in their history. From collecting a record minimum number of points that year, the club's fortunes deteriorated significantly and the *Gialloblu* were demoted to the fourth division, Serie D, for the first time. Parma were in dire need of financial assistance and ultimately went into liquidation on 2 January 1968. Six months later, a group of local businessmen financed the formation of a new club in the city, called AC Parmense.

In only their first season, Parmense won their divisional title in the semi-professional leagues and advanced to Serie D. They merged with Parma's former club for the start of the next campaign and played under Parmense's title. On New Year's Day in 1970, the club were officially renamed Associazione Calcio Parma, as they are known today, and were promoted from Serie D that same season. They spent the next 15 years switching between the second and third divisions.

In 1985, Parma heralded the arrival of Arrigo Sacchi, who used the club as a stepping stone for greater things. In his first season, Sacchi steered Parma into Serie B and did enough in the subsequent campaign (Parma finished the season in seventh place) to attract the attentions of Silvio Berlusconi, President of mighty Milan. Sacchi relinquished his position and went on to lead Milan to glory in the league championship and the European Champions' Cup. In November 1991, Sacchi was appointed the national team coach.

Club Name:

Associazione Calcio Parma

Founded: **1913 (Officially 1968)**

Address:

Via Partigiani d'Italia 1, 43100 Parma

Ground:

Stadio Ennio Tardini (Capacity: 27,500)

Club Colours:

White Shirts, with Yellow and Blue Trim, White Shorts, White Socks (Away Colours: Yellow Shirts, with Blue Trim, Yellow Shorts, Yellow Socks)

Major Honours:

Italian Cup Winners (1992), Cup Winners' Cup (1993)

Cup glory for Parma in the 1992 *Coppa Italia* (left) and the 1993 Cup Winners' Cup at Wembley (above).

GEORGES GRUN

(b: 25/1/62 Schaerbeek, Belgium) The defender spent his entire career with Anderlecht prior to his transfer to Parma after the 1990 World Cup finals staged in Italy. He has represented the Belgian national team on more than 60 occasions, playing in two World Cups. Grun settled quickly in Italy and his wealth of experience proved invaluable to the club's ambitions. He is one of the cornerstones of Parma's success.

ALBERTO DI CHIARA

(b: 29/3/64 Roma) Di Chiara is one of the most talented defenders in Italian football. He began his career as a winger with his hometown team, Roma, but was sold to Reggiana after making just four league appearances. Di Chiara moved on to Lecce and then Fiorentina, where he was converted to the left-back position. He joined Parma in 1991 and the following year he became the first *Gialloblu* to play for Italy.

1987 was to prove a pivotal year for Parma. Parmalat began its association with the *Gialloblu*, buying a 25 per cent stake in the club. The dairy company's President, Calisto Tanzi, who founded Parmalat in 1961, had previously displayed his company name in countless sporting events. From the national skiing championships to Formula One motor racing, Parmalat's logo could be seen from far and wide. The name appeared to act as a lucky charm for the teams it sponsored. In the early 1980s, it backed the Italian teams who became national and European champions at both volleyball and baseball. In 1986, Real Madrid were victorious in their domestic league and the UEFA Cup with Parmalat proudly printed on their jerseys.

Events in their first year as Parma's sponsors did little to inspire a repeat of past achievements. The Czech-born Zdenek Zeman took over the reins from Arrigo Sacchi, but he was dismissed after only seven matches in charge as a result of his side's dismal start to the 87/88 season. Giampiero Vitali replaced Zeman and he guided Parma to a respectable mid-table position in each of his two years at the club. In 1989, Vitali was asked to step aside by the Parma President, Ernesto Ceresini, as he enticed one of Italy's most promising coaches, Nevio Scala, from little Reggina (not to be confused with Reggiana) after he had almost led the southern Italian club to Serie A the previous year. Scala, the former Milan and Inter midfielder, was a novice in the coaching profession, but he was still in demand. Parma's encouraging prospects inspired Parmalat's President, Calisto Tanzi, to invest a portion of his own personal fortune in 1989, increasing Parmalat's interest in the club by a further 20 per cent. Tanzi believes the publicity generated from sponsorship is essential to Parmalat's growth. He also paraded his corporation logo in South America, where the shirts of Brazilian side Palmeiras, Uruguay's Penarol and Boca Juniors from Argentina all sported the company name.

In his first season with Parma, Nevio Scala managed to lead the *Gialloblu* to an unprecedented promotion to Serie A. Sadly, the achievement was marred by the death of the club President, Ernesto Ceresini, in

February. Having served Parma for 14 years, Ceresini was denied the pleasure of sharing the club's finest hour. Giorgio Pedraneschi took over the President's mantle after spending many years as a club director. Parma clinched promotion on the penultimate day of the 89/90 season, defeating – of all teams – their bitter rivals Reggiana.

In 1990, Parma explored the transfer market for the three permitted overseas players and the club's scouts passed their summer vacations observing the World Cup Finals staged in Italy. By the end of the tournament, Belgium's experienced defender Georges Grun, the goalkeeper of the Brazilian national team Claudio Taffarel, and the brightest prospect in Swedish football, Tomas Brolin, were added to an already gifted first team squad. Parma began their inaugural season in Serie A without offering any indication of the success they would later achieve. However, victories against Milan, Napoli and Fiorentina forced the rest of Serie A to take notice. By the spring of 1991, Parma were in sight of a UEFA Cup place and the race for Europe was not decided until the final day of the season. Inter had already qualified, so the *Gialloblu* joined the distinguished company of Torino, Genoa and Juventus, who were all vying for the three remaining places. On that final day, Genoa and Juventus were drawn together in a match Juve needed to win to avoid their first ever exclusion from European competition. Torino entertained Atalanta at home and Parma faced the daunting trip to the San Siro Stadium to play Milan. In a dramatic climax to the 90/91 season, Juventus were defeated in Genoa, while Parma fought out a goalless draw against Milan and joined Inter, Torino and Genoa in the UEFA Cup placings.

The following year, Parma silenced the cynics who had insisted that the element of surprise was the key to their first extraordinary season in Serie A. Once again, the club started its second campaign in Italy's premier division at a rather sluggish pace and were unfortunately eliminated in the first round of the UEFA Cup by the Bulgarians from CSKA Sofia, albeit on the away goals rule. Parma recovered sufficiently from their disappointment and by the end of the season equalled their previous year's tally of 38 points. This time, they failed to qualify for the UEFA Cup, but found glory in the form of the *Coppa Italia*, the Italian Cup. En route to the final, the *Gialloblu* defeated Fiorentina and the three-times-winners Sampdoria to earn a dream two-legged confrontation with Juventus. Parma were defeated by a disputed penalty in the first match in Turin, but their positive display filled the players with confidence for the return leg the following week. Goals by their golden boy, Alessandro Melli, and the man they call the Mayor, Marco Osio, overturned the deficit in the return leg as Parma lifted their first major trophy. Parma had qualified for Europe again and would contest the Cup Winners' Cup.

During the summer preceding the 92/93 season, the stylish left-back, Alberto Di Chiara, became the first Parma player to be capped by the Italian national team. Di Chiara was selected for a three-match tour of the United States and he made his debut in a goalless draw against Portugal. Since that warm afternoon in New Haven, Di Chiara has been a fixture in Arrigo Sacchi's squad. But for the presence of one of the world's finest defenders, Paolo Maldini, he would doubtless command a regular place in the *Azzurri*'s starting line-up.

The fans' expectations for the next campaign were now very different. The club responded with another memorable season, again after their customary slow start. Parma added the silky skills of the Colombian Faustino Asprilla to the side and his contribution proved invaluable, especially in the Cup Winners' Cup. While the *Gialloblu* maintained their position among Serie A's front-runners, Asprilla orchestrated the club's impressive run in Europe. The Hungarian side, Ujpest Dosza, Boavista of Portugal, Sparta Prague and the prestigious Spanish club Atletico Madrid were all

eliminated as Parma marched on to Wembley Stadium for a showdown with the Belgians, Royal Antwerp. In one of the most one-sided European finals ever witnessed, Parma, without the injured Asprilla, outclassed Antwerp and the 3-1 scoreline failed to reflect Parma's overwhelming superiority. The match could quite easily have produced the biggest victory in a European final since Real Madrid's 7-3 demolition of Eintracht Frankfurt in the 1960 Champions Cup.

Parma's success story has proved that a small, yet highly ambitious provincial club can live with the elite of Italian football. Sound financial backing, a capable coach and a squad of hardworking and talented players have all contributed to the club's fairy tale rise.

From the humble days of Verdi Foot Ball Club and their blue and yellow chequered shirts, Parma progressed to seize a notable chapter in *calcio*'s history.

NICOLA BERTI

(b: 14/4/67 Salsomaggiore Terme, Parma)

The outspoken midfielder is the most successful player in Parma's history to have come from the club's youth ranks. At the age of 18, Berti was transferred to Fiorentina after just one season in Parma's first team. He made 15 appearances for the Italian Under-21 side while in Florence, before joining Inter in 1989. He has since earned more than 20 full international caps.

ALESSANDRO MELLI

(b: 11/12/69 Agrigento, Sicily)

Following three dazzling years in Serie A, Melli blossomed into one of Italy's most sought after strikers. Although born in Sicily, he was raised in Parma, where his career was launched by Arrigo Sacchi in 1986. He spearheaded Italy's 1992 European Championship conquest at Under-21 level and he made his full international debut the following season.

Above: Golden boy Alessandro Melli celebrates his goal in Parma's 2-0 second-leg victory over Juventus in the 1992 *Coppa Italia*.

PIACENZA

Of all Serie A's teams, the little northern club from the Emilia Romagna region has the briefest of histories. Although Piacenza were founded more than 70 years ago, the club has spent much of that time fighting to escape from the lower divisions, so their sudden burst into the top flight in June 1993 was more than a touch surprising. Just ten years ago, Piacenza were in Serie C2, Italy's fourth division. They now hold a place among Italy's leading teams, facing the likes of Juventus and Inter for the first time in league competition. All this, for a team which has taken part in only eight Serie B championships.

Piacenza Football Club was formed in June 1919. The founder members, including the earliest president, 18-year-old student, Giovanni Dosi, gathered in a tavern in the centre of the city and decided on white and red colours for their team, which gave rise to their nickname, the *Biancorossi*. Piacenza's early years were promising and in 1931, they almost achieved their first promotion to Serie B. Unfortunately their progress was halted when, astonishingly, the league decided to force the club to replay two games which they had already won, as a result of refereeing errors. In the 1930s, two Piacenza players, Puppo and Girometta, were called up by Vittorio Pozzo for the national squad which took part in the 1936 Berlin Olympics, but neither managed to break into the first team. A player from the provincial club has never been summoned for the *Azzurri* since.

After World War II, and as a result of the restructuring of the league, Piacenza were able to participate in Serie B for the first time. Still, they were relegated to their customary position in Serie C within two years. A year later, the *Biancorossi* went into Italy's fourth division and their prolonged spell in the bottom two divisions lasted through to 1969, when they were promoted to Serie B for a second time. Piacenza inaugurated their new Galleana stadium and also met their regional rivals, Reggiana, in the second division, following an absence of more than 20 years. Sadly, both clubs were reunited in Serie C at the end of the season.

The *Biancorossi's* return to Serie B, in 1975, coincided with the appointment of coach, Giovan Batista Fabbri. He later guided Lanerossi Vicenza, the club which launched Paolo Rossi, into Serie A in his first season. Although G.B. Fabbri failed to prevent Piacenza from their immediate demotion to Serie C, he did enough to secure a position with Vicenza. By the summer of 1983, the *Biancorossi* found themselves in Italy's fourth division once again. Leonardo Garilli took over the club's presidency and it was his arrival which stimulated Piacenza's recovery. The following year, under the guidance of 'Titta' Rota, Atalanta's coach in

Serie A in the mid-1970s, the club won promotion to the third division and missed a second consecutive promotion to Serie B a year later. Piacenza were defeated in a play-off, but managed to secure a place in Serie B in 1987. This time their adventure lasted two years and their relegation was made all the more biting when Reggiana gained promotion from Serie C.

In 1990, President Garilli appointed 40-year-old coach Luigi Cagni. He had only one previous season's experience of coaching at professional level, with Centese in Serie C2, prior to his arrival in Piacenza. Cagni steered the *Biancorossi* to Serie B in his first season and in his second managed to consolidate Piacenza's place in the second division, a feat the club had managed only twice before. Their 11th place finish was the highest in the club's history, yet they waited until the very last day of the season before assuring their survival.

Piacenza's target for the 92/93 campaign was, inevitably, survival once again. However, the *Biancorossi's* uninspired start brought the fans out in protest against Luigi Cagni. After a goalless draw with promotion hopefuls Padova, Cagni confronted the fans who had waited for him outside the Galleana stadium. Bold he may have seemed, but he trusted his convictions implicitly. His philosophy of playing open, attacking football saw Piacenza develop into surprising front-runners for a coveted place in Serie A.

The race for promotion carried onto the last day of the season. Piacenza needed a victory away at Cosenza in order to guarantee at least a

Club Name:
Piacenza Football Club
Address:
Via Gorra 25, 29100 Piacenza
Founded: **1919**
Ground:
Stadio Galleana (Capacity: 12,000)
Club Colours:
Red Shirts, Red Shorts, Red Socks
(Away Colours: White Shirts, White
Shorts, White Socks)

Left: Antonio De Vitis sports Piacenza's away strip.
Below: Coach Luigi Cagni.

ARMANDO MADONNA

(b: 5/7/63 Alzano Lombardo, Bergamo)
The right winger enjoyed seven years with Piacenza, in two spells, helping the club rise from the fourth to the second division in the 1980s. Madonna began his career with his hometown team, Atalanta, before moving to Piacenza for the first time in 1983. In November 1988, he rejoined Atalanta and two years later, he signed for Lazio, only to return to Piacenza on loan after one season in Rome. Lazio sold Madonna to Spal in December 1992.

ANTONIO DE VITIS

(b: 16/5/64 Lecce)
'Toto' joined Piacenza from Udinese in 1991 and was one of Serie B's leading strikers, finishing in the runners-up spot in the goalscorers' charts for two consecutive seasons in his two years at Piacenza. De Vitis failed to fulfil his potential with Napoli at the start of his career and spent most of his early years playing in the lower divisions with four provincial southern teams, before moving to the north.

play-off berth, with either Ascoli or Padova, who played each other, or Lecce. A goal from Fulvio Simonini secured a victory for Piacenza, although their defence had to withstand a furious second half onslaught from Cosenza's attack to hold onto their slight advantage. Subsequent events in Padova brought jubilant scenes on the south coast as the *Biancorossi* clinched a place among Italy's glamour clubs without the need for a play-off.

It wasn't so much the promotion which filled coach Cagni with pride, but the manner in which his players carried out this most unexpected feat. Cagni demands a skilful game from his teams. This stems from his time as a defender in the days he played with Brescia, when he rarely savoured the role he was asked to perform.

'For most of my career, coaches told me just to think about clearing the ball and that's all,' he said. 'So, I did as I was told, but can't really say that I enjoyed it. I then thought that if I ever became a coach, I would want my team to do everything I wasn't able to do as a player and that means play football and not just concentrate on destroying it.'

Piacenza certainly delivered the attractive game Cagni preaches and more importantly 'played' their way out of the lower reaches of the league to earn a place on the most alluring stage in world football.

Those who follow Italian football from abroad usually do so because of the Serie A and the exciting, talented footballers to be found playing there. However, there is more to Italian football than just those top 18 teams, since without the lower divisions there would be no newly-promoted sides at the start of each season, nor would there be the terrible threat of relegation.

For football supporters familiar with the British-style league structure, the Italian system may, at first, seem a little surprising. Essentially, the Italian divisions are built like a pyramid with more sections the further down the game's echelons a side travels. The Serie A, as is well known, is an 18-team division with four relegation spots to Serie B. In turn, the Serie B contains twenty sides with a further four relegation and promotion places. However, when teams reach the Serie C1, third division, things begin to get a little more interesting. The division is split into the Girone A and Girone B, Group A and Group B, which both hold 18 sides.

These two sections are not divided merely at random but rather according to geographical distinctions. The Girone A sees the northern clubs at that level fight it out, while the Girone B is for teams from the south of the country. The reason behind this separation is fairly obvious to those who know Italian football and have some knowledge of Italian politics and economic history. Northern Italy has always been more wealthy and therefore more powerful than the south and this was, and still is, equally true for football clubs, making southern sides financially disadvantaged compared with their northern rivals. This was so much so that in the late 1950s the so called 'Zauli reform', named after its inventor, attempted positive discrimination in favour of the southern teams. By dividing Serie C1 into two parts, northern and southern sides would be guaranteed an equal number of new representatives in the Serie B, thereby maintaining some sort of equilibrium. Some would point to championship successes by Cagliari, Lazio,

Roma and Napoli (twice) in the past 25 years as a sign of the value of this reform. Certainly, it helps to give the southern sides a larger representation than they might otherwise have in the top two divisions.

Naturally, this split has implications for the divisions below. The Serie C2 is sliced in three, Girone A, Girone B and Girone C, with the top two teams in each 18-strong group gaining promotion to Serie C1. Once again, these *Gironi* are divided geographically into northern, central and southern sections which help ensure that there is a steady supply of sides to the both of the divisions above.

The final division to which the major sports' press accords some coverage is a sort of fifth division known as the *Dilettanti* (Amateurs). Until recently, these were called the *Interregionali* (Interregionals), which gave a clearer idea of how these nine sections were divided. Essentially, each 18-team group covers a couple of the 20 regions of Italy with only the top team in each division guaranteed a spot in Serie C2.

From the *Dilettanti* down, this regionalized pyramid continues from the *Eccellenza* (sixth division), through to the *Terza Categoria* (tenth division). What this means is that virtually every town in Italy, even those with more goats than they have inhabitants, can dream of reaching the Serie A since, in theory at least, the only obstacle to their progress is the ability of their players. In truth, the divide between the 'haves' and 'have-nots' in Italian football remains immense. Although the changes in structure have done much to try and even out the imbalances in Italian football, it is almost impossible to stop the traditionally big clubs from rising to the top and leaving the others in their wake. It could be quite a while, therefore, before we have the pleasure of seeing Dicomano fighting it out with the likes of Inter or Milan.

Left: The skills – and salaries – of players like Lentini at the top of the football pyramid are technically within reach of any amateur, but in reality are just a distant fantasy.

REGGIANA

In the summer of 1993, Serie A extended a warm and belated welcome to Reggiana, its latest addition. The provincial club required three-quarters of a century to make the jump up to Serie A after moving constantly up and down the lower divisions. Reggiana achieved their first ever promotion with style, reaching their milestone as the 1993 Serie B Champions.

REGGIANA

Reggiana secured the country's second division championship at the least expected time. Immediately before the start of the 92/93 season, many soccer pundits predicted nothing more than mid-table security for the club from the northern city of Reggio Emilia. The city, famed for its agriculture and dairy produce, is one of the country's most affluent, but it has struggled to produce a successful team to match its current opulence. Over the last decade, Reggiana have lived in the shadow of their neighbours from the Emilia Romagna region – Parma – who have won the Italian Cup and the European Cup Winners' Cup since their promotion to Serie A in 1990. By contrast, Reggiana's trophy cabinet is devoid of any major honour.

In the past, Reggiana appeared reluctant to take the giant step into Serie A. It was even suggested that the club President, Ermete Fiaccadori, had deliberately thrown away opportunities to lead his club into the top flight, some claiming he was not prepared to finance a Serie A campaign. This might explain why the club had finished in seventh place in each of the three seasons prior to their promotion, in addition to the club's amazing collapse in the closing stages of the 91/92 Serie B championship. In 1990, Reggiana finished six points behind their rivals Parma, who earned the last promotion berth in fourth place. The following year, they missed out by a mere three points to promoted Ascoli, winning just one of their remaining nine fixtures. The club seemed destined for promotion again in 1992, until they slipped into a curious decline in the final four months of the season. Reggiana had lost only five league fixtures from September to February, but then managed just one victory in their last 16 games, which included defeats in four of their last five. In almost identical fashion to the 89/90 season, Reggiana ended the campaign six points behind the team in fourth place, this time Udinese.

Reggiana were formed on 25 September 1919 and they took part in the national league before the top flight assumed its Serie A title in 1929. The club was, in fact, relegated the year before Serie A's inauguration – conceding 103 goals, which is still a record today.

Since then, Reggiana have been competing in Italy's second and third divisions – mainly in the second where the club has spent 30 years – and have also made the odd appearance in the fourth. It was during their early years that the club produced its only Italian international. Between 1921 and 1924, Felice Romano, a native of Buenos Aires in Argentina, represented Italy on five occasions. Romano was unfortunate in making his last appearance for the *Azzurri* in the spring of 1924 when Italy were defeated 7-1 against Hungary in Budapest.

League records in Italian football are normally recognized after 1929, the year when the league's current structure was formed. During the opening Serie B season, Reggiana conceded 75 goals – another club record – and were relegated to Italy's third division. In addition, they registered a club record minimum number of points as they suffered the first of seven relegations from Serie B to Serie C, which included a 9-1 defeat at the hands of Novara, the heaviest in their history.

Despite the wealth circulating within Emilia Romagna, the region never had a club strong enough to challenge their illustrious neighbours from Milan and Turin. Reggiana seemed reasonably content with their humble existence and have often provided players with a launching pad from which to progress to greater heights. Gianfranco Matteoli and Andrea Carnevale, who each won league titles with Inter and Napoli respectively, developed into Italian internationals after maturing with the club.

As with most Italian teams, Reggiana's nickname, the *Granata,* refers to the club colours; literally translated, it means garnet. The *Granata* enjoyed their most successful period in the 1960s. Following a spell in the mid-1950s in Serie D, Italy's fourth division, Reggiana climbed up the lower divisions and a decade later, came within a whisker of reaching Serie A. In 1964, they gained promotion from Serie C as champions with a club record of 55 points. They then just missed promotion to Serie A in three consecutive seasons.

Club Name:
Associazione Calcio Reggiana
Address:
Via Mogadiscio 1, 42100 Reggio Emilia
Founded: **1919**
Ground:
Stadio Mirabello (Capacity: 12,400)
Club Colours:
Dark Red Shirts, Dark Red Shorts, Dark Red Socks (Away Colours: White Shirts, White Shorts, White Socks)

Left: Reggiana enjoy a well deserved lap of honour after making it to Serie A.
Above: The man who delivered the dream: coach Pippo Marchioro.

REGGIANA

GIANFRANCO MATTEOLI

(b: 21/4/59 Nuoro, Sardinia)

The Sardinian played a vital role during Reggiana's promotion to Serie B in 1982. He left for Como, where he won the first of 14 Under-21 caps and, in 1985, inspired them to promotion to Serie A. Then, after one season with Sampdoria, the playmaker enjoyed three successful years with Inter. Matteoli represented the national team six times and, in 1989, won the Scudetto with the *Neroazzurri*.

ANDREA CARNEVALE

(b: 12/1/61 Monte San Biagio, Latina)

The much travelled striker is the best-known player to have worn Reggiana's jersey. He joined from Avellino, then a Serie A side, in 1981 and spent two years in Reggio Emilia before moving on to receive greater recognition. Carnevale won the *Scudetto* twice with Napoli, in 1987 and 1990, and collected ten full international caps. He played in the 1990 World Cup finals, before leaving Napoli for Roma.

Inevitably, as a provincial outfit, Reggiana had by this time exhausted its resources and so suffered a decline. By 1970, the *Granata* found themselves in Serie C once again.

Reggiana's seesaw ride through the lower reaches of the league continued throughout the 1970s and 1980s. Their fans were not asked to wait long for an upturn in fortune following their demotion in 1970, as the club won the Serie C championship in the next season to bounce back up to Italy's second division. In 1975, they were relegated from Serie B again after a play-off against Alessandria. The match was staged on neutral ground and Alessandria edged the tight affair in Milan by two goals to one. When a play-off determines a club's future, it is always much harder to accept demotion. One fixture settled the outcome of an entire campaign. Reggiana failed to recover sufficiently and endured the next six years in Serie C.

In true Reggiana tradition, they went up to Serie B as champions again 1981, only to drop down two years later for another six-year stretch in the third division. It was almost predetermined that Reggiana should celebrate their next promotion by winning the Serie C championship, which they achieved in 1989 under the guidance of Giuseppe – or Pippo – Marchioro. The 57-year-old Milanese coach has enjoyed considerable success with minor clubs. He steered Cesena to a UEFA Cup spot for the first time in their history in 1977. Sadly, Cesena were eliminated in the first round by Magdeburg, but it was still an achievement for the unfashionable northern club. That season, the UEFA Cup was captured by another Italian club, Juventus, scraping a victory on the away goals rule against the Spanish side, Atletico Bilbao. A year later, Marchioro was appointed coach of Como and he guided the lakeside club from Serie C to Serie A in successive seasons.

Despite losing two of his most prized players during his first three years in Serie B with Reggiana, it took him only an extra year to realize the club's ambition of promotion to Serie A. In 1990, Reggiana sold Andrea

Silenzi, their own top scorer and the divisions leading scorer, to Napoli for £3 million. For a club of Reggiana's stature and limited resources, it was an offer they could not refuse. The giant marksman had set a club record that season with his 23 goals. A year later, in November 1991, President Fiaccadori sold the fans' favourite Fabrizio Ravanelli to Juventus, but at least ensured the grey-haired young striker stayed until the end of the season. Ravanelli – perhaps foolishly – disclosed his burning desire to move immediately to Juventus and consequently felt the wrath of his 'former' fans for more than six months. Ravanelli's departure swelled Reggiana's bank account by a further £3 million.

Pippo Marchioro masterminded Reggiana's promotion without a prolific goalscorer in his ranks, placing the emphasis of his tactics on the team's function as as a unit. He adopts the zonal system and his players have regularly executed the tactic almost to perfection. Their performances during their promotion year earned the club the distinguished nickname, *Il Piccolo Milan* – Little Milan. Indeed, Marchioro coached Milan during the 1970s and he is vehement about the strengths of Milan's style of play. Yet it might all have been so

different had Marchioro accepted an offer to coach Udinese before the start of the 92/93 season. Udinese had dismissed Adriano Fedele – the man who had just steered them into Serie A – a mere week before the opening day of the season. Marchioro's aversion to a move came as something of a surprise. After all, he felt Reggiana were hardly on the verge of rewriting history following a less than encouraging pre-season.

As the 92/93 season unfolded, more and more pieces began to fit Marchioro's tactical jigsaw. Reggiana had won ten consecutive matches at their tight Mirabello stadium and by Christmas, they were proudly perched at the top of Serie B. Marchioro's defence provided the backbone for the club's success. In their young goalkeeper, Luca Bucci, Reggiana had unearthed an enormous talent. Following the introduction of the new back pass law, Reggiana's defenders took great comfort in the knowledge that Bucci is extremely comfortable

with the ball at his feet. He also has the ability, as most great goalkeepers have, to make even the most difficult saves look easy.

The club's attractive game was orchestrated by the midfield playmaker, Giuseppe Scienza. Science by name, he was rather the architect of Reggiana's promotion. The club captain had fulfilled his potential late in his career, but finally stepped up to the higher division more deserving of his talent. One player felt especially proud of his return to the top flight. Marco Pacione almost suffered a premature end to his career with a knee injury while at Genoa; they had declared the striker unfit for the rigours of Serie A football. His injury problems had hit the headlines in the summer preceding the *Campionato,* but Reggiana came to his rescue and he did not let them down. The 30-year-old from Pescara had never quite lived up to expectation and after one season with Juventus in the mid-1980s, Pacione's career had been travelling in a downward spiral. His striking partner, Francesco De Falco, was also rewarded with a return to Italy's first division after an absence of 12 years. Toto displayed the enthusiasm of a player half his age and his contribution in his second season in Reggio Emilia, on and off the field, proved invaluable to coach Pippo Marchioro.

After three-quarters of a century, Reggiana eventually found a winning formula, which Pippo Marchioro expertly carried out. Coaches come and go in football and like many of them, Marchioro has lived through some difficult moments. 'I only ever remember the good times', he said. 'The bad I forget.'

Reggiana's fans will always remember Marchioro for delivering their long awaited dream of promotion to Serie A.

MARCO PACIONE

(b: 27/7/63 Pescara) After three promising years with Atalanta, great things were expected from the striker early in his career. Pacione was snapped up by Juventus in 1985, but he failed to make an impact in Turin, where he made just 12 league appearances. He left for Verona and earned two international caps for Italy's B team, before his journey took him via Torino and Genoa to the city of Reggio Emilia in 1992.

ANDREA SILENZI

(b: 10/2/66 Rome) The towering striker began his career with Rome's fourth division side, Lodigiani, and moved to Reggiana in 1987 after one season with little Arezzo. In 1990, Silenzi topped the Serie B goalscorers charts with 23 goals. His achievement was rewarded with a lucrative transfer to Napoli, but his two years in Southern Italy were beset by injury problems and he was offloaded to Torino.

Reggiana's successful 1992/3 campaign owed much to the talents of goalkeeper Luca Bucci (above) and forward Dario Morello (left).

ROMA

By far the most consistent team from southern Italy, Roma have only ever known one season in the Serie B and can boast a proud cup record that is rivalled only by Juventus. They also have a record of being one of the most consistent clubs when it comes to producing players at youth level. They have picked up five Italian youth league titles as well as winning the prestigious Viareggio youth tournament on three occasions. Their continued supremacy over Lazio has led them to be considered as the capital's first team. Moreover, their 19 seasons in European competition have given their red and yellow shirts far greater international recognition than the light blue colours of their bitter rivals.

Associazione Sportiva Roma is a relatively young club having been formed on 22 July 1927 when the four Roman clubs of Alba, Fortitudo, Roman and Pro Roma decided to merge into one. It was an association that bore fruit almost immediately as A.S. Roma became recognized as one of the top teams in Italy. For seven consecutive seasons between 1929 and 1936 they were never outside the top six places in Serie A and twice managed to take second place in the title race (1930-31 and 1935-36).

Among the stars of that period were goalscorers like Rodolfo Volk and Enrico Guaita – an Argentinian winger who, due to his Italian ancestry, picked up ten caps for Italy. The side also contained the legendary *mediano* (centre-half) Attilio Ferraris who represented Fortitudo and then Roma for over a decade, going on to pick up a World Cup winner's medal with Italy in the 1934 competition.

The arrival of international goalkeeper Enrico Masetti and the prolific goalscorer Amadeo Amadei helped to strengthen the squad further and by the 1941-42 season they had formed the strongest team in Italy. They won the title finishing three points ahead of the great Torino side that would go on to win five championships in a row. This was something of a boost to the ailing Fascist dictatorship which had placed so much emphasis on re-establishing links with ancient Rome. A victory for the capital was an important part of putting the city back ahead of Turin and Milan.

The interruption of the war had an adverse effect on Roma's fortunes as they failed to reproduce the form that had kept them near the top of the table. Things got so bad that in 1950-51 they were relegated to the Serie B for the only time in their history. It was a miserable season that included no fewer than 20 defeats in the 38 match season. They were joined in the drop by another great pre-war club, Genoa. However, Roma remained in Serie B for just one season and returned to Serie A ready for the stern questions that it can pose. That Serie B campaign was one which they dominated along with Brescia but ended up taking by just one point.

It was a point that took them back to the top and helped to assure that they never returned to the lower divisions.

The side managed consistent form throughout the 1950s but failed to set the domestic scene alight. They hoped for good luck in signing Knut Nordahl, brother of the successful Gunnar Nordahl, but he proved to be a flop. Instead, they invested more wisely on the Uruguayan Alcide Ghiggia who was to play over 200 times for the club, becoming one of their most loyal foreign servants. The side struggled throughout the 1950s to achieve truly competitive form but by 1961 they were ready for European competition and – thanks to the goals of two Argentinians, Francisco Lojacono and Pedro Manfredini – they won the second edition of the Fairs Cities' Cup. Manfredini, in particular, was a peculiar character who was labelled *Piedone*, meaning 'Big Foot', because of his size 13 football boots. This led the sports press to criticize the big forward despite his grabbing a hat-trick on his debut for the club. Still, he played his part in what was the first Italian success in Europe when Roma overcame Birmingham City in the final and, with Fiorentina taking the Cup Winners' Cup in the same year, 1961 was a good year for Italian football on the European front.

At home, Roma continued to be a mid-table side with little realistic hope of taking the Serie A title. Their best chance of success appeared to be in the Italian Cup which has always been treated by the bigger clubs as a minor competition and therefore leaves the door open to other sides.

By 1964, a long love-affair between Roma and the *Coppa Italia* had begun. On no fewer than five occasions they have met fellow *Coppa Italia* specialists, Torino, in the final. This cup expertise has also stood them in good stead for European competition where they have been represented on an impressive total of 19 occasions placing them behind only Juventus, Inter and Milan in terms of seasons played in these major competitions.

Club Name:

Roma Associazione Sportiva

Address:

Via di Trogoria km. 3,600, 00128 Roma

Founded: **1927**

Ground:

Stadio Olimpico (Capacity: 82,656)

Club Colours:

Red Shirts with Yellow Trim, Red Shorts, Red Socks with Yellow Trim (Away Colours: White Shirts, White Shorts, White Socks)

Major Honours:

League Champions (1941-42, 1982-83), Italian Cup Winners (1964, 1969, 1980, 1981, 1984, 1986, 1991), Fairs Cities' Cup (1961)

Left: 'The Prince', Giuseppe Giannini makes a point to French referee Joel Quiniou during the 1991 UEFA Cup Final against Inter, second leg.
Above: Roman fireworks.

ROMA

By the time the 1980s came around, Roma had finally built a side that looked capable of winning the Serie A as well as challenging for cup glory. They won back to back Italian Cups in 1980 and 1981 and also managed two top three finishes in the league. Eventually, in 1982-83, over forty years after their last success, the *Giallorossi* (yellow and reds) won their second championship.

The side was guided by the wily old Swede, Nils Leidholm, who has spent no fewer than four spells at the helm of the club. This was by far his most successful term in charge. The signing of Brazilian star Paolo Roberto Falcao for 1,700 million lire in 1980, just after the ban on foreign players had been lifted, proved to be a wise move. Long-time servants like lively winger Bruno Conti and midfield general Agostino Di Bartolomei combined well with hard men Carlo Ancelotti and Pietro Vierchowod. In attack were the combined skills of Austrian Herbert Prohaska and Roma's greatest ever goal-scorer, Roberto Pruzzo. It was a victory gained in some style with no fewer than four points' lead over second-placed Juventus. With Lazio languishing in Serie B, the celebrations went on for days in one half of the capital.

The following season, Roma headed into Europe with the dream of another European title seeming to grow with every success. Having won through the first three rounds with some ease, it seemed that their run had been brought to an abrupt halt by a 2-0 defeat at the hands of Dundee United. However, the Roma players – and Roberto Pruzzo in particular – had other ideas. Perhaps fuelled by the insults they had received from Dundee United manager Jim McLean during the first leg, Roma won 3-0 in the Stadio Olimpico and could easily have had more. The match ended with some ugly scenes as the Roma players crowded around the Scottish manager to return some of the abuse they had suffered in Dundee.

The day before the final with Liverpool in Rome, local singing star and diehard Roma fan Antonello Venditti staged a concert to wish his favourites good luck but it was not to be enough. The final itself is part of European Cup history. The early goal by Phil Neal, the equalizer by Roberto Pruzzo and then the tension as time began to tick away and the game headed into extra time. The game reached a climax as Bruce Grobelaar performed his 'spaghetti legs' routine and helped cause the penalty misses by World Cup winners Bruno Conti and Francesco Graziani that cost Roma the Cup in their own stadium. It was, perhaps, the symbol of the end of an era. The last instance of English dominance in Europe, accompanied by the arrival of Italian clubs on the scene.

From that moment on Roma returned to their habitual mid-table security. They have won the Italian Cup again as well as running Inter close for the UEFA Cup in 1991. Following a doping scandal involving Angelo Peruzzi and Andrea Carnevale – which saw them both banned for a year (although they both insisted that they had only taken a pill that Peruzzi's mother had given to them to help them digest after eating too much pasta) – Peruzzi was sold on to Juventus while the ex-Napoli striker remained at the club.

The signing of Thomas Hassler from Juventus proved to be an intelligent acquisition as the diminutive midfielder developed still further in Rome. His stunning free-kicks were of great service to the club and his partnership with Sinisa Mihaijlovic began gradually to bear fruit. Although Vujadin Boskov's coaching was seriously questioned at the start of the 1992-93 season as Roma plunged to the bottom of the table, his work took time to have effect and Roma began to turn into a better organized team than they had been under Ottavio Bianchi's 'reign of terror'. Bianchi is notorious for his harsh training methods and his disputes with club captain and fans' idol, Giuseppe Giannini, reputedly cost him his job.

Giannini, for his part, dropped out of international contention after having seemed to be Azeglio Vicini's 'golden boy'. Having reached 47 caps and equalled the club record of Bruno Conti, he came to the end of the line with the arrival of Arrigo Sacchi. Giannini was just

coach the side had was the Swede, Nils Liedholm, whose biggest successes as a coach came with the club from the capital. His insistence on a modern zonal defence marked him out as a coach with clear ideas and his ability to take the sting out of any potential crisis made him ideal management material.

The success enjoyed under Liedholm and the continued presence of their favourites in the national side has given the Roma supporters on the Curva Sud plenty to cheer about. They view themselves as by far the capital's top team (and history proves them right about this) as well as being the strongest side in Southern Italy (Napoli might have a few things to say about

the latest in a long line of players that Roma have given to the national side. Ferraris and Guaita played in Italy's first World Cup triumph and Pietro Serantoni took part in their second. Even in 1982, Bruno Conti made sure that Roma were not without representation in the final. In between these wins, players like Egisto Pandolfini, full-back Giacomo Losi, wingers Giampaolo Menichelli and Paolo Barison, Francesco Rocca, and – perhaps less often than his talents merited – Roberto Pruzzo all played for their country. The latest additions to this list were striker Ruggiero Rizzitelli and left-back Amedeo Carboni, neither of whom commanded a regular spot in the side.

Roma have often picked up coaches who have enjoyed greater success at other clubs and this has certainly not helped the side's cause. Coaches like Helenio Herrera, Alfredo Foni and even recent acquisition, Vujadin Boskov, were all very successful with other sides before coming to Rome. Undoubtedly, the most truly 'Roman'

that). The matches with Lazio are traditionally tight and often ill-tempered with some fans displaying banners proclaiming such things as 'Una sedia a rotelle per il vostro straniero' (A wheelchair for your foreigner) to greet the newly arrived Paul Gascoigne. Such behaviour is typical of the ill-will between the two sets of supporters. Sometimes this bad feeling goes sadly beyond the bounds of sport as, in October 1979, when a Lazio supporter was killed by a flare launched before the Derby match. Groups like the Mods and the Commando Ultra Curva Sud are among the most famous followers of the Giallorossi who draw their support more from the city centre than the suburban following of Lazio. The Roma fans also have the additional rivalry of Il Derby del Sud (The Derby of the South) with Napoli which can be an equally heated affair. With these important fixtures every season and a successful history, Roma can proudly stand as one of the strongest and most important teams in the history of Italian football.

BRUNO CONTI

(b: 13/3/55, Nettuno)
A quick-witted winger with both good crossing and shooting ability. Conti was with Roma for over 15 years with just two short spells with Genoa in the Serie B. He won the nation's hearts with probably the best Italian performances during the World Cup victory in Spain in 1982. Undoubtedly the quality of crosses and passes that he provided in his 47 international appearances helped Paolo Rossi and Francesco Graziani to shine. At club level he was also part of Roma's title-winning side of 1983 and will be remembered more for his dribbling skills than for his unfortunate penalty miss against Liverpool in the 1984 European Cup Final.

GIUSEPPE GIANNINI

(b: 20/8/64 Rome)
Bought by Roma when he was just 15, this elegant midfielder has been loyal to the club despite overtures from Juventus and other northern clubs. Nicknamed Il Principe ('The Prince') because of his dashing good looks and style of play, he was a regular in the Italian national team under Azeglio Vicini. Recently, his public arguments with coach Ottavio Bianchi reputedly led to the coach being removed, such is Giannini's popularity with the Roma faithful.

Above: Völler and Rizzitelli – from Roma's 1990/91 squad.

SAMPDORIA

One of the youngest clubs in the Serie A, Sampdoria have made a big impression on the top flight in the last ten years. Initially thought of by many as *bella ma sprecona* (beautiful but wasteful) because of their impressive attacking play but lack of trophies, they have now changed most people's minds. Winning the league title in 1991 helped to dispel this myth as did their earlier Cup Winners' Cup triumph. However, defeat by Barcelona in the European Cup Final in a match they might easily have won served only to underline, for some people at least, just how Samp always seem to slip up on the really big occasions.

Although the club has only been in existence under its current name for less than fifty years, the actual origins of the side go back much further. The two clubs that eventually combined to create the *Blucerchiati* (literally the 'hooped blues') were both founded before 1900. The elder of the two by a few years, Andrea Doria, was founded as a local reaction to the 'foreign' team that had been formed in the city largely by English ex-pats (i.e. Genoa). Later came the catchily named Sampierdarenese from Sampierdarena in the city of Genoa. It must indeed have been a relief for football pundits when the two sides merged on 1 August 1946. Taking the club colours of both sides (Andrea Doria's blue and white along with Sampierdarenese's red and black) the new and distinctive strip, now known the world over, was created.

In truth, the merger was the best thing that could have happened for both clubs as neither was particularly successful. The one real claim to fame that Andrea Doria could have was that of having provided the Italian national team with their first ever captain back in 1910. Francesco Cali, a rugged defender, wore the captain's armband during the 6-2 demolition of France. It was to be more than 75 years until another player from the club would receive this honour when Gianluca Vialli led the *Azzurri* in their 4-0 drubbing of Hungary in a friendly in Taranto.

Both sides struggled for domestic success of any sort and it was only in 1922 (the year in which there were two titles played for in Italy) that Sampierdarenese came close to taking the league title. By 1927 it had become obvious that the clubs would have greater chances of success if they were to combine forces and this they did under the name of Dominante. Although the name was impressive, the side dominated very little and ended up going down to Serie B in its first season. The name was to change to Liguria, then to Sampierdarenese, then back to Liguria before World War II brought about a break in proceedings. It was, in fact, under the name Liguria that the club achieved its best pre-war league finish in 1939. The side ended up in fifth position in the Serie A along with Napoli and

Roma. However, this team could not be held together and the following season it dropped into Serie B. They returned to Serie A immediately only to finish last in the final championship before the Italian league ceased to play because of the war.

Soon after World War II was over, the two clubs were reborn under their separate names but this was to prove short-lived and, eventually, the side that is now known as Sampdoria Unione Calcio was born. While the two clubs had almost always played second fiddle to Genoa, the new side helped make the so called *Derby della Lanterna* (the Lighthouse Derby, named after the giant lighthouse in this major port) a much more balanced affair. Finally, Genoa, just like Milan and Turin, was a divided city in footballing terms. However, Genoa remain the better supported side within the city to this day, despite the poor fortunes of the club since the War.

In their first season, Sampdoria scored home and away victories over Genoa but this was not enough to put them above tenth place in the Serie A. Indeed, these early years of the club's history were characterized by a process of establishing themselves as the main side in Genoa without really challenging for the league title.

Of the first 12 post-war Serie A campaigns containing both Genoa sides, Sampdoria finished the season ahead on no fewer than ten occasions. Moreover, for four seasons in the 1950s and early 1960s Sampdoria were the city's only representatives in the first division as Genoa suffered relegation to Serie B. One of the best Sampdoria sides of the period was that of the 1948-49 season which managed a good fifth place finish in the Serie A with its so-called 'atomic attack' (a strike force of Lucentini, Prunechi and Baldini), which managed to score 74 goals in 38 matches.

Another of the stars of that attack was the forward Adriano Bassetto nicknamed Nano (the Dwarf). In seven seasons at the club he struck 93 Serie A goals making him the club's top scorer with a record that not even Vialli or Mancini could catch in the 1980s.

Club Name:

Sampdoria Unione Calcio

Address:

Via XX Settembre 33/3, 16121 Genova

Founded: **1946**

Ground:

Stadio 'Luigi Ferraris' (Capacity: 43,868)

Club Colours:

Blue Shirts with Red, White and Black Hoop, White Shorts, Blue Socks (Away Colours: White Shirts, White Shorts, White Socks)

Major Honours:

League Champions (1990-91), Italian Cup Winners (1984-85, 1987-88, 1988-89), Cup Winners' Cup Winners (1989-90)

Left: Sampdoria's Mauro Bertarelli in pain.

Above: Waving the flag for Samp.

ANTONIO 'TONINO' CEREZO

(b: 21/4/55 Belo Horizonte, Brazil) Signed by Sampdoria in 1986 from Roma when he was already 31 years old, few believed that he would play in Genoa for very long. However, six seasons at Samp and a major part in their championship and cup triumphs proved all the sceptics wrong. A gangly midfielder with great ball control, he gave an eye-catching performance during the 1982 World Cup and Roma snapped him up. However, he soon won a place in the hearts of the Sampdoria supporters, so much so that they recorded a song, The Tonino Cerezo Samba, as a tribute to his skills.

PIETRO VIERCHOWOD

(b: 6/4/59 Calcinate) Nicknamed 'The Tsar' because of his Russian origins and also his imperious defensive qualities, Vierchowod arrived in Genoa after spells with Como, Fiorentina and Roma. He has now spent over ten seasons with Sampdoria and seems to have improved with age as one of the last of the great man-markers in Italy. He was actually a part of the World Cup winning squad of 1982 and looks to be determined to make a trip to the United States in 1994. His speed, fitness and decisive tackling make him able to 'snuff out' even the best strikers and his tussles with Marco Van Basten have become almost legendary.

Sampdoria's best league campaign in this period came in 1960-61 when they managed a fourth place finish which was to be their best ever right up until they took the title. It was no fluke that this coincided with the signing of Sergio Brighenti from Padova. Brighenti struck 27 times in that first season with Samp and this is still a club record. He finished top of the goalscorers table and still, to this day, claims that he should have been credited with 28 goals since a deflected shot of his would have gone in anyway. Another stalwart of the time was stopper Gaudenzio Bernasconi who went on to play 335 games for the club.

However, this peak was to be followed by a long slump that saw Doria dip down into Serie B for one season in 1966-67. One bright light in this darkness came from star of the future Romeo Benetti, who passed one season with the club in 1969 which helped to put his career back on the right track and attracted the interest of Milan and Juventus.

By 1977 things had become so bad that the Genoese giants spent five seasons in the lower division. It was at this stage that Paolo Mantovani took over as club president. With sensible investment and stubborn resistance to the offers of the bigger clubs, he helped build a team capable of challenging for major honours.

In 1982, the side returned to Serie A and Roberto Mancini arrived at the club. Following a couple of mid-table finishes and the arrival of other important elements in the side like Pietro Vierchowod (from Roma in 1983) and Gianluca Vialli (from Cremonese in 1984) as well as Graeme Souness and Trevor Francis, the first of three Italian Cups was won in 1985.

Home and away victories over Milan in the two legs of the final were enough to take the trophy. In the first leg no fewer than four British players took part (Wilkins, Hateley, Souness and Francis) with the Scot scoring the only goal of the game. The goal-scorers in the return tie, Vialli and Mancini, announced the shape of things to come for Sampdoria.

When a second cup win followed in 1988, Sampdoria were obviously well prepared for European competition as well. An impressive run in the 1988-89 Cup Winners' Cup competition ended in a 2-0 defeat to Barcelona in Berne. However, another domestic cup success guaranteed them entry to the same European trophy in 1989-90. This time they did not slip up and two goals by golden boy, Vialli, gave Samp their only European trophy to date. It was seen by many as a major indication that the side that had entertained the crowd so often had come of age and was finally ready for victory at the highest level. This can only be understood in view of the fact that the *Coppa Italia* is not considered such a major competition as the F.A. Cup is in England and that to win that trophy was never likely to gain the same respect for the club as a major European victory or some sort of Serie A success.

The cycle of success which Mantovani had started had still to reach its climax. In 1990-91, the Serie A title was taken under the guidance of Yugoslav Vujadin Boskov. Milan and Inter trailed home five points adrift as a 3-0 win over Lecce (including an incredible strike by Moreno Mannini) gave Sampdoria their deserved glory in front of their home crowd with one game still to play. To celebrate this success Vialli, Ivano Bonetti and Tonino Cerezo bleached their hair with most entertaining results, particularly in the case of the Brazilian. The *Blucerchiati* came close to crowning their achievements with a European Cup win the following season. However, a Ronald Koeman free-kick in extra-time ended this dream in a final which Gianluca Vialli might have won for them had he taken the excellent chances which came his way.

The 'three musketeers' Mancini, Vialli and Vierchowod, who had seen all of Sampdoria's significant victories and resisted the temptation to move on to bigger clubs, were finally broken up in the summer of 1992 when Vialli made a £12 million move to Juventus. Moreover, influential coach Vujadin Boskov was replaced by Sven Goran Eriksson. Boskov had continued the work of Renzo Ulivieri and Eugenio Bersellini and honed his side into one of the most stylish attacking teams in

SAMPDORIA

GIANLUCA VIALLI

(b: 9/7/64 Cremona)

Initially an immensely talented 'wide' player, Vialli was another great youth product from Cremonese. Sampdoria signed him in the hope that he could continue his good partnership with Under 21 team-mate Roberto Mancini. It proved to be a wise move as Vialli became increasingly inspirational to the side, ready to cover the whole pitch to help their cause. He soon broke into the international scene where he has played over 50 times to date. The Sampdoria fans were heartbroken to hear of his transfer to Juventus, where he failed to produce the same magic as he did in Genoa.

All of this is in stark contrast with city rivals Genoa, who have spent a large part of the last ten years down in Serie B. The history of Derby games shows a clear supremacy for Sampdoria since they were founded just after the war – long after Genoa's greatest days had ended. Sampdoria's 29 victories to just 17 for Genoa is a fair reflection on the two sides' fortunes between 1946 and 1993. Sampdoria have shown what is possible for a club to achieve without being the most wealthy team in Italy or even the best supported side in their own city. Supporters like the famous *Ultras Tito Cucchiaroni* (named after Samp's Argentine star of the 1950s) have seen their ranks swollen through the recent success of the club. Traditionally, Sampdoria draw their support from areas like Sampierdarena where half of the original club was born.

However, for many years supporters of the club were outnumbered by about ten to one in the city of Genoa by followers of the club bearing the city's name. Paolo Villaggio, a famous comedian and Sampdoria sympathizer, used to joke that if you wanted to know how Sampdoria were faring away from home you were better off pretending to be a supporter of their opponents – such was the strength of Genoa support in the city. Nowadays, Samp have made up ground in terms of local following, (around 170,000 fans paraded through the streets when they won the title in 1991), thanks to the quality of their play and their league and Cup triumphs. Their success is a tribute to the vision of coaches and chairmen who have held onto their best players and encouraged an attacking, skilful style of play that was bound to bring success. In the post-Vialli era it remains to be seen if the side can continue at the highest level, although the quality of Roberto Mancini's play is almost better than it was before Vialli's departure. They certainly hope to give Genoa plenty to aim at.

ROBERTO MANCINI

(b: 27/11/64 Jesi)

A creative attacking midfielder and one of the greatest Italian talents of recent years. His understanding with Gianluca Vialli often seemed to border on the telepathic. A tremendous bending free-kick as well as incredible volleying technique were amongst the abilities that pushed him into the national side where he never quite managed to produce his outstanding league form. Unlike Vialli, Mancio – as Mancini is called – remained faithful to Sampdoria and also found a regular place in national team coach Arrigo Sacchi's plans.

Serie A. Perhaps his finest hour came in what was virtually a championship decider in the San Siro against Inter in 1991. Soaking up the constant pressure of Inter's attacks, Sampdoria struck twice with stunning counter-attacking play. It was probably the finest game of the season and a fitting tribute to the tactical insight of the much travelled Yugoslav coach. Gianluca Vialli's deadly rounding of Zenga to take the second goal was pure perfection and, despite the Inter goalkeeper's protests, Sampdoria had taken a major step towards their first title.

The loss of a striker of Vialli's quality meant that Sampdoria had given up the player who had won the most international caps in their history. Over 50 appearances place him well clear of Pietro Vierchowod and Roberto Mancini. In truth, it is only this recent success that has thrown Sampdoria players into the national team with any regularity. Goalkeeper Gianluca Pagliuca and right-back Moreno Mannini became regular stars at the highest level although a bad neck injury in a car crash forced Pagliuca to the sidelines at the end of the 1992-93 season. Even balding genius Attilio Lombardo, defender Marco Lanna and young playmaker Eugenio Corini have featured in the plans of the *Azzurri*.

Above: Sampdoria-Roma in January 1956 - Firmani shoots at goal.

TORINO

Torino Calcio, more than any other club in Italy, seem to have had to struggle against fate and then with the ghosts of their own glorious past. One of the toughest teams in Italy to beat on their home soil, they sometimes become victims of their own commitment away from home. With seven league titles, they could rightfully claim membership to the top level of Italian football with only Milan, Inter and bitter rivals Juventus above them.

The story of Torino Calcio begins, as is the case for so many clubs in Italy, as a fusion of other clubs and a group of dissidents from their local rivals. F.C. Torinese and Internazionale Torino along with a group of dissidents from Juventus came together to form Torino Calcio in 1906. In their first season, they came close to a memorable victory as a scoreless draw with Andrea Doria in Genoa left them one point adrift of champions Milan.

There followed a period that was not a particularly happy one for Torino. They managed some consistent league finishes without ever really threatening to win the league title. However, by 1927 the side seemed to be ready to take the title and this they duly did. Celebrations had to be cut short, though, when accusations were made that Torino officials had tried to bribe the Juventus defender, Luigi Allemandi, before their Derby encounter. Despite the fact that Allemandi actually played a blinder, the accusations were upheld and Torino found themselves without their first title.

Still, Torino did not have to wait long for a chance to clear their name since they picked up the title the following year. They won by two clear points with a side that contained some of the finest players of the day, such as Adolfo Baloncieri and Argentinian Julio Libonatti, who would also be capped 17 times for Italy.

Although it was bad to have the title taken away and then lose out to Bologna in 1929, nothing hurt the Torino faithful more than watching Juventus win five titles in a row between 1930 and 1935. Torino's form tailed off badly in this period, almost as if they were becoming discouraged by the success of their rivals and in 1935 they came within one point of relegation.

However, in 1936 Torino returned to more respectable levels finishing in third place – finally ahead of Juve. There followed another second place to Bologna in 1939. The stars of Venezia's 1941 Italian Cup-winning side were two of the hottest 21-year-old properties of the day, Valentino Mazzola and Ezio Loik, and both were soon snapped up by Torino. Under the presidency of Ferruccio Novo and with a little help from national coach, Vittorio Pozzo – a known Torino sympathizer, the *Granata* (clarets) finished in second place behind Roma and were starting to construct a powerful squad.

By 1942-43, the first season in which both Mazzola and Loik played regularly for the club, Torino were ready for the title. Giuseppe Grezar, Romeo Menti and Guglielmo Gabetto were part of the side which completed the league and Cup double by beating Venezia 4-0 in the Cup final (Mazzola grabbing one goal against his old club). Although they had not dominated the championship, they had some of the best young players in Italy and they would soon add several more.

During World War II, the team was kept together by all being given 'jobs' with FIAT. This was surprising because the Agnelli family, who owned FIAT, also owned Juventus and yet they were prepared to help the Torino side maintain its strength. By the time the War was over, no side in Italy could compete with Torino in terms of players or technical organization.

It took one season for Torino to get their side working to perfection as they won another championship in 1945-46, this time by one point from Juventus. The following season they swept all before them, finishing with a massive ten point margin over a stunned Juventus. In May 1947, the Italian national team defeated Puskas' Hungary 3-2 with no fewer than ten Torino players in the side. Only Valerio Bacigalupo, the goalkeeper, missed out to the Juventus goalkeeper Lucidio Sentimenti, though he would be capped later in his career.

If 1946-47 had been an impressive season, then 1947-48 was positively breathtaking. They won 19 of their 20 home games (one draw with Juventus) and took the Serie A by a clear 16 points from Milan. They outscored their nearest rivals by almost 50 goals and along their way thrashed Alessandria (10-0), Salernitana (7-1), Lucchese (6-0) and even joint second place finishers Triestina (6-0).

Club Name:
Torino Calcio
Address:
Corso Vittorio Emanuele II 77, 10128 Torino
Founded: **1906**
Ground:
Stadio Delle Alpi (Capacity: 70,012)
Club Colours:
Claret Shirts, White Shorts, Black Socks with Claret Trim (Away Colours: White Shirts, White Shorts, White Socks with Claret Trim)
Major Honours:
League Champions (1927-28, 1942-43, 1945-46, 1946-47, 1947-48, 1948-49, 1975-76), Italian Cup Winners (1936, 1943, 1968, 1971,1993)

Left: Torino's Brazilian striker Walter Casagrande.
Above: The Stadio Delle Alpi.

VALENTINO MAZZOLA

(b: 26/1/19 Cassano d'Adda – d: 4/5/49)
The captain of the great Torino side of the 1940s and father of Inter's superstar Alessandro. A strong but skilful midfielder, he was rated by those who saw him play as the finest post-war Italian player. A sign of his character came in one famous match while he was still playing with Venezia before signing to Torino. The crowd knew of his imminent sale and showered him with insults when Torino took the lead. Mazzola knuckled down and inspired Venezia to a 3-1 win, thus silencing the crowd before his transfer at the end of the season. Described by Giampiero Boniperti as 'like a bull with perfect ball control', he was killed in the Superga air disaster.

EZIO LOIK

(b: 26/1/19 Fiume – d: 4/5/49) Midfield partner of Valentino Mazzola, their careers seemed intertwined from their days at Venezia, to Torino and then to the Italian national team. He played an important role in Venezia's Italian Cup win in 1941 and then transferred to Torino alongside Mazzola. The pair guaranteed Torino the sort of quality that was always likely to provide success and they helped take Torino to five league titles. Although never quite as prolific as Mazzola, he did manage an admirable 62 goals for the club in those five title winning seasons before he, too, met his death at Superga.

Fate, however, was not to permit the 'Great Torino' side to carry on much further. They were well on their way to an incredible fifth title in a row when disaster struck. With just four games of the season remaining and the title all but sewn up, they were flying back from a friendly with Benfica in Portugal on 4 May 1949 when their plane crashed into the Basilica at Superga on the hills just above Turin. None of the 18 players on board nor the crew had survived. On 6 May, Torino were declared Italian champions and the remaining four games of the season were played by their youth team against the opposing youth sides. All these games were won but, for Torino, an era had ended.

It proved impossible for Torino to replace the players they had lost and the side slumped to the lower reaches of the Serie A before collapsing into Serie B in 1959. Although they returned after just one season in the lower division, the side was still far from truly competitive. A respectable third place finish in 1965 hinted that better times might be around the corner.

Finally, in 1967-68, Torino returned to their winning ways as they picked up the *Coppa Italia* again. Even this win, however, was clouded with sadness. In 1967, one of Torino's most promising young players, Gigi Meroni, was killed. Capped six times by Italy already, he was just 24 years old when he was run down by a car. Once more it seemed that Torino were having to battle against more than just the other sides around them.

Another *Coppa Italia* win in 1971 showed that the team was definitely on its way back. The next season they finished second in Serie A. Eventually, in 1976, the heirs of the legendary side from the Stadio Filadelfia were found. Under the guidance of Gigi Radice, the *Granata* took the title thanks, above all, to their incredible home form. They won fourteen of their fifteen games at the Stadio Comunale. The vast majority of Torino's goals came from the strike force of Paolino Pulici and Francesco Graziani. To finish two points ahead of Juventus and beat them twice in the season was more than most of their followers could

ever have hoped for. The celebrations in Turin were so great that the mayor of the city, Diego Novelli, called them the biggest since the Liberation.

Sadly for Torino this joy was short-lived as, once more, Juventus returned to the top of Italian football and left their local rivals sliding down the table. There was a moment's respite in 1984-85 when Gigi Radice returned to the helm and took the club to a fine second place finish under the presidency of rich industrialist Sergio Rossi. This was to prove to be a false dawn, as certain sections of the Torino faithful accused Rossi of being linked with FIAT (and, therefore, arch-rivals Juventus) and the president eventually became sick of this and left the club soon after. The side then slumped to Serie B in 1989.

Perhaps this was the ideal tonic for the team as they appeared to sharpen up their ideas and begin, once again, to build a team. Torino won Serie B with ease and amongst the players who won promotion were promising young players like Luca Marchegiani in goal, Gianluca Sordo in the midfield and a gangly winger called Gianluigi Lentini. Not only did Torino have some good players, but they were playing some nice football.

Immediately on their return to Serie A, Torino proved good enough to win a place in the UEFA Cup and in the 1991-92 season they came within a whisker of their first European triumph. Having defeated Real Madrid in the semi-final, they lost out to Ajax on away goals in the final. A third place league finish confirmed that coach Emiliano Mondonico knew how to do his job while players like Silvano Benedetti, Roberto Cravero, Enrico Annoni and the Belgian Enzo Scifo provided the backbone of the team.

Once more, though, Torino were to be robbed of many of their greatest players in the summer of 1992, although this time it was by the transfer market. Club president Borsano, who had dragged the club out of Serie B, destroyed his image with the fans by selling off Benedetti to Roma, Cravero to Lazio, Policano to

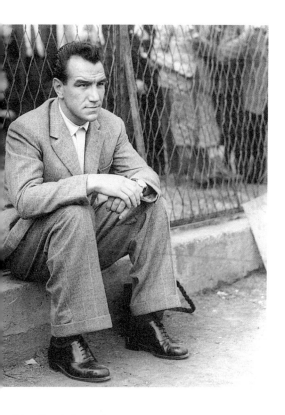

Napoli and above all, Gianluigi Lentini to Milan. This last sale enraged the Torino faithful who had developed an intense love of Lentini as a symbol of the new Torino. However, Juventus and Milan started to make rival bids for the player and when the price reached £13 million, Lentini signed for Milan. The Torino supporters began a string of protests and near-riots through the streets of the city. It was a bitter pill for the fans to swallow.

Without Lentini, and despite the signing of Carlos Aguilera from fellow sell-off specialists Genoa, the 1992-93 season was a subdued one for Torino. However, Lentini's up-and-down form for Milan must have been something of a comfort to the club's owners who could justifiably argue that they got value for money when they sold the young star off.

Lentini was just the latest example of what Torino do best. Their record for bringing through youth players is second to none. In recent years this has brought through the likes of Giuseppe 'Beppe' Dossena, Dino Baggio, Roberto Cravero, Diego Fuser, Marco Osio,

Roberto Rambaudi, Gianluigi Lentini and Gianluca Sordo. Noticeably, only Sordo remains at the club and this seems to be Torino's fate – to produce the quality players that will then help to make other sides great.

This has not always been the case and, in the 1940s in particular, Torino held onto their best products, some of whom helped the team occupy ten of the 11 places in the national team. However, their most capped player came from the 1976 title-winning side as Francesco Graziani picked up 47 caps with the club (64 caps in all). Others to have played significant roles for the national team include Argentinian star Julio Libonatti in the late 1920s and stylish midfielder Giuseppe Dossena, who was an important part of the 1982 World Cup winning side, particularly during qualification.

Obviously, the biggest influences on Torino were during that glorious period in the 1940s under the presidency of Ferruccio Novo, who was instrumental in building up that particular side. More recently, Luigi Radice played an important part, as coach, in re-building the credibility of the Torino team and turning them into a competitive side.

Perhaps the most important influence on Torino, however, has been the success of their local rivals Juventus. Rarely have Torino found themselves consistently ahead of Juventus in the Serie A and this has given added intensity to Derby matches. Indeed, the Turin Derby is the most balanced in Italy. Although well supported by neutrals during Derby games, Torino have a relatively small support outside their own city and must count on locals for the vast majority of their support, whereas Juventus draw fans from all over the peninsula. Rivalry between the two sides is fierce as witnessed by Pasquale Bruno having to be man-handled from the pitch when sent off in a recent Derby. With feelings running so high among the players, it is true to say that supporting Torino is as much about wanting to see Juventus lose as it is about wishing to see the *Granata* win.

PAOLO PULICI

(b: 27/4/50 Roncello) Capped on 19 occasions for Italy, Pulici was one of the main reasons that Torino finally regained the championship in 1976. He played for 15 seasons with the Granata after being signed from Legnano in 1967. His swift wing skills down the left led him to many goal-scoring situations and his 21 strikes in 30 games put him top of the goal-scorers' table in 1976 bettering the 18 goals which had given him the same title the previous season. He finally left the club in 1982 and played for Udinese and Fiorentina before hanging up his boots.

GIANLUIGI LENTINI

(b: 27/3/69 Carmagnola) Brought through Torino's youth ranks, the young winger firmly established himself in the first team as his side fought to get out of Serie B. His first two seasons in Serie A brought him into the limelight as his dribbling skills and ability to cut inside defenders worried even the best defences. A quietly-spoken individual, much loved by the Torino fans, his transfer to Milan provoked fierce protests and left a gap in the team which they found very hard to fill.

Above: A pensive Ezio Loik at Atalanta in 1948.

UDINESE

Udinese are the northernmost club in the Serie A, and one of the oldest. Although they have never won any major Italian titles, they have spent over 20 seasons in the top Italian division, which is an impressive record for a city of just 126,000 inhabitants. The club also has a good record with players imported from South America starting back in 1957 with Luis Pentrelli from Argentina up to 1989 with the arrival of his fellow countryman Abel Balbo.

UDINESE

Udinese started their footballing history with success in 1896 when they were crowned the unofficial Italian champions in Treviso, two years before the first official championship was played for in Turin. This proved to be something of a false start for the side from the Friuli-Venezia Giulia region of Italy (after which their stadium is named). Indeed, it was not until 1911 that the team began to take any regular part in the Italian championship. The years prior to World War I were to be singularly unsuccessful ones for the team as in their only outings at the top level they finished near the bottom of their regional section of the national championship.

By 1919, when competitive football resumed after the war, Udinese appeared in slightly better shape to take on their rivals in the Venetian section of the championship. Their second place finish in 1922 was the best position that they ever achieved against the other sides from their region and they also progressed to the final of the first ever *Coppa Italia* in the same season only to lose out to Vado in extra time. The following season, however, they found themselves in a new league section containing sides from other regions and were immediately relegated to the second division.

There followed one short season back in the top flight in 1925-26 before Udinese tumbled into the lower divisions where it took them almost 25 years to force their way back into the top flight. The side spent several seasons in the newly created Serie C (third division) during the 1930s before finally winning promotion to Serie B in 1939. The struggle to remain in Serie B proved difficult for the *Bianconeri* (black and whites, just like Juventus) and in 1943 they would have been relegated but for the interruption of World War II and a new league structure helping to keep them afloat.

Although they did drop into Serie C in 1948, Udinese appeared to be stronger than their league position suggested and soon won two promotions in successive seasons to take the side into the Serie A in 1950 for the first time in their history. Despite heavy away defeats against Inter and Milan, Udinese managed a more than respectable ninth place finish in their first season at the very top of the game. Soon the side began to find it something of a struggle to remain in Serie A and in 1954 it took play-off matches with Spal and Palermo to help keep Udinese in the top flight. As if spurred on by this result, the 1954-55 season turned out to be the best in the club's history.

Having brought in the Swedish striker Arne Selmosson to partner Italian goal-scorer Lorenzo Bettini, Udinese found a strike force capable of scoring 34 Serie A goals between them. Hard-working attacking midfielder Enzo Menegotti and winger Ercole Castaldo also helped the side to take an incredible second place in Serie A – a result few had thought the side capable of after they had lost their first three matches of the season. The team even managed a memorable 3-2 home win over the eventual champions Milan but were given little time to celebrate their historic championship finish. An official enquiry found the side guilty of bribery during the previous season and they were relegated to Serie B despite their impressive form.

Selmosson was sold on to Lazio but Udinese still proved strong enough to return to Serie A after one season in the lower division. Giuseppe Secchi led the front line for the 1956-57 season, back in the top flight, with 18 goals and was ably assisted from the midfield by a new Swede at the club, Bengt Lindskog. The side's fourth place finish demonstrated that the runners-up spot of 1955 had been no fluke. The arrival of the Argentine star Luis Pentrelli promised much for the following season but the team failed to find the same form and fell to the lower reaches of the Serie A. They narrowly avoided relegation in three successive seasons from 1958 to 1961 and in 1961-62, despite the return of Selmosson, Udinese finished a miserable season at the bottom of the Serie A.

Having seen champions like Lindskog, Pentrelli and, for a second time Selmosson, depart, Udinese could not reverse the negative trend that their relegation had started. The 1963-64 season ended in their descent to Serie C where the side would remain for a depressing

Club Name:

Udinese Calcio

Address:

Via Cotonificio 94, 33100 Udine

Founded: **1896**

Ground:

Stadio 'Friuli' (Capacity: 42,247)

Club Colours:

Black and White Striped Shirts, White Shorts, White Socks (Away Colours: Yellow Shirts, Black Shorts, Yellow Socks)

Left: Francesco Dell'Anno takes on Lazio's Thomas Doll.

BENGT ARNE SELMOSSON

(b: 29/3/31 Sil, Sweden) Despite his six seasons played in Rome, Raggio di Luna ('Moonbeam', due to his blonde hair) was at his happiest and most successful in his two spells at Udinese. A midfielder of great class with an eye for goal, his talents were described by his fellow countryman, Kurt Hamrin, as 'more like those of a South American than a Swede'.

FRANCO CAUSIO

(b: 1/2/49, Lecce) Inextricably linked with Juventus where he won six championships, Causio finished his career in tranquil Udine where he found the fresh lease of life which guaranteed him a World Cup winner's medal in 1982. His dribbling and passing skills both on the wing and in the midfield helped Udinese to their fine sixth place Serie A finish in 1983.

14 seasons. A moment's hope came in 1973 when they finished on top of their division but lost out in a play-off with Parma. Finally, in 1977-78, Udinese won promotion to the Serie B and also took the Anglo-Italian Cup for Serie C sides. Just as they had in the 1940s, Udinese followed their promotion from Serie C to Serie B with immediate promotion to the Serie A in 1978-79. The team won Serie B by six clear points from Cagliari and suffered just four defeats along the way. The following season they were fortunate to stay up as Lazio's relegation for their part in the game-fixing scandal of 1980 meant that, despite finishing second bottom of Serie A, Udinese kept their place in the top flight. In the same season, Udinese picked up their only European honour as they won the Mitropa Cup – a tournament still played for by sides from Italy, Austria, Hungary, Czechoslovakia and Switzerland (and occasionally from Yugoslavia and Romania), although seriously undermined in value by the arrival of the European Cup in 1955.

Having avoided the drop, Udinese set about building a side that might actually manage to make an impact on the top half of the Serie A. The experienced Brazilian sweeper, Edinho, was brought to the club in 1982 to join the likes of ex-Juventus star winger cum midfielder Franco Causio, prolific striker Pietro Virdis and promising youngsters Massimo Mauro and Manuel Gerolin. The side managed an incredible 20 draws in their 30-match season to finish sixth in Serie A just a few points away from a place in Europe. Earlier in 1982, Causio brought immense honour to the club by appearing in the World Cup final – even if it was for just one minute as a sign of affection from manager Enzo Bearzot.

Udinese added still further to their credibility as a top level side in the summer of 1983 when they brought back the young Luigi De Agostini from Catanzaro and stunned their Serie A rivals with the signing of Brazilian genius Zico from Flamengo. Due to the restrictions on the signing of foreign players in operation at the time, the team from Udine avoided the competition of the major clubs who had already filled their foreign player

quota and were thus unable to sign the Brazilian. Their £3 million investment was immediately justified as he struck 19 goals for the club and helped them to ninth place finish in the league.

Zico's second season at the club proved much less profitable due to injury and Udinese saw themselves head closer to the relegation zone. The Brazilian was sold in 1985 and his replacement, Geronimo Barbadillo from Peru, failed to match the Brazilian's high standards. He was, however, one of the few foreign players to remain in Italy after his career ended, opening his own clothes shop in the country. Then the 1986-87 season saw Udinese finish bottom of the Serie A once more and slip into Serie B, despite the signing of the star Argentinian, Daniel Bertoni.

Although they fought their way back to the Serie A for a season in 1989 thanks to the goals of Antonio De Vitis, Udinese fell back into Serie B despite 11 goals from their new South American star Abel Balbo. Eventually the side snatched fourth spot in Serie B in 1991-92 which was enough to return them to Serie A.

Balbo proved to be a revelation in Serie A for the 1992-93 season as he struck no fewer than 21 goals and helped earn his side a play-off with Brescia for the honour of remaining in the Serie A. In a match played in Bologna, yet another Balbo goal contributed to a 3-1 victory that assured them of another Serie A season and relegated their opponents, Brescia.

Udinese may have seen several seasons in the Italian first division but their players have very rarely managed to battle into the Italian national team. The most notable exception to this was the ex-Juventus star, Franco Causio, who chose to end his career with Udinese in the early 1980s. Causio won just six caps whilst with the club – but this still makes him their most capped international. Other full international call-ups came in the 1950s for right-winger Amos Mariani and midfielder Enzo Menegotti. Neither was to have a particularly a lengthy international career. In recent seasons, Udinese have provided Under-21 internationals like Stefano Rossini and Fabio Rossitto for the Italian team but only midfielder Francesco Dell'Anno was seriously considered for full international duty. When Argentine striker Abel Balbo became a naturalized Italian citizen in 1993, rumours began that he might become part of a new generation of *oriundi* to play in the Italian national team but these voices were soon silenced by the Italian football federation.

Because of their relatively lowly position in Italian football, Udinese have never had the chance to compete in major European competition and their only successes have come in minor tournaments such as the Anglo Italian Inter-League Cup and the Mitropa Cup. This lack of genuine success has also led to difficulties in attracting any top quality coaches to the side. Recent

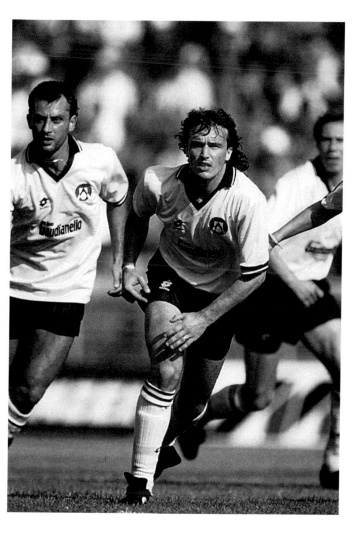

occupants of the hot seat include Corrado Orrico, Giancarlo De Sisti, Adriano Fedele and Albertino Bigon. None of them, however, has been able to take Udinese to the heights of that second place achieved in 1954-55.

The fate for Udinese's most loyal supporters, like that of followers of all Italy's provincial clubs, is to see their most successful players swiftly poached by the richer clubs. This often leaves sides like Udinese struggling to avoid relegation and, only occasionally, pulling off the shock of staying up and managing a finish amongst the top clubs of the Serie A. Still, a battling season to keep a place in the Serie A has a sweet taste that few of the bigger clubs will ever know.

ZICO

(b: 3/3/53 Rio de Janeiro, Brazil) In just two seasons with Udinese (one cut short by injury), Arthur Coimbra Antunes, to give him his full name, won the hearts of the club's supporters with his incredible skills. His 55 goals in just 77 appearances for his country attest to the quality of his play, as do the comparisons with Pelé that followed him throughout his career.

ABEL EDUARDO BALBO

(b: 1/6/66 Villa Constitución, Argentina) Signed from River Plate at just 23 years of age, the tall, powerful Argentine was an immediate success at the club. In his first four seasons with the club he struck 65 league goals and his 21 strikes in the 1992-93 season left him second only to Giuseppe Signori in the goalscorers' table as well as attracting interest from several larger clubs.

Far left: Although keeper Giuliano Giuliani has over 200 Serie A appearances to his name, he made just the one in the 92/93 championship.
Above: Abel Balbo in full flight.

Chronicle of Italian Football

From its origins in the 1890s - heavily influenced by the British game - through the development of what we now know as Serie A, to the highs and lows of international glory and disaster, Italian football has created its own dramatic history.

This chronicle captures some of the key moments of the early days and each decade from the 1940s (above: Milan play Torino in May 1945) to the 1980s (right: Dino Zoff holds the World Cup aloft in 1982), including heroic victories, farcical defeats, genuine tragedy and off-pitch scandal.

the early years

Although some historians have tried to trace the roots of Italian football back to the ancient game of *calcio fiorentino* played in Renaissance Florence, there are few who would deny that the true origins of the game in the peninsula came from England.

Edoardo Bosio, a Turin businessman, set up Internazionale Football Club in Turin in 1891 following numerous visits to England where he saw the game being played. Just two years later, the oldest club still in existence was born. The Genoa Cricket and Athletic Club began its life on 7 September 1893 – under the watchful eye of the Englishman Dr. Spensley. Indeed, even by the time the first championship was organized in 1898, Genoa retained a strong English influence. The team that took that first title (the other competing sides were F.C. Torinese, Internazionale di Torino and the Società Ginnastica di Torino) was Spensley, Leaver, Bocciardo, Dapples, Bertollo, Le Pelley, Ghiglione, Pasteur, Ghigliotti, De Galleani, Baird. Obviously there were no limitations on *stranieri* (foreigners) in those days. So strong was the Genoa side in comparison with the other clubs in Italy at the time that they won no fewer than six of the first seven Italian titles – with Spensley in goal on every occasion. There were other clubs born around this time – Juventus in 1897 and Milan in 1899. They are two of the three most profoundly influential clubs in the development and continuation of football in Italy.

THE AZZURRI ARE BORN

Although competitive football started in Italy at the end of the nineteenth century, it was not until 1910 that a full international side played for the first time. On 15 May 1910 at the Arena di Milano, playing in white strips, Italy took on France. The now famous blue strips were only adopted in 1911 – as a tribute to the House of Savoy who carried this blue on their coat of arms.

It may seem odd that in the eleven that took to the pitch that day, there were no representatives of the Piedmontese side Pro Vercelli who were dominating the championship of the day. The reason for this was simple.

The championship final for 1910 had been scheduled for 24 April but, since many of their players were involved in a military tournament, Pro Vercelli asked for the game to be played on 1 May. Their request was turned down and Pro Vercelli sent their youth team (beaten 10-3 by Inter) in protest. As a result their players were banned for a year. Instead, U.S. Milanese supplied most players to the side (three) although team captain was Francesco 'Franz' Cali of Andrea Doria. Italy emerged victorious by the resounding margin of six goals to two. Pietro Lana struck a hat-trick for Italy with Fossati, Rizzi and De Benardi getting the others. Around 4,000 spectators were there to see the birth of one of the greatest international sides in football.

THE YEAR OF THE TWO TITLES

The Italian Football Federation (FIGC) has governed the often tempestuous affairs of *calcio* since its birth. There have, of course, been many controversial moments along the way and none more so than the 1921-22 season which saw two championship titles awarded.

The giants of the day, such as Pro Vercelli, Genoa, Bologna and Juventus, felt that the smaller clubs had too big a say in the running of football. The bigger clubs broke away to run their own championship – won by Pro Vercelli – while the 'official' title went to little Novese. Fortunately for the sake of the credibility of the growing game of football, the breakaway group was persuaded to return to the fold the following season and since then the threat of such a farcical situation has never again arisen.

TITLE TALES OF TORINO

Torino's first ever title victory, in the 1926-27 season, is, to this day, surrounded by scandal and intrigue which has never been fully resolved. Having brilliantly taken the championship by two points from Bologna, certain Torino officials were then accused of trying to bribe the Juventus defender Luigi Allemandi before a Derby match. The accusations came from a journalist and a student who shared Allemandi's hotel. They stated that the Juventus player had been paid 50,000 lire – half before the game and half after. What added to the mystery was the fact that Allemandi was thought by many observers to be the best player on the park in the game in question. Although Torino lost the title (and Allemandi was banned), Leandro Arpinati, then president of the Italian federation, refused to award the title to his own favourites, Bologna, who had finished in second place. Instead, the title remains in the record books as never having been won. Fortunately for Torino, they went a long way towards restoring their reputation the following season when they won the league with ease and made accusations of corruption seem more than a little ridiculous.

CAMPIONI DEL MONDO

One of the major boosts to the credibility of the Fascist régime in Italy came from footballing triumphs at the World Cups of 1934 and 1938 with an Olympic victory sandwiched in between. However, there was very little of a Fascist nature about the team that won the first of the two trophies. Under the almost invincible leadership of Vittorio Pozzo (87 matches in charge with 60 wins and just 11 defeats) a side was assembled full of *oriundi* (Italians born abroad), usually players from Latin America who conveniently found Italian ancestors so as to be able to don the blue shirts of Italy. Although outwardly Fascism was firmly against such foreign imports, those in power realized the propaganda value of a strong football team and so took a kind view of these 'patriots' who were only, after all, coming back home. Of the 1934 side, victorious 2-1 after extra time over Czechoslovakia, three were Argentinians – the towering defender Luisito

Monti, goalscorer Raimondo Orsi and speedy winger Enrico Guaita. By 1938, however, a truly Italian line-up had been found built around Giuseppe Meazza, the 'brains' of the side, and Silvio Piola, the 'brawn'. Victory over Hungary by a margin of four goals to two was a glorious moment for Italian football and one they would have to wait no fewer than 44 years to repeat.

JUVENTUS TAKE COMMAND

When the Italian championship finally switched to a single league format in 1929, it was because it was felt that football had become such a national phenomenon that it was no longer appropriate to continue to use regional divisions.

At precisely the same moment Juventus had begun to build up one of the strongest sides in Serie A history. They took five titles in a row from 1930-35, a period which profoundly marked the development of Italian football. Juventus put themselves firmly at the top of the game in Italy and began to create the kind of popularity for their black and white strips that no other club in Italy has ever been able to match.

Above: The 1902 Genoa squad – the club took six out of the first seven Italian championships.

the 1940s

The interruption of World War II means that it is hard to describe the 1940s in general terms – and yet one team so dominated the years that it is hard not to think of it as their decade.

The *Grande Torino* (Great Torino) team won five Serie A titles – one before the war and four after it – thereby setting new standards for the quality of football in Italy. The team was kept together throughout the war thanks to 'jobs' invented for them with FIAT in Turin and they emerged after the conflict to find themselves with little opposition.

Sadly for Italian football, the team which could have formed the basis of a successful national team and perhaps thwarted Real Madrid's early European dominance was to be lost due to a tragic air crash in the hills near Turin. For a country emerging from defeat in the war, it was hard to come to terms with.

CAPITAL GAINS

Since the first championship in 1898, no side from further south than Genoa had ever taken the title until Roma picked up the championship in 1942. Some felt that the victory was something which the Fascist régime was keen to see as it would cement Rome's position as the capital. However, the truth was that Roma had a fine side containing one of the season's top scorers, Amedeo Amadei, and two foreign stars, the Argentinian, Pantò, and the Albanian, Krieziù. Krieziù was one of the few players from his country to prove successful in Italy. Roma took the title by three clear points ahead of Torino, a side that would control the rest of the decade.

A PLAYER FOR ALL POSITIONS

The extraordinary record of all-purpose player, Piero Magni, began in 1942 when he first played for Juventus. In a career which included 106 games with the club, Magni played with ten different numbers on his back – including the goalkeeper's jersey. Having been denied the full set of eleven, Magni moved on to Genoa and finally got to wear the number five shirt which he had never before played in – against Juventus in Turin!

What makes Magni's achievement all the more remarkable is that in the 1940s each number referred to a specific position rather than allowing the choice today's players have when it comes to shirt numbering.

FOREIGN INVASION

When World War II was over, Italy found itself submerged beneath an enormous rush of foreign players. From 1946 to 1949, over 120 *stranieri* (foreigners) came into the Serie A from all over Europe and began to have a big impact on the game.

There were many flops in this time but there were also a few players who would go on to affect Italian football deeply. A large number of promising foreigners were spotted at the 1948 Olympic football tournament in London where the Scandinavian nations met with particular success. This led to the arrival of the Danes John Hansen and Karl Praest at Juventus and the Swedes Gunnar Nordahl, Nils Liedholm and Gunnar Gren at Milan.

Although some of these early imports proved to be wise investments, the vast majority had very short careers. Indeed, it was said of the Juventus Czech star, Jan Arpas, that 'he appeared and disappeared like a cat in a sitting room', so infrequent were his games for the club. With the post-war era came the Italian obsession with foreign talent, an obsession which continues to this day.

A STEP IN THE WRONG DIRECTION

The 1945-46 championship, the first after the end of World War II, saw Italy once again divided in footballing terms. Both a Northern championship and a Central/Southern title were played. Only the top four sides from each division went on to the final play-off league. Fortunately, this situation lasted only one season and the following year the Serie A returned to the single league format which had proved so successful since its foundation in 1929.

DISASTER AT SUPERGA

Just when it seemed that Italian football was beginning to find some shape after the interruption caused by the War, it was struck by the greatest disaster in its history.

On 4 May 1949, Torino were well on their way to a fifth successive championship, sweeping all before them. With one of the most complete players in the history of Italian football, Valentino Mazzola, as captain, the Bulls had taken the 1947-48 title by an amazing 16 points. Torino showed just how powerful their new WM formation could be as it permitted them to be both tight at the back and immensely strong in attack.

With an array of stars like goalkeeper Valerio Bacigalupo, defenders Aldo Ballarin and Virgilio Maroso, Mario Rigamonti, Ezio Loik and Giuseppe Grezar in midfield and Guglielmo Gabetto up front, Torino gave no fewer than ten players to the Italian national team in the 3-2 win over Hungary in 1947.

The team also compiled the biggest ever win in Serie A when they dished out a terrible 10-0 defeat to poor Alessandria in 1948. Indeed, the 1947-48 season proved to be particularly memorable as Torino struck home no fewer than 125 goals; this worked out to be an incredible average of one goal every 28 minutes of competitive football.

Club president Ferruccio Novo seemed to have built a team that nobody could compete with as they pulled into a clear lead in the title race of 1948-49. Over the four post-war seasons that Torino won the title they did not lose a single home game and drew just eight times in Turin.

However, tragedy struck this greatest of sides on their way back from a friendly in Portugal with Benfica when their plane crashed into the Basilica of Superga in the hills above Turin. There were no survivors and as Gianni Brera, one of Italy's greatest sports writers, was to say later, 'Italian football lost about ten true champions and, with them, about ten years of football or maybe more.'

Left: The Superga air disaster of 4 May 1949 and (above) the funeral for the Torino players who perished.

the 1950s

After the Superga disaster which had destroyed the legendary Torino side and many Italian internationals, it took Italy time to make up lost ground at both domestic and international levels.

The 1950s were years of poor international form and few truly outstanding club sides. Those which did emerge, such as Inter, Milan, Juventus and Fiorentina suffered in comparison with the Torino team that had gone before them. Moreover, when these sides ventured into Europe for the first time they found the obstacle of the mighty Real Madrid in their way. It was a time of coming to terms with the loss of so many great players and also of attempting to return to playing at the highest level. In this, the second influx of foreign players – most notably from Scandinavia and, once again, Latin America – did much to help the Italian game. As the Italian economy quickly recovered from the ravages of war, so Italian football began to be a more glamorous and star-studded phenomenon.

WORLD CUP FAILURES

Having lost so many great players in an air crash, the Italian squad decided in 1950 to travel to Brazil by ship. This proved to be a great mistake as the players lost fitness and were unable to train properly during the two week journey. All the footballs on board were lost after a couple of days and despite a crowd of 200,000 waiting to greet the team when they disembarked at Rio de Janeiro, the side failed to live up to expectations. A 3-2 defeat by Sweden was enough to send them home again. If this was bad, then worse was to follow with two defeats by the host nation Switzerland eliminating the Italians in 1954.

The final humiliation came with a failure to qualify in 1958, mainly due to a 2-1 defeat by Northern Ireland. This was another team crammed with *oriundi* like Alcide Ghiggia, Miguel Montuori, Dino Da Costa and

Top: **Gunnar Nordhal scores for Milan against Rapid in September 1956.**
Above: **Another Scandinavian import, Lennart 'Nacka' Skoglund.**

Juan Alberto Schiaffino. In the end the skills of the South Americans could not save the Italian side. It was not a good decade for the national team as they struggled to rebuild after Superga.

FIORENTINA TAKE FIRST TITLE

When asked to pick the best Italian club side of the 1950s, most people would have little hesitation in handing the award to Fulvio Bernardini's record-breaking Fiorentina side of 1955-56. Winning the title from Milan by no fewer than 12 points (still a Serie A record) they lost just one game in the entire season – to Genoa on the last day of the league programme. It was the first post-war title to go outside of Turin and Milan and the side would go on to finish as league runners-up in the following four seasons. Stars of the side included super striker Giuseppe 'Pecos Bill' Virgili, left-sided midfielder Armando Segato, stern defender Sergio Cervato, lively goalkeeper Giuliano Sarti and South American Miguel Montuori. The team was so strong that throughout the late 1950s the so-called *blocco della Fiorentina* (block from Fiorentina) came into use with as many as nine players from the Florence club being pulled into the national side. In the season following their championship win, Fiorentina came close to taking the European Cup before succumbing to Real Madrid (playing in Madrid) in the final.

FOREIGN BAN

With the national team performing so badly and seemingly falling behind the Serie A title race in crowd-pulling terms, many sought to lay the blame on the number of foreigners in the Italian game. Following World War II, there had been a major influx of foreign players – particularly Scandinavians such as Nordahl, Gren and Liedholm at Milan – and the presence of these stars meant that people were drawn to the Serie A grounds as never before. In contrast, the national team, naturally deprived of the wide choice they would have

liked because of the presence of these foreign players, turned in such poor performances that attendances began to decline.

In an attempt to solve both of these problems, Giulio Andreotti – at that time a secretary in the ruling Christian Democrat party – decided that no more resident's permits would be given to foreign footballers unless they had Italian nationality, thereby leaving the door open for *oriundi*. One of the main reasons this law was passed was the humiliating 3-0 defeat of Rome by Hungary on 27 May 1953, at the inauguration of the Olympic Stadium in Rome. The standard of play was so poor that many, like Andreotti, sought to lay the blame on the foreigners – in fact, it all sounds vaguely familiar for Italian football followers in the 1990s.

A STAR IS BORN

Juventus have almost always been the pacesetters in Serie A. They were one of the first teams to pay for a transfer when they signed Virginio Rosetta from Pro Vercelli. Equally, they made the first 100,000 lire signing in 1928 when they bought the Argentinian, Raimondo Orsi.

In 1957-58 it was as a result of remarkable feats on the pitch that Juventus once again hit the headlines. Taking their tenth title was obviously an achievement which required some sort of special recognition. As a result, the 'gold star' was invented; this now also adorns the strips of Milan and Inter. Juventus, however, went one step further when they added a second star to their badge in 1982 for picking up title win number 20.

CONFUSION AT THE TOP

While the 20 years prior to the 1950s had been deeply marked by the powerful influence of Vittorio Pozzo as sole coach of the Italian national side, his departure left the way clear for the same sort of chaos that had reigned in the early days of the *Azzurri*. There were no fewer than eight different managerial combinations during the 1950s with an average of four men being in charge on each occasion. The height of this confusion was reached in 1957-58 when no fewer than six men were involved in the training and team selection of the national side: Foni, Pasquale, Schiavio, Tentorio, Marmo and Biancone. Not surprisingly, this particular reign produced four defeats in seven games and soon came to an end. The 1950s proved to be Italy's least successful years.

Above left: Milan-Genoa action from their March 1954 meeting – Nordhal on target again.
Below: Giampiero Boniperti scores for Juventus, October 1951.

the 1960s

The 1960s was the decade of Milan and Inter, of Mazzola and Rivera, of European success and international disaster. The emergence from the shadow of the crash at Superga in 1949 which had wiped out the great Torino team had taken a long time. However, particularly at club level, these years saw a significant growth in the stature of Italian teams around Europe – and the world.

It is curious, perhaps, that despite the 1960s being one of the periods of major growth in FIAT's history it was not Juventus (owned by FIAT bosses, the Agnelli family) but rather Milan and Inter that ruled the roost both at home and on the continent. Once again, it was seen that club success and international success did not necessarily go hand in hand and the most strict and longest-lasting ban in the history of the Italian game was placed on foreign players in the middle of the decade. Maybe it was this that helped the *Azzurri*'s fortunes improve as the decade drew to a close, but perhaps it also cost Italy any chance of European Cup success in the decade to come.

WITH FRIENDS LIKE THESE ...

Poor Catania goalkeeper, Gaspari, found himself on the receiving end of one of the worst pieces of misfortune ever seen in the Serie A on Sunday 29 January, 1961 when his side took on Inter in the Serie A. It was not so much the result, a heavy 5-0 defeat, which shocked the unfortunate goalie but rather the scorers of four of the five goals.

Grani, Corti and Giavara – who grabbed two – were playing for Catania that day as they all struck own goals past the despairing Gaspari.

Top: Giovanni Trapattoni as a player in the 1960s – for Milan.
Above: Trap leaves the Wembley turf after Milan's 1963 European Cup victory over Benfica.

THE BATTLE OF SANTIAGO

Over the years, Italy have been involved in plenty of tough matches, but few more so than in the World Cup of 1962 when they faced host nation Chile in Santiago. The Chilean crowd had already been turned against the Italian side after Italian newspaper reports on the poverty they had seen in Chile filtered back there. Moreover, the inclusion of South American 'traitors' such as Omar Sivori, Jose Altafini and Humberto Maschio did little to endear the *Azzurri* to the home crowd.

Early in the match, Maschio was punched by a Chilean player. Giorgio Ferrini retaliated by kicking out at an opponent. The English referee, Aston, saw fit to send off Ferrini but took no action against the Chileans. Later, with half-time approaching, Mario David was continuing a running battle with the Chilean left-winger when he, too, was sent off. Nine men held out until the 74th minute but ended up going down 2-0 and surrendering another World Cup.

EUROPEAN CHAMPIONS

Finally, in 1963, Milan broke the Real Madrid-Benfica stranglehold on the European Cup when they defeated the Portuguese side at Wembley. Having gone behind to a strike from the legendary Eusebio, Milan reacted well and struck back twice through Jose Altafini. It was the first Italian win in the European Cup (Roma had already won the Fairs Cities' Cup and Fiorentina the Cup Winners' Cup back in 1960-61).

Milan were followed in their European triumph by city rivals, Inter, who beat the other great side of the day, Real Madrid, to take the title in Vienna in 1964. Inter went one better by going on to beat Independiente and win the World Club Cup. The following season, Inter repeated their successes both in Europe and on the World stage. However, not to be outdone, Milan

returned to European glory in 1969, thrashing Cruyff's Ajax to win the title before they, too, managed to emulate Inter and beat Estudiantes for the World Club Cup.

FOREIGN BAN – PART TWO

The attitude of the Italian Football Federation (and the Italian people) towards *stranieri* – the foreign players who help to make Serie A so entertaining – has always been decidedly ambivalent. It is, of course, in the best interests of the championship to have the best players in the world on show every Sunday. On the other hand, the foreign stars make easy scapegoats whenever an Italian side fails in Europe, since they are viewed as caring less for their clubs than their Italian counterparts. Moreover, they stand in the way of homegrown Italian talent. It was with this in mind that a total ban was placed on the buying of foreign players in 1964.

Those already in the country could continue to play and some, such as the Brazilians Amarildo and Nene, or West German World Cup star Karl-Heinz Schnellinger, carried on right into the 1970s. Some would seek to attribute the improved World Cup performances of 1970, 1978 and 1982 to this ban. Whether or not this can be believed is another matter. The ban was eventually lifted in 1980.

NATIONAL DISASTER

When Pak-Doo Ik slammed the ball home for North Korea against Italy in 1966, little did he know he would be writing his name in the record books as part of one of the biggest shocks in World Cup history (rivalled only by England's 1-0 defeat at the hands of the United States amateurs in 1950). Having fielded an under-strength team, believing they would cruise through against the Asians, Edmondo Fabbri's team were left to go home and face the music. Unfortunately, when they landed back in Genoa they had something a little more solid than mere music to face. A hail of rotten tomatoes greeted the returning failures who had headed off with such high hopes of victory. Perhaps the thought of this sort of welcome has helped spur on the Italian side in subsequent moments of crisis.

MAZZOLA VERSUS RIVERA

Having picked up the 1968 European Championship with the help of two young attacking midfielders, Gianni Rivera and Alessandro Mazzola, Italian national team coach, Ferruccio Valcareggi found himself in the unenviable position of having to choose between arguably the two biggest talents in Italian football.

Knowing that he could never have a balanced team with both in the side, Valcareggi concocted a typical Italian compromise, *la staffetta* (the relay baton), which allowed each player to play half a game and increased their rivalry. This was to reach a peak in the 1970 World Cup final when Rivera played for just a few minutes, despite his outstanding performances earlier in the tournament.

Left: Napoli's South Americans Jose Altafini and Omar Sivori.
Above: North Korean players can't believe they've just beaten Italy 1-0 at Middlesborough in the 1966 World Cup.
Below: The best of rivals – Gianni Rivera and Sandro Mazzola.

the 1970s

Because of the ban on foreign players and the dominance of Juventus, the 1970s will be best remembered for the performances of Italian stars like Franco Causio, Roberto Bettega or Pietro Anastasi. Juve picked up five league titles during this time and began to exert an enormous influence on the national team as well. Some fans would see the foreigners' ban as contributing to an up-turn in Italy's international form, as seen both in Mexico and Argentina. However, the truth may be that after the disasters of Chile and England, the only way was up as far as the *Azzurri* were concerned.

THE MIRACLE IN MEXICO

Having come through their opening round matches by scoring just one goal (by Domenghini against Switzerland) and having defeated the mediocre host nation, few would have expected Italy to produce one of the most thrilling encounters in World Cup history in their semi-final with West Germany in 1970. Roberto Boninsegna gave Italy the lead after only eight minutes and from that point on it seemed that the Azzurri would be content to hold onto their lead. This they managed until the final minute of the game when Schnellinger shot through a crowd of players to take the game into extra time. It looked as though the German refusal to give up had paid the same rewards it did against England in the quarter-final.

However, Italy refused to admit defeat and showed the strength of character and physique they had so often been accused of lacking in the past. Gerd Muller gave West Germany a 2-1 lead only for veteran defender Tarcisio Burgnich to equalize. Just before the close of the first half of extra time Luigi 'Gigi' Riva struck a thunderous left-foot shot which once again gave Italy the lead. It appeared that the match might finally have been decided until Gerd Muller popped up once more to head the goal that took the score to 3-3. The final twist of the match came when Gianni Rivera, who some thought was to blame for West Germany's third goal which he failed to clear off the line, struck an unstoppable shot past Sepp Maier. The drama was complete and Italy were through to the final.

The final itself was a disappointment for Ferruccio Valcareggi's team. Many blamed exhaustion or Rivera's absence because of the inclusion of Sandro Mazzola for defeat. Anyone who saw the Brazilian vintage of 1970 would recognize, however, that there was no shame in defeat by a side playing such sparkling football.

INTER'S GREAT ESCAPE

One of the most controversial incidents of the 1970s took place in the 1971-72 European Cup tie between Inter and Borussia Münchengladbach. Trounced 7-1 in Germany, it appeared that Inter were sure to go out of the competition but towards the end of the match Roberto Boninsegna was struck by a beer can. The match was already lost but a replay was ordered and this time around, Inter battled for a 0-0 draw in West Berlin. The 4-2 victory achieved in Milan in the meantime suddenly became enough to carry Inter through, although they eventually lost out in the final to Ajax.

ENGLAND FINALLY BEATEN

In 1973, to celebrate the 75th anniversary of the Italian Football Federation, the past two World Champions, England and Brazil, were invited to Italy to play. Surprisingly, in the previous 63 years of competitive football the Italian national side had never beaten England. This was soon to change.

Goals by Pietro Anastasi and Fabio Capello gave Italy a 2-0 victory in Turin on 14 June, and they were offered the chance to complete an historic double exactly five months later. Around 100,000 people packed into Wembley Stadium to see Peter Shilton parry out an 86th minute Giorgio Chinaglia shot which, once again, landed at the feet of Juventus star Fabio Capello. He gratefully accepted the gift. This remains the only Italian victory against England at Wembley.

DISASTER IN GERMANY

If the Mexico World Cup had been a case of doing better than expected, then 1974 in West Germany was certainly a case of failing to live up to expectations. The opening signals were bad as Dino Zoff, unbeaten in 1143 minutes at international level, was unable to save a shot by the Haitian Sanon. Memories of North Korea in 1966 came flooding back but goals by Rivera, Anastasi and an own-goal from Auguste saved Italy's blushes. In the meantime, the temperamental Chinaglia had hurled his shirt at Valcareggi's feet in disgust when substituted in the 69th minute. The atmosphere was bad and it was only going to get worse after a mediocre draw with Argentina. Finally, a 2-1 defeat at the hands of Poland sent Italy homeward to think again.

THE RETURN OF THE GREAT TORINO?

While Juventus dominated Italian football in the 1970s (taking five league titles) there was a moment's joy for the other half of Turin in the 1975-76 season when Torino picked up their first title in 27 years. It was an emotional moment, naturally bringing back memories of the all-conquering side of the 1940s which perished so tragically in the Superga air disaster. The joy was doubled by the fact that the Juventus team of Zoff, Gentile, Scirea, Bettega and Causio had been left, for once, in second place. Stars for the *Granata* were Paolino Pulici, Francesco 'Ciccio' Graziani and the two Salas, Claudio and Patrizio.

EUROPEAN JUVENTUS AT LAST

After no fewer than 16 unsuccessful attempts, Juventus finally managed to pick up a European trophy by beating Athletic Bilbao on away goals in the UEFA Cup Final. Having won 1-0 in Turin thanks to a Marco Tardelli strike, Roberto Bettega got the vital away goal that helped the *bianconeri* to the trophy despite going

down to a 2-1 defeat. It was the Turin giants' fourth major European Final after previously losing out to Ajax in the European Cup Final in 1973 and to Ferencvaros and Leeds United in the Fairs Cities' Cup (now the UEFA Cup). Despite their domestic dominance, they had to wait longer for European triumph than Milan, Inter, Roma and Fiorentina who all picked up silverware before them.

BEARZOT STARTS TO BUILD

The poor performances of 1974 were soon forgotten as the so-called *blocco Juve* (Juve block) helped Italy to achieve fourth place in the 1978 World Cup. No fewer than nine Juventus players were used in the games against Hungary, Argentina, Austria and Holland. The effects were positive, especially against Argentina where a classic counter-attack gave Roberto Bettega the goal that forced the host nation to play away from Buenos Aires. However, the team that had started the tournament so well, winning three games out of three, began to run out of steam and missed vital chances in a 0-0 draw with West Germany. Finally two long-range strikes past Dino Zoff gave Holland a 2-1 victory and allowed them to enter the final against the host nation whom Italy had already beaten. Although there was disappointment in the Italian camp (especially after losing the third/fourth place play-off to Brazil to two more long-range goals) the foundations had been laid for 1982 in Spain.

Top: Brazilian defender Brito blocks an Italian attack during Brazil's 4-1 victory in the 1970 World Cup Final – for Italy, honour in defeat.
Above: Enzo Bearzot, whose development of the national side in the 1970s would bear rich fruit in 1982.

the 1980s

Like every other period in Italian football, the 1980s had their fair share of excitement and scandal. They began badly with the match-fixing scandal that threatened to bring down a lot more players and clubs than it eventually did.

With the ban on foreigners having been lifted, the best players in the world returned once again to ply their trade in the Serie A. Their effectiveness was seen as the decade drew to a close and Italy picked up all three European trophies in one season. Platini inspired Juventus, Maradona raised Napoli to two titles and the Gullit-Van Basten-Rijkaard trio elevated Milan to new levels. In between times, of course, the *Azzurri* proved the Italian press wrong by achieving their greatest success of modern times. In 1982, after a 44-year wait, Italy picked up the World Cup for the third time in their history on a magical July night in Madrid.

THE FIX

A scandal which had already been brewing in late 1979 finally came to a head in March 1980 following the declarations made by businessman Massimo Cruciani to Rome magistrates. Cruciani claimed that he had, with the collaboration of certain players, agreed to place bets with illegal bookmakers on the outcomes of certain matches in Serie A and B. However, the results that the players had agreed to 'fix' had not gone as intended. Cruciani ended up losing a fortune and so decided to denounce the players and clubs involved.

Among those cited by Cruciani were Paolo Rossi, Bruno Giordano, Enrico Albertosi, Giuseppe Wilson, Lionello Manfredonia, Giuseppe Dossena, Stefano Pellegrini and Giuseppe Zinetti. He also named Juventus, Milan, Lazio, Avellino, Bologna, Perugia, Napoli, Lecce, Taranto, Palermo, Vicenza and Genoa as the clubs involved in the fixing. Milan's 2-1 win over Lazio in particular was put under the microscope as

Cruciani claimed to have lost hundreds of thousands of pounds. One Lazio player, Montesi, confirmed that matches had been fixed but that he had never wished to take part. Following the stunning arrest of some players after matches on 23 March, the following decisions were reached in May of the same year. Lazio and Milan were both relegated to Serie B while Albertosi, Wilson, Giordano, Manfredonia and Rossi, among others, were all banned from the game for periods of up to four years. Felice Colombo, the Milan president, was banned for life and his Bologna counterpart was banned for a year. It was a day of disaster for Italian football, the marks of which continue to this day with rumours of *Totonero* (the black market football pools) still rife, particularly in southern Italy.

WORLD CHAMPIONS – AGAIN

It required something pretty special to take away the bitter taste of the football scandal of 1980 and that was just what Italy got in Spain in 1982. Having been branded the 'worst team ever' by a large section of the sports press, the Italian squad refused to speak to journalists throughout the tournament. Much has been made of the resolve and team spirit that resulted from this – perhaps too much. As it was, Italy did just enough to get through the first round and land themselves in a section with Argentina and the tournament favourites, Brazil.

In the match with Argentina, Gentile cancelled out Maradona in his own uncompromising fashion and goals by Tardelli and Cabrini gave Italy the win. Against Brazil, it was time for Paolo Rossi to come out of hibernation. Once again, the Brazilians made the mistake of pushing on for the win when a draw would have put them through. Twice they pulled back from behind but they could not manage it a third time. Suddenly, from tournament underdogs, Italy had

become the only credible winners of the tournament. With greater self-belief, the *Azzurri* defeated Poland and then West Germany to win the World Cup, even allowing themselves the luxury of a missed penalty in the final. Sandro Pertini, the Italian President, was seen waving his arms in the air beside King Juan Carlos of Spain. The rest of Italy was celebrating too.

DISASTER AT HEYSEL

What should have been one of Italian football's finest moments, Juventus at last winning the European Cup, was tragically marred by one of the greatest disasters ever to hit Italian supporters. Thirty-nine fans (32 of them Italian) were killed as they attempted to flee from advancing Liverpool fans. When the supporting wall collapsed behind the retreating fans, there was little that could be done to save them from being crushed to death.

Anyone who watched that night would have been sickened to see what football could become in the hands of a few mindless idiots. It seems foolish to try to lay the blame on any particular group of people, rather it would be better to concentrate on making sure such a disaster never takes place again. With a typical knee-jerk reaction, UEFA banned English clubs from Europe and that tragic night at Heysel became a turning point in European football. English football, for reasons other than simply not being allowed to compete, was about to find that its period of European supremacy had come to an end.

VIVA DIEGO

The fact that Napoli remained, until 1987, without a single league title to their credit was a sign of Italy's division. Without the resources and often, they felt, their northern rivals' advantage of 'friends in high places', Napoli continually missed out on the biggest prizes despite enormous support from their fans. One man, however, did more than any other to change that. Diego Armando Maradona came to Naples in 1984 and helped to transform a mid-table side into title contenders. By 1986-87, the time had come for Napoli to bring the Serie A title to the heart of Southern Italy.

They finished three points clear of Juventus and joyous celebrations engulfed Naples. Without the division of loyalties existing in most major Italian cities, the whole of Naples was behind their *Azzurri*, who were to take the title once again in 1989-90.

SACCHI'S REVOLUTION

While Napoli president Corrado Ferlaino was looking to build his own super-squad, Silvio Berlusconi was undertaking similar operations at AC Milan. Under the guidance of Arrigo Sacchi – the coach brought from progressive Parma – Milan had thrown off the old cautious style of Italian football and now adopted a 'pressing' tactic that virtually suffocated opponents by surrounding the man with the ball.

This tactic came to fruition in the 1988-89 European Cup competition when Real Madrid were utterly humiliated 5-0 in the San Siro at the semi-final stage and saw their dreams of regaining the trophy in tatters. Steau Bucharest fared little better as they were trounced 4-0 in the final, barely managing to get out of their own half throughout the match and conceding all the goals in the space of just half an hour's play.

Far left: The triumphant 1982 World Cup-winning team.
Above: A fan appeals for help during the tragedy at Heysel.

crossover

From the important role that Britons played in the foundation of clubs such as Genoa, Milan, Juventus and Napoli to the birth of rival clubs set up by Italians, the footballing relationship between Italy and the British Isles has known plenty of ups and downs. The erstwhile 'home of football' appeared for a long time to have put a jinx on Italy both at club and international level but this seems to have faded, especially in recent years. The fortunes of British players in the Italian league have seen more total failure than shining success, although there have been just enough successful UK players to keep the top clubs coming back for more.

The story goes back to the very origins of Italian football when Genoa dominated Italian football taking six of the first seven titles with the famous Englishman, Dr. Spensley, in goal. However, these first *stranieri* (foreigners) were not 'imports' in the way we think of them today, but rather ex-patriots who felt a certain nostalgia for the game they had loved in their home country. The arrival of the first British players actually signed while playing abroad did not take place until almost half a century later.

The only British import of note to arrive in Italy before World War II years was the Scottish-Italian, Giovanni 'Johnny' Moscardini, born in Falkirk in 1897. Moscardini joined the Italian army in World War I, during which time he sustained an injury which he did his best to hide for the remainder of his career. His left arm was about eight inches shorter than his right but Moscardini developed a special pose for pictures in which this problem was

well concealed. He was spotted playing football in his father's home town of Barga just after the War. As a result, he was called for a trial with Lucchese where he would later be called up to the Italian national team as one of the first *oriundi* (players of Italian descent born abroad). 'Johnny' played nine times for Italy, scoring seven goals, and his team-mates noted how, as a striker, he played *all'inglese* (in the English style) – a term still used to describe a physical, courageous player who may be somewhat lacking in technique. It was this style that would mark out the likes of John Charles and Joe Jordan in the future – even though neither of them were actually English!

After Moscardini retired from the game and returned to Scotland in 1925, no more Britons ventured to Italy despite the first 'boom' of imports in the 1930s. At this stage, Italy still preferred to look to South America for its foreign stars while England, in particular, still believed itself to be the home of the real world champions who had nothing to learn by playing football outside their own country.

All this was to change, however, after England's miserable World Cup showing of 1950 and the dreadful hammering received at Wembley by Puskas, Hidegkuti and the rest of that outstanding Hungarian side. Suddenly it appeared that perhaps there might be something to be gained by playing the game abroad. Equally, the Italian fascination with South American players had begun to wane a little and the physically stronger Scandinavians such as John Hansen, Gunnar Nordahl and Nils Liedholm came to Italy. This expanded view of possible sources of foreign talent led the Italian eyes to be cast towards the British Isles.

The first real success story of this new-found interest in all things British was the tall Welshman, John Charles, signed by Juventus from Leeds United for £65,000 in

1957. Prior to the gentle giant's arrival, only Englishmen Norman Adcock at Padova, Triestina and Treviso and Frank Ratcliffe at Alessandria, along with Irishman Paddy Sloan at Milan, Udinese and Brescia had made the long trip south to Italy.

It was Charles who proved arguably to be the most successful British player of all time in his five seasons with Turin's most famous club. His record of 93 league goals with the club has never been approached, let alone equalled, by any other Briton and his three Italian titles and two Italian Cup Winners' medals are a record that any Serie A player would be proud of.

Charles was such a hero at the club that he even went so far as to release records, such as 'Love in Portofino', which sold well among the Juventus faithful. He was a shining example for all those Britons who followed in his footsteps. If a player could settle into the Italian lifestyle and learn the language, there was much to be enjoyed from playing football in Italy.

As often happens in Serie A, if one particular nationality proves successful at a certain club then it is certain that others sides will follow suit. Having seen Charles succeed at Juventus, three other clubs (Torino, Milan and Inter) moved into the British market place in 1961. Torino made the double signing of Denis Law from Manchester City and, in the hope of keeping Law company, Joe Baker from Hibernian. Meanwhile, Milan brought in Jimmy Greaves from Chelsea and Inter took Gerry Hitchens. Of the four, only Hitchens lasted more than a season as the others failed to adapt to what they saw as the 'monastic' lifestyle demanded of Italian players at the time. This was a stern warning to Serie A sides of one of the unfortunate aspects of buying even the best British players. Law, Greaves and Baker had been reasonably successful on the pitch but it took more than just goals to make a worthwhile import – the player really had to feel at home in the country. Only Hitchens succeeded in this respect and indeed played for eight seasons in Italy, moving from Inter to Torino and then to Atalanta and finally

British imports (clockwise from bottom left): John Charles, Gerry Hitchens and Jimmy Greaves.

Above: Graeme Souness and Trevor Francis in Sampdoria's colours at the Luigi Ferraris Stadium, Genoa in July 1984.

Cagliari. These eight seasons made him the longest serving Briton in the history of the Italian game.

By 1964 when the major ban was imposed on foreign players (partly caused by Italy's particularly poor performance in the 1962 World Cup and failure to qualify in 1958), only Hitchens was left in Italy and he finished his Italian adventure in 1969 bringing the first chapter of British involvement in Italian football to a close. In the 1970s, the only 'British connection' came from Darlington-born Italian Giuseppe Wilson and Tuscan Giorgio Chinaglia who was brought up in South Wales. Both played for Lazio in their championship-winning side and only got around the ban thanks to their Italian ancestry.

The ban was lifted in 1980, since it was felt by many that there was a need for foreign talent to strengthen the Serie A sides. Immediately, the Arsenal midfield star Liam Brady was taken on by Juventus where he helped the side to two championships, scoring the last-match penalty which guaranteed his side the league title ahead of Fiorentina in 1982. He followed this with two season spells at emerging Sampdoria and old giants Inter. Finishing his Italian career with Ascoli was a sign of just how much Brady enjoyed his Italian experience. Once again the flood gates were set to open on imports from the UK.

Joe Jordan arrived at Milan in 1981 and helped them out of Serie B in 1983 before moving on to Verona. Nicknamed *Lo squalo* (The Shark) after the movie success of the period, 'Jaws', Jordan never really reproduced his Serie B form in Serie A and spent just three seasons in Italy. Soon after Jordan's arrival, Trevor Francis arrived at Sampdoria where he was joined by Graeme Souness. Ray Wilkins and Mark Hateley came to Milan and Gordon Cowans and Paul Rideout went from Aston Villa to Bari for three seasons.

This surge of interest in British players took place despite the total flop of Milan's signing of Watford's top scorer, Luther Blissett. Blissett had struck 27 league goals for Watford in 1982-83 but followed this up with an abysmal total of five strikes in 30 games for Milan. Once again, another painful lesson had been learned – just because a player can score plenty of goals in Britain there is no guarantee he will even score once in the Serie A.

Francis and Souness proved to be a good combination at Sampdoria in 1985 as they took the side to a fourth place Serie A finish and the Italian Cup.

'Here is Samp's new leader,' the press said of Souness, 'he looks like Tom Selleck, the actor who plays Magnum.'

He marshalled Samp's midfield well but in 1986 some in-fighting led to the Scot proving less influential and he went back to Scotland while Francis moved on for one season at Atalanta before he, too, returned home.

Paul Elliott spent a happy two year spell with Pisa from 1987-89 but he was joined in Italy by a player who would prove a terrible disappointment in the Serie A. Juventus had picked out a Welsh striker, Ian Rush, to follow in John Charles' footsteps. They had hoped Rush would take them back to the top but in this, he certainly failed.

'It's like being in a foreign country,' he allegedly moaned, and rumours abounded that he missed home comforts and could not pick up the language.

It was to be an experience which warned Serie A clubs once more of just how risky an investment a British player could be. Germans, Dutch and South Americans seemed more reliable.

It was not until 1991 that a club chose to take the British route again when Bari signed David Platt. Despite his side going down to Serie B, Platt impressed enough to catch the attention of Juventus. Obviously enjoying life in Italy, Platt had made up his mind early that he was going to make a serious effort to fit in. Italian lessons and a desire to live as an Italian saw to it that Platt won much acclaim and even in his long spells in the stands for Juventus he was praised for the way he comported himself as a perfect professional.

By 1992, Platt was joined by pacy defender Des Walker and midfield talent Paul Gascoigne. Walker struggled as he was often played out of position at left-back and many wondered about the wisdom of buying a British defender when Italy has always managed to produce so many good defenders of her own. Gascoigne, for his part, was coming back after a season's lay-off due to injury and had an up-and-down first season which flickered with brilliance and controversy without ever fully taking off. By Summer '93, Walker was heading back home, Platt across to Sampdoria, and Gazza was still with Lazio.

If the story of the British player in Italy is full of highs and lows, so is the history of encounters at club and international level between the two countries. On some occasions, most notably during the 1970s, it seemed that Italian sides could do nothing against the might of Britain, especially England, in Europe. However, that situation has changed greatly and recent seasons seem to show that Italian football has improved and adapted to cope with what the British Isles has to offer in terms of football competition.

The first official meeting between the Italian national team and a side from the British Isles took place in Rome on 20 May 1931 when Scotland were the visitors. Easily dispatched 3-0 by a large part of what would become the 1934 World Cup-winning team, it was a promising start for the *Azzurri* but one which was not to continue in such style. Their first game with England ended a 1-1 draw in Rome and soon after they lost 3-2 to England at Highbury. Italy had to wait until 1973 to beat England – which they did both at Turin and Wembley – thereby ending a poor sequence of results. Recent meetings have seen Italy reverse this form and they have not lost to England since 1976,

the last meeting between the two sides being Italy's 2-1 win in the third and fourth place play-off in the 1990 World Cup.

Italy's meetings with the rest of the British Isles have been relatively few. They have twice tangled with Scotland in World Cup qualification (for the 1966 and 1994 competitions) and have suffered just one defeat, thanks to a late John Greig goal at Hampden Park in 1965. Wales have met Italy on four occasions losing all but one surprise away win in Brescia in 1988. Northern Ireland's 2-1 home win helped put Italy out of the 1958, although they, too, have lost more than they have won. The Republic of Ireland, for their part, have never beaten or even managed a draw with the Italian national side in their six meetings.

In European competition, meetings have been much more regular and tell a most interesting story. The early meetings between the two sides tended to go in favour of the Italians but by the late 1960s and throughout the 1970s and early 1980s, British sides proved to be some of the Italian's most difficult adversaries. Recently, however, the tide appears to have turned and the

Above: Ian Rush in his only season with Juventus.
Below: Luther Blissett at the San Siro after signing for Milan in July 1983.

CROSSOVER

Serie A stars have progressed much further in Europe and won most of the direct battles with sides from the British Isles.

The first major meeting between the two sides (Inter had lost out to Birmingham City in the inaugural Fairs Cities' Cup) took place when Milan played both Glasgow Rangers and Manchester United in the 1957-58 European Cup. The Italian side dismissed the Scots' challenge with a resounding 6-1 aggregate win and proceeded to the semi-finals stage where they met Manchester United. A 2-1 home win gave a slight advantage to the Red Devils but Milan, with two goals from Schiaffino, and one each for Liedholm and Danova, won 4-0 in the San Siro and went on to miss out narrowly in a 3-2 defeat to Real Madrid in the final.

Other notable encounters in these formative years of European competition came in two major finals of 1961. In the Fairs Cities' Cup, which would become the UEFA Cup, Roma beat Birmingham City who had earlier put Inter out of the competition. Meanwhile, in the Cup Winners' Cup Final, Fiorentina took on Glasgow Rangers over two legs. A 2-0 win at Ibrox virtually guaranteed the Florence outfit their one and only European trophy and Swedish winger, Kurt Hamrin, did much to cement international relations between Scotland and Italy by dribbling down the wing while making rude gestures to the Rangers faithful. A 2-1 home win was enough to make sure of the cup.

By 1965, it was noticeable that a subtle change had begun to occur in battles between Italian and British sides. Perhaps the ban on foreign players was already weakening Italian club sides or maybe British clubs had learned to play against the Italians. Whatever the reason, Liverpool's win against Juventus thanks to goals from Lawler and Strong proved to be a turning point in the story of European ties between Britain and Italy. Milan were eliminated by Chelsea in the Fairs Cities' Cup of the same season after the London club had already disposed of Roma. Leeds United also put an end to Torino's involvement in the same tournament, confirming the fact that British clubs, especially those from England, had found the measure of many of the Italian giants.

Although Italian sides did score some wins over British clubs in the ensuing years, they were not as frequent as they had previously been. Glasgow Celtic staged their momentous fight back against Inter in 1967 to become the first British side to take the European Cup. Later, their arch-rivals, Rangers, knocked Torino out of the Cup Winners' Cup on their way to winning the trophy in 1972. Moments like Milan's win over Manchester United on their way to the 1969 European Cup or their win over Leeds United in the 1973 Cup Winners' Cup Final were few and far between. Other matches, like Juventus's win over Derby County in 1973, were clouded with Brian Glanville's accusations of the 'golden fix' which saw the Italian club's officials accused of attempting to bribe the referee.

It was not until the 1980s that Italian football finally seemed able to compete once again with sides from the other side of the English Channel. Juventus led the way with their impressive 5-2 aggregate win over Aston Villa in the 1983 Champions Cup and eliminated Manchester United from the Cup Winners' Cup the following year. At the same time, Roma were progressing in the European Cup thanks to a remarkable comeback after losing out 2-0 to Dundee United away from home. In another good advert for Italo-Scottish relations, Roma won 3-0 in the Stadio Olimpico and surrounded United manager Jim McLean at the end of the match to return the insults they had received in Scotland. In that 1984 final, Roma lost out to Liverpool on penalties but it was to be the last time a British club would put an Italian team out of Europe.

Certainly, the ban on English clubs following Juventus's European Cup win over Liverpool at Heysel had a profound effect on matches between the two nations. When Inter met Aston Villa in 1990 it was an important occasion as it was the first time Italian and English sides had met since the ban had been lifted. It would be a sign of whether Italy's new-found

confidence in Europe would continue with the return of the English teams. A 2-0 home win seemed to guarantee Villa their passage to the third round but a rousing home performance saw Inter grab a 3-0 win which demonstrated both immense character and just how much the Italian game had improved.

At precisely the same time, Bologna were performing a similar comeback (having lost 3-1 away) against Heart of Midlothian. In 1992, with Liverpool back in Europe, they met Genoa in the UEFA Cup but the Italian side illustrated just how much things had changed in European football with home and away wins over what had once been the most feared side in Europe.

The footballing conflicts between Italy and the UK have been numerous both at club and international level with the balance swinging from one side to another through the decades. This history has been complemented by more than twenty British stars coming to try their luck in Italy. In the opposite direction, the likes of ex-Pisa goalkeeper Alessandro Nista are among the few who have tried the experience – and he lasted just a few months under the stern training régime at Leeds United. With the now greatly improved salaries in Italy, there seems no reason for any Italian to try to come and play in Britain. As far as club and national matches between the two sides are concerned, Italy are enjoying a degree of supremacy at the moment, although with the Italian economy under a certain amount of strain and the anxiety of the British sides to recapture former glories, there is no saying how long this situation will last.

Above: Torino's Denis Law indulges in post-match analysis with Milan's Mario David after their match in December 1961.

Serie A Statistics

SCUDETTO WINNERS

Juventus	22
Inter	13
Milan	13
Genoa	9
Torino	7 (+ 1 revoked)
Bologna	7
Pro Vercelli	7
Fiorentina	2
Napoli	2
Cagliari	1
Lazio	1
Sampdoria	1
Verona	1
Casale	1
Novese	1

MOST GOALS FROM A PLAYER IN ONE MATCH

6 GOALS
Silvio Piola
PRO VERCELLI vs Fiorentina (7-2 1933/34)
Omar Sivori
JUVENTUS vs Inter (9-1 1960/61)

5 GOALS
Italo Rossi
PRO PATRIA vs Roma (6-1 1929/30)
Giovanni Vecchina
PADOVA vs Pro Patria (7-0 1929/30)
Cesare Fasanelli
ROMA vs Livorno (7-1 1930/31)
Giuseppe Meazza
AMBROSIANA INTER vs Bari (9-2 1937/38)
Guglielmo Gabetto
JUVENTUS vs Bari (6-2 1939/40)
Romano Penzo
INTER vs Genoa (9-1 1945/46)
Istvan Mike
BOLOGNA vs Livorno (6-2 1948/49)
Bruno Ispiro
TRIESTINA vs Padova (9-1 1948/49)
Em. Del Vecchio
VERONA vs Sampdoria (5-3 1957/58)
Carlo Galli
MILAN vs Lazio (6-1 1957/58)
A. Valentin Angelillo
INTER vs Spal (8-0 1958/59)
Kurt Hamrin
Atalanta vs FIORENTINA (1-7 1963/64)
Roberto Pruzzo
ROMA vs Avellino (5-1 1985/86)

SCUDETTO ROLL OF HONOUR

1898 Genoa	1948 Torino
1899 Genoa	1949 Torino
1900 Genoa	1950 Juventus
1901 Milan	1951 Milan
1902 Genoa	1952 Juventus
1903 Genoa	1953 Inter
1904 Genoa	1954 Inter
1905 Juventus	1955 Milan
1906 Milan	1956 Fiorentina
1907 Milan	1957 Milan
1908 Pro Vercelli	1958 Juventus
1909 Pro Vercelli	1959 Milan
1910 Inter	1960 Juventus
1911 Pro Vercelli	1961 Juventus
1912 Pro Vercelli	1962 Milan
1913 Pro Vercelli	1963 Inter
1914 Casale	1964 Bologna
1915 Genoa	1965 Inter
1916-1919 Suspended	1966 Inter
1920 Inter	1967 Juventus
1921 Pro Vercelli	1968 Milan
1922 Pro Vercelli (C.C.I)	1969 Fiorentina
Novese (F.I.G.C)*	1970 Cagliari
1923 Genoa	1971 Inter
1924 Genoa	1972 Juventus
1925 Bologna	1973 Juventus
1926 Juventus	1974 Lazio
1927 Torino (revoked)	1975 Juventus
1928 Torino	1976 Torino
1929 Bologna	1977 Juventus
1930 Ambrosiana Inter	1978 Juventus
1931 Juventus	1979 Milan
1932 Juventus	1980 Inter
1933 Juventus	1981 Juventus
1934 Juventus	1982 Juventus
1935 Juventus	1983 Roma
1936 Bologna	1984 Juventus
1937 Bologna	1985 Verona
1938 Ambrosiana Inter	1986 Juventus
1939 Bologna	1987 Napoli
1940 Ambrosiana Inter	1988 Milan
1941 Bologna	1989 Inter
1942 Roma	1990 Napoli
1943 Torino	1991 Sampdoria
1944-5 Suspended	1992 Milan
1946 Torino	1993 Milan
1947 Torino	

* F.I.G.C. Federazione Italiana Giuoco Calcio
C.C.I. Confederazione Calcistica Italiana

COPPA ITALIA ROLL OF HONOUR

1922 VADO-Udinese	1-0
1936 TORINO-Alessandria	5-1
1937 GENOVA-Roma	1-0
1938 JUVENTUS-Torino	3-1
1939 AMBROSIANA INTER-Novara	2-1
1940 FIORENTINA-Genova	1-0
1941 VENEZIA-Roma	3-3, 1-0
1942 JUVENTUS-Milano	1-1, 4-1
1943 TORINO-Venezia	4-0
1958 LAZIO-Fiorentina	1-0
1959 JUVENTUS-Inter	4-1
1960 JUVENTUS-Fiorentina	3-2
1961 FIORENTINA-Lazio	2-0
1962 NAPOLI-Spal Ferrara	2-1
1963 ATALANTA-Torino	3-1
1964 ROMA-Torino	0-0, 1-0
1965 JUVENTUS-Inter	1-0
1966 FIORENTINA-Catanzaro	2-1
1967 MILAN-Padova	1-0
1968 TORINO (Winners in final group of 4)	
1969 ROMA (Winners in final group of 4)	
1970 BOLOGNA (Winners in final group of 4)	
1971 TORINO-Milan	0-0 (5-4 pens)
(Winners of play-off in final group of 4)	
1972 MILAN-Napoli	2-0
1973 MILAN-Juventus	1-1 (6-3 pens)
1974 BOLOGNA-Palermo	1-1 (5-4 pens)
1975 FIORENTINA-Milan	3-2
1976 NAPOLI-Verona	4-0
1977 MILAN-Inter	2-0
1978 INTER-Napoli	2-1
1979 JUVENTUS-Palermo	2-1
1980 ROMA-Torino	3-2 (AET)
1981 ROMA-Torino	1-1, 1-1 (5-4 pens)
1982 INTER-Torino	1-0, 1-1
1983 JUVENTUS-Verona	0-2, 3-0
1984 ROMA-Verona	1-0, 1-1
1985 SAMPDORIA-Milan	2-1, 2-1
1986 ROMA-Sampdoria	2-0, 1-2
1987 NAPOLI-Atalanta	3-0, 1-0
1988 SAMPDORIA-Torino	1-0, 1-2 (AET)
1989 SAMPDORIA-Napoli	0-1, 4-0
1990 JUVENTUS-Milan	0-0, 1-0
1991 ROMA-Sampdoria	3-1, 1-1
1992 PARMA-Juventus	0-1, 2-0
1993 TORINO-Roma	3-0, 2-5

COPPA ITALIA WINNERS

Juventus	8
Roma	7
Torino	5
Fiorentina	4
Milan	4
Inter	3
Napoli	3
Sampdoria	3
Bologna	2
Atalanta	1
Genoa	1
Lazio	1
Parma	1
Vado	1
Venezia	1

MOST PROLIFIC STRIKERS

	GOALS
Silvio Piola	290
Gunnar Nordahl	225
Giuseppe Meazza	218
José Altafini	216
Kurt Hamrin	190
Amedeo Amedei	188
Guglielmo Gabetto	187
Giampiero Boniperti	177
Giuseppe Savoldi	168
Roberto Boninsegna	163
Adriano Bassetto	158
Luigi Riva	156

MORE SERIE A RECORDS

The fewest number of goals scored on one day of Serie A play is 6 (1969 & 1979).

The Sicilian side, Catania, hold the record for collecting the fewest number of points in a Serie A season: 12 (1983/84).

Varese (71/72) and Catania (83/84) managed just one victory in Serie A during their respective seasons.

During the 1949/50 season, Venezia conceded a record 89 goals in Serie A.

SERIE A TOP SCORERS

SEASON	PLAYER	TEAM	GOALS
1929/30	Giuseppe Meazza	Ambrosiana Inter	31
1930/31	Rodolfo Volk	Roma	29
1931/32	Angelo Schiavio	Bologna	25
	Pedro Petrone	Fiorentina	
1932/33	Felice Borel	Juventus	29
1933/34	Felice Borel	Juventus	32
1934/35	Enrico Guaita	Roma	28
1935/36	Giuseppe Meazza	Ambrosiana Inter	25
1936/37	Silvio Piola	Lazio	21
1937/38	Giuseppe Meazza	Ambrosiana Inter	20
1938/39	Aldo Boffi	Milan	19
	Ettore Puricelli	Bologna	
1939/40	Aldo Boffi	Milan	24
1940/41	Ettore Puricelli	Bologna	22
1941/42	Aldo Boffi	Milan	22
1942/43	Silvio Piola	Lazio	21
1944-45	Suspended		
1945/46	Eusebio Castigliano	Torino	13
1946/47	Valentino Mazzola	Torino	29
1947/48	Giampiero Boniperti	Juventus	27
1948/49	Istvan Nyers	Inter	26
1949/50	Gunnar Nordahl	Milan	35
1950/51	Gunnar Nordahl	Milan	34
1951/52	John Hansen	Juventus	30
1952/53	Gunnar Nordahl	Milan	26
1953/54	Gunnar Nordahl	Milan	23
1954/55	Gunnar Nordahl	Milan	27
1955/56	Gino Pivatelli	Bologna	29
1956/57	Dino Da Costa	Roma	22
1957/58	John Charles	Juventus	28
1958/59	A. Valentin Angelillo	Inter	33
1959/60	Omar Sivori	Juventus	27
1960/61	Sergio Brighenti	Sampdoria	27
1961/62	José Altafini	Milan	22
	Aurelio Milani	Fiorentina	

SEASON	PLAYER	TEAM	GOALS
1962/63	Harald Nielsen	Bologna	19
	Pedro Manfredini	Roma	
1963/64	Harald Nielsen	Bologna	21
1964/65	Sandro Mazzola	Inter	17
	Alberto Orlando	Fiorentina	
1965/66	Luis Vinicio	L.R. Vicenza	25
1966/67	Luigi Riva	Cagliari	18
1967/68	Pierino Prati	Milan	15
1968/69	Luigi Riva	Cagliari	20
1969/70	Luigi Riva	Cagliari	21
1970/71	Roberto Boninsegna	Inter	24
1971/72	Roberto Boninsegna	Inter	22
1972/73	Giuseppe Savoldi	Bologna	17
	Gianni Rivera	Milan	
	Paolino Pulici	Torino	
1973/74	Giorgio Chinaglia	Lazio	24
1974/75	Paolino Pulici	Torino	18
1975/76	Paolino Pulici	Torino	21
1976/77	Francesco Graziani	Torino	21
1977/78	Paolo Rossi	L.R. Vicenza	24
1978/79	Bruno Giordano	Lazio	19
1979/80	Roberto Bettega	Juventus	16
1980/81	Roberto Pruzzo	Roma	18
1981/82	Roberto Pruzzo	Roma	15
1982/83	Michel Platini	Juventus	16
1983/84	Michel Platini	Juventus	20
1984/85	Michel Platini	Juventus	18
1985/86	Roberto Pruzzo	Roma	19
1986/87	Pietro Paolo Virdis	Milan	17
1987/88	Diego Maradona	Napoli	15
1988/89	Aldo Serena	Inter	22
1989/90	Marco Van Basten	Milan	19
1990/91	Gianluca Vialli	Sampdoria	19
1991/92	Marco Van Basten	Milan	25
1992/93	Giuseppe Signori	Lazio	26

MOST APPEARANCES

Dino Zoff	**570**
(Udinese, Mantova, Napoli & Juventus)	
Silvio Piola	**565**
(Pro Vercelli, Lazio, Juventus & Novara)	
Enrico Albertosi	**532**
(Fiorentina, Cagliari & Milan)	
Gianni Rivera	**527**
(Alessandria & Milan)	
Pietro Ferraris	**506**
(Pro Vercelli, Napoli, Am.Inter, Torino & Novara)	
Tarcisio Burgnich	**494**
(Udinese, Juventus, Palermo, Inter & Napoli)	
Giancarlo De Sisti	**477**
(Roma & Fiorentina)	
Giacinto Facchetti	**475**
(Inter)	
Sergio Cervato	**466**
(Fiorentina, Juventus & Spal)	
Franco Causio	**460**
(Lecce, Palermo, Juventus, Udinese & Inter)	

MOST LOYAL SERVANTS

		APPEARANCES
Gianni Rivera	Milan	501
Giacinto Facchetti	Inter	475
Giampiero Boniperti	Juventus	444
Sandro Mazzola	Inter	417
Mario Corso	Inter	413
Giorgio Ferrini	Torino	405
Giacomo Bulgarelli	Bologna	391
Giuseppe Bruscolotti	Napoli	387
Giacomo Losi	Roma	386
Gaetano Scirea	Juventus	377
Carlo Reguzzoni	Bologna	377
Giuseppe Furino	Juventus	361
Nils Liedholm	Milan	359
Tarcisio Burgnich	Inter	358
Antonio Juliano	Napoli	355

MORE SERIE A RECORDS

The 48 goals scored on October 4 1992 represent the highest total on one day for an 18-team Serie A. The record for the highest ever total remains the 54 scored in a 21-team Serie A in the 50/51 season.

Milan hold the Serie A record for consecutive matches without defeat: 58 (beaten 1-0 by Parma on 21 March 1993 – goal from Asprilla).

In the 1947/48 season, Torino claimed the Serie A Championship with a record 65 points – albeit in a 21-team Serie A. The Granata also scored a record 125 goals.

Torino hold the Serie A record for totalling the highest number of points at home in one season: 39 of a possible 40 (1947/48).

In the 1949/50 season, Juventus claimed a record number of points away from home. La Signora collected 32 of a possible 38 points.

Varese hold the record for the longest run without a win in Serie A: 28 consecutive games (1971/72).

Natale Faccenda is the the youngest ever Serie A debutant. On 28 September 1930, he played for Livorno in a goalless draw against Milan aged 15 years, 9 months and 3 days.

PENALTY EXPERTS

PLAYER	SCORED	TAKEN
Giuseppe Savoldi	45	56
Istvan Nyers	36	50
Roberto Baggio	33	38
Diego Maradona	30	34
Roberto Boninsegna	29	34
Gianni Rivera	27	34
Paolino Pulici	26	31
Roberto Pruzzo	26	35
Nils Liedholm	25	32
Mario Maraschi	24	26

ATALANTA

Highest Placing: 5th in Serie A (47/48)
Highest Points Total: 51 (Serie B 58/59)
Lowest Points Total: 16 (Serie A 37/38)
Biggest Home Victory: 7-1 vs Triestina (Serie A 52/53)
Heaviest Home Defeat: 1-7 vs Fiorentina (Serie A 63/64)
Biggest Away Victory: 6-2 vs Bologna (Serie A 49/50)
Heaviest Away Defeat: 1-9 vs Torino (Serie A 41/42)
All-time Top Scorer: Severo Cominelli 62 goals
Season's Top Scorer: Hans Jeppson 22 (Serie A 51/52)
Most Appearances: Stefano Angeleri 319
Biggest Signing: £3 million Maurizio Ganz from Brescia (92/93)
Biggest Sale: £6 million Claudio Caniggia to Roma (92/93)

CAGLIARI

Highest Placing: Serie A Champions (69/70)
Highest Points Total: 49 (Serie B 63/64, 76/77, 78,79)
Lowest Points Total: 14 (Serie B 33/34)
Biggest Home Victory: 5-1 vs Sampdoria & Lecce (Serie B 77/78 & 78/79)
Heaviest Home Defeat: 1-5 vs Roma (Serie A 75/76)
Biggest Away Victory: 6-1 vs Varese (Serie A 68/69)
Heaviest Away Defeat: 1-5 vs Torino (Serie A 75/76)
All-time Top Scorer: Gigi Riva 156 goals
Season's Top Scorer: Gigi Riva 21 (Serie A 69/60)
Most Appearances: Mario Brugnera 328
Biggest Signing: £2.5 million Francesco Moriero from Lecce (92/93)
Biggest Sale: £6 million Daniel Fonseca to Napoli (92/93)

CREMONESE

Highest Placing: 16th in Serie A (84/85)
Highest Points Total: 55 (Serie C 76/77)
Lowest Points Total: 15 (Serie A 84/85)
Biggest Home Victory: 5-0 vs Triestina & Jnr Casale (Serie C 72/73 & 74/75)
Heaviest Home Defeat: 0-5 vs Roma (Serie A 84/85)
Biggest Away Victory: 4-0 vs Padova (Serie C 74/75)
Heaviest Away Defeat: 0-9 vs Roma (Serie A 29/30)
All-time Top Scorer: Emiliano Mondonico 97 goals
Season's Top Scorer: Emiliano Mondonico 20 (Serie C 74/75)
Most Appearances: Cesini 419
Biggest Signing: £1.5 million Ruben Pereira from Danubio (91/92)
Biggest Sale: £4 million Giuseppe Favalli to Lazio (92/93)

FOGGIA

Highest Placing: 9th in Serie A (64/65 & 91/92)
Highest Points Total: 51 (Serie B 90/91)
Lowest Points Total: 24 (Serie A 66/67 & 73/74)
Biggest Home Victory: 5-0 vs Cosenza & Avellino (Serie B 90/91) & Verona (Serie A 91/92)
Heaviest Home Defeat: 2-8 vs Milan (Serie A 91/92)
Biggest Away Victory: 7-2 vs Udinese (Serie B 62/63)
Heaviest Away Defeat: 0-6 vs Juventus (Serie A 77/78)
All-time Top Scorer: Vittorio Nocera 101 goals
Season's Top Scorer: Vittorio Nocera 24 (Serie B 62/63)
Most Appearances: Attilio De Brita 415
Biggest Signing: £2 million Oberdan Biagioni from Cosenza (92/93)
Biggest Sale: £8 million Igor Shalimov to Inter (92/93)

GENOA

Highest Placing: Serie A Champions (9 times)
Highest Points Total: 56 (Serie C 70/71)
Lowest Points Total: 17 (Serie A 73/74)
Biggest Home Victory: 7-1 vs Padova (Serie A 48/49)
Heaviest Home Defeat: 0-8 vs Milan (Serie A 55/55)
Biggest Away Victory: 6-2 vs Venezia (Serie A 39/40)
Heaviest Away Defeat: 1-8 vs Juventus (Serie A 33/34)
All-time Top Scorer: Enrico Sardi 87
Season's Top Scorer: Roberto Pruzzo 18 (Serie B 75/76 & Serie A 76/77)
Most Appearances: Fosco Becattini 423
Biggest Signing: £4 million Igor Dobrovolski from Dy. Moscow (90/91)
Biggest Sale: £5 million Davide Fontolan to Inter (90/91)

INTER

Highest Placing: Serie A Champions (13 times)
Highest Points Total: 58 (Serie A 88/89)
Lowest Points Total: 26 (Serie A 41/42)
Biggest Home Victory: 9-0 vs Casale (Serie A 33/34)
Heaviest Home Defeat: 1-4 vs Venezia & Napoli (Serie A 42/43 & 54/55)
Biggest Away Victory: 6-0 vs Udinese & Bologna (Serie A 60/61 & 88/89)
Heaviest Away Defeat: 1-9 vs Juventus (Serie A 60/61)
All-time Top Scorer: Giuseppe Meazza 197 goals
Season's Top Scorer: Antonio Valentin Angelillo 33 (Serie A 58/59)
Most Appearances: Giacinto Facchetti 475
Biggest Signing: £8 million Igor Shalimov from Foggia (92/93)
Biggest Sale: £4.5 million Vincenzo Scifo to Torino (91/92)

JUVENTUS

Highest Placing: Serie A Champions (22 times)
Highest Points Total: 51 (Serie A 76/77)
Lowest Points Total: 29 (Serie A 38/39 & 61/62)
Biggest Home Victory: 9-1 vs Inter (Serie A 60/61)
Heaviest Home Defeat: 1-7 vs Milan (Serie A 49/50)
Biggest Away Victory: 7-0 vs Pro Patria (Serie A 50/51)
Heaviest Away Defeat: 0-6 vs Inter (Serie A 53/54)
All-time Top Scorer: Giampiero Boniperti 178 goals
Season's Top Scorer: Felice Borel 32 (Serie A 33/34)
Most Appearances: Gampiero Boniperti 444
Biggest Signing: £12 million Gianluca Vialli from Sampdoria (92/93)
Biggest Sale: £4 million Massimo Orlando to Fiorentina (91/92)

LAZIO

Highest Placing: Serie A Champions (73/74)
Highest Points Total: 50 (Serie B 68/69)
Lowest Points Total: 15 (Serie A 84/85)
Biggest Home Victory: 9-1 vs Modena (Serie A 31/32)
Heaviest Home Defeat: 0-5 vs Fiorentina (Serie A 59/60)
Biggest Away Victory: 6-2 vs Palermo (Serie A 56/57)
Heaviest Away Defeat: 1-8 vs Inter (Serie A 33/34)
All-time Top Scorer: Silvio Piola 143 goals
Season's Top Scorer: Giuseppe Signori 26 (Serie A 92/93)
Most Appearances: Aldo Puccinelli 339
Biggest Signing: £5.5 million Paul Gascoigne from Tottenham Hotspur (92/93)
Biggest Sale: £3.5 million Paolo Di Canio to Juventus (90/91)

LECCE

Highest Placing: 9th in Serie A (88/89)
Highest Points Total: 50 (Serie B 84/85)
Lowest Points Total: 16 (Serie A 85/86)
Biggest Home Victory: 8-0 vs Scafatese (Serie B 46/47)
Heaviest Home Defeat: 0-3 vs Inter & Milan (Serie A 88/89 & 90/91)
Biggest Away Victory: 6-1 vs Cosenza (Serie C 75/76)
Heaviest Away Defeat: 1-9 vs Marsala (IV Serie 56/57)
All-time Top Scorer: Anselmo Bislenghi 83
Season's Top Scorer: Anselmo Bislenghi 32 (Serie C 52/53)
Most Appearances: Michele Lorusso 417
Biggest Signing: £1 million Antonio Rizzolo from Palermo (92/93)
Biggest Sale: £3 million Antonio Conte to Juventus (91/92)

STATISTICS – 93/94 CLUB RECORDS

MILAN

Highest Placing: Serie A Champions (13 times)
Highest Points Total: 60 (Serie A 50/51)
Lowest Points Total: 27 (Serie A 81/82)
Biggest Home Victory: 9-0 vs Palermo (Serie A 50/51)
Heaviest Home Defeat: 1-5 vs Genoa & Inter (Serie A 57/58 & 73/74)
Biggest Away Victory: 8-0 vs Genoa (Serie A 54/55)
Heaviest Away Defeat: 1-6 vs Alessandria (Serie A 35/36)
All-time Top Scorer: Gunnar Nordhal 210
Season's Top scorer: Gunnar Nordahl 35 (Serie A 49/50)
Most Appearances: Gianni Rivera 501
Biggest Signing: £13 million Gianluigi Lentini from Torino (92/93)
Biggest Sale: £4.5 million Stefano Borgonovo to Fiorentina (90/91)

PIACENZA

Highest Placing: 3rd in Serie B (92/93)
Highest Points Total: 47 (Serie C 74/75)
Lowest Points Total: 26 (Serie C 82/83 & Serie B 88/89)
Biggest Home Victory: 5-0 vs Clodiasottomarina (Serie C 76/77)
Heaviest Home Defeat: 2-5 vs Vigevano (Serie C 74/75)
Biggest Away Victory: 4-1 vs Vigevano & Biellese (Serie C 74/75 & 79/80)
Heaviest Away defeat: 0-5 vs Reggiana (Serie C 80/81)
All-time Top Scorer: Armando Madonna 48 goals
Season's Top Scorer: Bruno Zanolla 23 (Serie C 74/75)
Most Appearances: Armando Madonna 196
Biggest Signing: £1.3 million Fabrizio Fioretti from Pescara (91/92)
Biggest Sale: £1.2 million Armando Madonna to Atalanta (88/89)

SAMPDORIA

Highest Placing: Serie A Champions (90/91)
Highest Points Total: 54 (Serie B 66/67)
Lowest Points Total: 20 (Serie A 73/74)
Biggest Home Victory: 7-0 vs Pro Patria (Serie A 55/56)
Heaviest Home Defeat: 0-5 vs Inter (Serie A 65/66)
Biggest Away Victory: 7-3 vs Venezia (Serie A 49/50)
Heaviest Away defeat: 1-7 vs Inter & Udinese (Serie A 55/56 & 60/61)
All-time Top Scorer: Adriano Bassetto 92
Season's Top Scorer: Sergio Brighenti 27 (Serie A 60/61)
Most Appearances: Gaudenzio Bernasconi 335
Biggest Signing: £4 million Eugenio Corini from Juventus (92/93)
Biggest Sale: £12 million Gianluca Vialli to Juventus (92/93)

NAPOLI

Highest Placing: Serie A Champions (Twice)
Highest Points Total: 51 (Serie A 89/90)
Lowest Points Total: 23 (Serie A 41/42)
Biggest Home Victory: 8-1 vs Pro Patria (Serie A 55/56)
Heaviest Home Defeat: 1-6 vs Bologna (Serie A 38/39)
Biggest Away Victory: 5-0 vs Modena (Serie A 29/30)
Heaviest Away Defeat: 1-11 vs Alessandria (Campionato Nazionale 27/28)
All-time Top Scorer: Attila Sallustro 106 goals
Season's Top Scorer: Antonio Vojak 21 (Serie A 33/34)
Most Appearances: Giuseppe Bruscolotti 387
Biggest Signing: £6 million Daniel Fonseca from Cagliari (92/93)
Biggest Sale: £4 million Luca Fusi to Torino (90/91)

REGGIANA

Highest Placing: Serie B Champions (92/93)
Highest Points Total: 55 (Serie C 63/64)
Lowest Points Total: 23 (Serie B 29/30)
Biggest Home Victory: 6-1 vs Olbia (Serie C 77/78)
Heaviest Home Defeat: 0-7 vs Roma (Serie B 51/52)
Biggest Away Victory: 4-1 vs Catania (Serie B 67/68) & Casale (Serie C 80/81)
Heaviest Away Defeat: 1-9 vs Novara (Serie B 29/30)
All-time Top Scorer: Flaviano Zandoli 42
Season's Top Scorer: Andrea Silenzi 23 (Serie B 89/90)
Most Appearances: Giampiero Grevi 284
Biggest Signing: £750,000 Dario Morello from Inter (90/91)
Biggest Sale: £3.2 million Andrea Silenzi to Napoli (90/91)

TORINO

Highest Placing: Serie A Champions (7 times)
Highest Points Total: 65 (Serie A 47/48)
Lowest Points Total: 23 (Serie A 58/59)
Biggest Home Victory: 10-0 vs Alessandria (Serie A 47/48)
Heaviest Home Defeat: 0-6 vs Fiorentina (Serie A 49/50)
Biggest Away Victory: 7-1 vs Roma (Serie A 58/59)
Heaviest Away Defeat: 0-7 vs Milan (Serie A 49/50)
All-time Top Scorer: Paolino Pulici 134 goals
Season's Top Scorer: Valentino Mazzola 29 (Serie A 46/47)
Most Appearances: Giorgio Ferrini 443
Biggest Signing: £4.5 million Vincenzo Scifo from Inter (91/92)
Biggest Sale: £13 million Gianluigi Lentini to Milan (92/93)

PARMA

Highest Placing: 3rd in Serie A (92/93)
Highest Points Total: 52 (Serie C 51/52 & 72/73)
Lowest Points Total: 23 (Serie B 64/65)
Biggest Home Victory: 6-0 vs Pro Sesto (Serie C 50/51)
Heaviest Home Defeat: 1-7 vs Padova (Serie B 31/32)
Biggest Away Victory: 4-1 vs Catanzaro (Serie B 89/90)
Heaviest Away Defeat: 1-7 vs Palermo (Serie B 58/59)
All-time Top Scorer: Bronzoni 78 goals
Season's Top Scorer: Massimo Barbuti 17 (Serie C 82/83)
Most Appearances: Ivo Cocconi 308
Biggest Signing: £3 million Faustino Asprilla from N.Medellin (92/93)
Biggest Sale: £3 million Enzo Gambaro to Milan (91/92)

ROMA

Highest Placing: Serie A Champions (Twice)
Highest Points Total: 53 (Serie B 51/52)
Lowest Points Total: 24 (Serie A 72/73)
Biggest Home Victory: 9-0 vs Cremonese (Serie A 29/30)
Heaviest Home Defeat: 1-7 vs Torino (Serie A 47/48)
Biggest Away Victory: 7-0 vs Reggiana (Serie B 51/52)
Heaviest Away Victory: 1-7 vs Juventus (Serie A 31/32)
All-time Top Scorer: Roberto Pruzzo 106 goals
Season's Top Scorer: Rodolfo Volk 29 (Serie A 30/31)
Most Appearances: Giacomo Losi 386
Biggest Signing: £6 million Claudio Caniggia from Atalanta (92/93)
Biggest Sale: £4 million Stefano Desideri to Inter (91/92)

UDINESE

Highest Placing: 4th in Serie A (56/57)
Highest Points Total: 55 (Serie B 78/79)
Lowest Points Total: 15 (Serie A 86/87)
Biggest Home Victory: 7-0 vs Napoli (Serie A 57/58)
Heaviest Home Defeat: 2-7 vs Foggia (Serie B 62/63)
Biggest Away Victory: 5-0 vs Carrarese (Serie B 47/48)
Heaviest Away Defeat: 0-7 vs Fiorentina & Milan (Serie A 58/59)
All-time Top Scorer: Lorenzo Bettini 67 goals
Season's Top Scorer: Abel Balbo 22 (Serie B 90/91)
Most Appearances: Dino Galparoli 191
Biggest Signing: £3.5 million Zico from Flamengo (83/84)
Biggest Sale: £3 million Marco Branca to Sampdoria (90/91)

Key:
G Goalkeeper D Defender M Midfield F Forward
( ) Apps as sub [ ] pens

ANCONA	Pos	D.O.B.	Apps	Gls	Serie A Total Apps	Gls
Massimo Agostini	F	20-01-64	33	12[1]	177	46
Luca Bertarelli	F	15-12-73	2(2)	-	2	-
Andrea Bruniera	D	10-02-64	27(2)	-	55	1
Nicola Caccia	F	10-04-70	26(21)	-	34	-
Felice Centofanti	M	23-05-69	18(14)	1	19	1
Lajos Detari	M	24-04-63	32(1)	9[2]	47	14
Franco Ermini	C	13-08-61	14(2)	2	44	4
Stefano Fontana	D	26-10-65	24(4)	-	24	-
Massimo Gadda	M	16-09-63	8(3)	-	21	-
Milos Glonek	D	26-09-68	23	-	23	-
Roberto Lorenzini	D	09-07-66	27	-	70	-
Fabio Lupo	M	11-10-64	23(1)	5	54	6
Salvatore Mazzarano	D	04-07-65	29(1)	-	29	-
Davide Micillo	G	17-04-71	8	-14	8	-14
Alessandro Nista	G	10-07-65	26	-59	64	-101
Marco Pecoraro	M	24-12-62	32	-	48	-
Oscar Ruggeri*	D	26-01-62	7	1	7	1
Sean Sogliano	M	28-02-71	29(2)	2	29	2
Sebastiano Vecchiola	M	23-05-70	26(3)	4	26	4
Sergio Zarate*	F	14-01-69	11(5)	2	11	2

*Ruggeri sold to Mexican side, America, in November.
 Zarate sold to Argentinian side, Velez Sarsfield in February.

BRESCIA	Pos	D.O.B.	Apps	Gls	Serie A Total Apps	Gls
Stefano Bonometti	M	30-12-61	28(1)	-	61	3
Edoardo Bortolotti	D	08-01-70	11(5)	-	11	-
Luca Brunetti	D	10-11-64	23(1)	-	24	1
Nello Cusin	G	12-03-65	8(1)	-8	90	-108
Luciano De Paola	M	30-05-61	25	-	28	-
Sergio Domini	M	11-03-61	26	1	130	5
Salvatore Giunta	C	13-04-67	31	1	93	13
Gheorghe Hagi	M	25-02-65	31	6	31	6
Marco Landucci	G	25-03-64	27	-36	153	-192
Nicola Marangon	M	14-04-71	8(8)	-	11	-
Dorin Mateut	F	05-08-65	4	4	-	-
Paolo Negro	D	16-04-72	26(3)	1	49	1
Massimo Paganin	D	19-07-70	30	1	30	1
Francesco Passiatore	F	22-07-71	1(1)	-	1	-
Marco Piovanelli	F	07-04-74	2(7)	-	12	-
Alessandro Quaggiotto	M	04-01-62	3(3)	-	3	-
Fiorin Raducioiu	F	17-03-70	29(1)	13[3]	89	20
Marco Rossi	D	09-09-64	30	2	32	2
Ioan Sabau	M	12-02-68	32	4	32	4
Giampaolo Saurini	F	13-11-68	15(5)	3	26	4
Marco Schenardi	M	03-03-68	30(22)	1	48	1
Paolo Ziliani*	D	10-06-71	3(1)	-	5	-

*Ziliani sent on loan to Napoli in November.

ATALANTA	Pos	D.O.B.	Apps	Gls	Serie A Total Apps	Gls
Ricardo Alemao	M	22-11-61	22(2)	2	115	11
Tebaldo Bigliardi	D	05-02-63	22(2)	-	112	-
Roberto Bordin	M	10-01-65	33	3	182	9
Maurizio Codispoti	M	04-07-64	18(4)	-	52	2
Stefano De Agostini	M	25-10-64	27	-	58	-
Fabrizio Ferron	G	05-09-65	30	-38	162	-174
Maurizio Ganz	F	13-10-68	32	14[1]	45	14
Oscar Magoni	M	22-09-67	18(10)	-	18	-
Claudio Mascheretti	D	31-01-70	6(5)	-	6	-
Giuseppe Minaudo	M	22-03-67	30(1)	2	85	4
Paolo Montero	D	03-09-71	27	2	27	2
Luigino Pasciullo	D	18-02-61	10(7)	-	170	7
Simone Pavan	M	29-04-74	1	-	1	-
Carlo Perrone	M	08-07-60	32(2)	5	125	17
Davide Pinato	G	15-03-64	5(1)	-7	7	-9
Federico Pisani	F	25-07-74	6(5)	1	12	1
Mirko Poloni	F	18-09-74	1(1)	-	2	-
Sergio Porrini	D	08-11-68	33	2	100	3
Roberto Rambaudi	F	12-01-66	31	6	64	15
Leo Rodriguez	M	27-08-66	19(13)	1	19	1
Alessio Tacchinardi	M	23-07-75	1	-	1	-
Emanuele Tresoldi	D	20-11-73	3(2)	-	9	-
Ivan Valenciano	F	18-03-72	5(4)	-	5	-
Mauro Valentini	D	04-01-64	22(1)	-	70	-

CAGLIARI	Pos	D.O.B.	Apps	Gls	Serie A Total Apps	Gls
Francesco Bellucci	D	23-02-73	4(2)	-	24	-
Pier Paolo Bisoli	M	20-11-66	32	2	65	3
Giorgio Bresciani*	F	23-04-69	4(1)	-	128	26
Massimiliano Cappioli	M	17-01-68	31(8)	7	66	9
Antonio Criniti	F	28-10-70	12(10)	1	33	3
Nicola Di Bitonto	G	01-05-66	1(1)	-	3	-1
Gianluca Festa	D	12-03-69	31(1)	-	90	-
Aldo Firicano	D	12-03-67	33	3	95	4
Enzo Francescoli	M	12-11-61	32	7	98	17
Gianluca Gaudenzi	M	28-12-65	8(3)	-	95	5
Jose Herrera	M	17-06-65	32(1)	1	89	8
Mario Ielpo	G	08-06-63	34	-33	101	-109
Gianfranco Matteoli	M	21-04-59	31(2)	-	265	10
Francesco Moriero	F	31-03-69	27(4)	4	113	8
Nicolo Napoli	D	07-02-62	31(1)	2	126	13
Luis Oliveira	F	24-03-69	29(3)	7	29	7
Luigi Pancaro	D	26-08-71	3(1)	-	3	-
Vittorio Pusceddu	D	12-02-64	32	7	114	14
Marco Sanna	M	27-12-69	17(15)	-	17	-
Marcelo Tejera	M	06-08-73	5(4)	-	5	-
Matteo Villa	D	23-01-70	10(8)	-	32	-

*Bresciani sold to Napoli in November.

MORE SERIE A RECORDS

The record for the longest winning streak belongs to Milan, who in the 89/90 season won 11 consecutive matches in Serie A.

In the 1991/92 season, Milan became the first team to win the Serie A Championship without losing a match.

In the 1978/79 season, Perugia remained undefeated but still finished in the runners-up spot behind Milan.

Cagliari hold the record for conceding the fewest number of goals in one Serie A season: 11 (1969/70).

Bari are the holders of the Serie A record for scoring the fewest number of goals in one season: 11 (1969/70).

Aged 34 years, 4 months and 26 days, Renato Nigiotti is the oldest ever Serie A debutant, playing in Palermo's 1-0 win over Torino on 19 March 1933.

On 9 May 1937, Amedeo Amedei became the youngest player to score in a Serie A fixture. Amedei was aged 15 years and 9 months when he scored Roma's consolation in their 5-1 defeat at Lucchese.

The record for the best goal per game average in a Serie A season belongs to Felice Borel. The former Juventus striker scored 29 goals in 28 games in 1932/33.

Paolino Pulici and Francesco Graziani enjoyed the most prolific striking partnership in Serie A history. The pair shared 200 goals playing for Torino from 1973 to 1981 (Pulici 103 & Graziani 97).

Kurt Hamrin holds the Serie A record for scoring the most goals in an away match. The Swede scored five in Fiorentina's 7-1 demolition of Atalanta on February 2 1964.

The sweeper, Francesco Janich, holds the Serie A record for playing the highest number of matches without scoring a goal: 426.

In the 1946/47 season, Torino's legendary Valentino Mazzola claimed the fastest hat-trick in Serie A, scoring 3 goals in 2 minutes (29', 30', 31') against Vicenza.

Ezio Pascutti is the only Serie A player to have scored in 10 consecutive Serie A matches, playing for Bologna during the 1962/63 season.

SERIE A STATISTICS – 92/93 PLAYERS

FIORENTINA	Pos	D.O.B	Apps	Gls	Serie A Total Apps	Serie A Total Gls
Francesco Baiano	F	24-02-68	32	10[2]	96	28
Gabriel Batistuta	F	01-02-69	32	16	59	29
Daniele Beltrammi	F	09-03-74	7(5)	1	9	2
Emiliano Betti	G	15-02-82	1(1)	-	1	-
Daniele Carnasciali	D	06-09-66	31	-	31	-
Stefano Carobbi	D	16-01-64	24(1)	-	177	3
Lorenzo D'Anna	D	29-01-72	5(3)	-	5	-
Antonio Dell'Oglio	M	19-06-63	12(7)	-	197	7
Fabrizio Di Mauro	M	18-06-65	29	6	142	13
Stefan Effenberg	M	02-08-68	30	5[1]	30	5
Mario Faccenda	D	23-11-60	23(2)	1	242	7
Danielè Giraldi	M	06-11-74	1(1)	-	2	-
Giuseppe Iachini	M	07-05-64	21(7)	1	190	
Diego Latorre	M	04-08-69	2(2)	-	2	-
Brian Laudrup	M	22-02-69	31	5	31	5
Gianluca Luppi	D	23-08-66	28	1	128	1
Alessandro Mannini	G	26-08-57	15(2)	-28	143	-166
Gian Matteo Mareggini	G	08-01-67	21	-28	76	-84
Massimo Orlando	M	26-05-71	29(1)	3	82	14
Stefano Pioli	D	19-10-65	31	-	176	1
Andrea Vascotto	F	21-09-71	5(5)	1	6	1
Rufo Emiliano Verga*	D	21-12-69	4(3)		-	39

*Verga sold to Venezia in November.

FOGGIA	Pos	D.O.B	Apps	Gls	Serie A Total Apps	Serie A Total Gls
Mauro Bacchin	G	27-10-69	4(1)	-9	4	-9
Oberdan Biagioni	M	17-10-69	24(5)	5[5]	24	5
David Bianchini	D	23-07-71	24(1)	1	24	1
Pierpaolo Bresciani	F	21-07-70	29(5)	6	29	6
Giordano Caini	D	28-03-69	22	-	22	-
Pasquale De Vincenzo	M	12-02-68	31	2	31	2
Giuseppe Di Bari	D	17-11-69	27(1)	-	27	-
Luigi Di Biagio	M	03-06-71	30(1)	5[1]	31	5
Giuseppe Fornaciari	D	27-07-67	18(3)	-	18	-
Donatello Gasparini	D	29-07-71	3	-	11	-
Gualtiero Grandini	D	06-10-67	9	-	26	-
Gianluca Grassadonia	D	25-05-72	9(3)	-	9	-
Igor Kolyvanov	F	06-03-68	26(1)	5[1]	41	8
Francesco Mancini	G	10-10-68	31	-46	61	-95
Paolo Mandelli	F	04-12-67	20(8)	2	21	2
Hernan Medford	F	04-12-67	12(8)	1	12	1
Pieluigi Nicoli	M	06-04-66	17(11)	-	17	-
Dan Petrescu	D	22-12-67	30(2)	3	55	7
Giovanni Pisano	F	05-10-68	1(1)	-	1	-
Brian Roy	F	12-02-70	20(2)	3	20	3
Nicolo Sciacca	M	24-11-68	15(5)	2[1]	15	2
Andrea Seno	M	01-02-66	30	2	30	2

GENOA	Pos	D.O.B	Apps	Gls	Serie A Total Apps	Serie A Total Gls
Roberto Arco	F	05-03-74	6(5)	1	6	1
Mario Bortolazzi	M	10-01-65	31	1	178	13
Claudio Branco	D	04-04-64	24(2)	1	96	11
Nicola Caricola	D	13-02-63	28	2	171	5
Luca Cavallo	M	19-05-73	7(2)	-	7	-
Fulvio Collovati	D	09-05-57	8(6)	-	368	8
Igor Dobrovolski*	F	27-08-67	4	1	4	1
Armando Ferroni	D	03-04-61	3(3)	-	264	4
Valeriano Fiorin	M	27-09-66	19(6)	-	99	2
Andrea Fortunato	D	26-07-71	33	3	33	3
Maurizio Iorio	F	06-06-59	13(8)	1	198	37
Roberto Onorati	M	05-02-66	20(6)	2	143	4
Michele Padovano	F	28-08-66	27(3)	9[2]	77	26
Christian Panucci	D	12-04-73	30(6)	3	31	3
Gennaro Ruotolo	M	20-03-67	31(1)	2	125	8
Elio Signorelli	M	07-03-70	2(2)	-	4	-
Gianluca Signorini	D	17-03-60	30	2	151	4
Tomas Skuhravy	F	07-09-65	31	10[2]	96	36
Giampaolo Spagnulo	G	26-09-64	24	-31	4	-31
Stefano Tacconi	G	13-05-57	11(1)	-24	355	-350
Vincenzo Torrente	D	12-02-66	26	-	114	2
Johnny Van't Schip	M	30-12-63	29(12)	2	29	2

*Dobrovolski sent on loan to Marseille in November.

INTER	Pos	D.O.B	Apps	Gls	Serie A Total Apps	Serie A Total Gls
Beniamino Abate	G	10-11-62	7(2)	-10	47	-63
Sergio Battistini	D	07-05-63	34	5	297	27
Giuseppe Bergomi	D	22-12-63	31	2	359	21
Nicola Berti	M	14-04-67	32	4	233	29
Alessandro Bianchi	M	07-04-66	17	1	166	11
Luigi De Agostini	D	07-04-61	31	1	317	31
Stefano Desideri*	M	03-07-65	4(2)	1	191	32
Riccardo Ferri	D	20-08-63	20	1	274	6
Davide Fontolan	F	24-02-66	25(9)	2	86	14
Antonio Manicone	M	27-10-66	20	1	29	2
Marcello Montanari*	D	25-09-65	1	-	12	-
Angelo Orlando	M	11-08-65	19(4)	-	68	2
Antonio Paganin	D	18-06-66	25(9)	-	141	1
Darko Pancev	F	17-09-65	12(3)	1	12	1
Stefano Rossini	D	02-02-71	3(3)	-	24	-
Matthias Sammer*	M	05-09-67	11	4	11	4
Salvatore Schillaci	F	01-12-64	21(1)	6[1]	111	32
Igor Shalimov	M	02-02-69	32	9	65	18
Ruben Sosa	F	25-04-66	28	20[3]	151	60
Mirko Taccola	D	14-08-70	6(5)	-	8	-
Paolo Tramezzani	D	30-07-70	13(9)	-	13	-
Simone Veronese	D	08-07-74	1(1)	-	1	-
Walter Zenga	G	28-04-60	29	-26	296	-251

*Desideri sold to Udinese in November.
*Montanari sold to Bari in November.
*Sammer sold to Borussia Dortmund in January.

JUVENTUS	Pos	D.O.B	Apps	Gls	Serie A Total Apps	Serie A Total Gls
Dino Baggio	M	24-07-71	32(1)	1	84	4
Roberto Baggio	M	18-02-67	27(1)	21[3]	186	93
Massimo Carrera	D	22-04-64	29	-	120	3
Pierluigi Casiraghi	F	04-03-69	18(8)	1	98	20
Antonio Conte	M	31-07-69	31	2	123	3
Alessandro Dal Canto	D	10-03-75	3(2)	-	3	-
Marco Antonio De Marchi	D	08-09-66	18(6)	1	103	5
Paolo Di Canio	F	09-07-68	31(12)	3	131	11
Roberto Galia	M	16-03-63	21(5)	-	291	15
Massimiliano Giacobbo	M	15-07-74	1(1)	-	1	-
Julio Cesar Silva	D	08-03-63	16	1	78	3
Jurgen Kohler	D	06-10-65	29	1	56	4
Giancarlo Marocchi	M	04-07-65	23(11)	1	151	11
Andreas Moeller	M	02-09-67	26(1)	10	26	10
Angelo Peruzzi	G	16-02-70	29	-44	80	-106
David Platt	M	10-06-66	16	3	45	14
Michelangelo Rampulla*	G	10-08-62	7(2)	-3	68	92(1)
Fabrizio Ravanelli	F	11-12-68	22(14)	5[1]	22	5
Luigi Sartor	D	30-01-75	1	-	1	-
Moreno Torricelli	D	23-01-70	30(2)	-	30	-
Gianluca Vialli	F	09-07-64	32(2)	6	255	92

*Rampulla is the only Serie A goalkeeper ever to score from open play.

LAZIO	Pos	D.O.B	Apps	Gls	Serie A Total Apps	Serie A Total Gls
Roberto Bacci	M	15-06-67	31(3)	-	86	-
Cristiano Bergodi	D	04-10-64	16(3)	1	167	3
Mauro Bonomi	D	23-08-72	10(1)	-	38	-
Luigi Corino	D	26-04-66	20(6)	-	40	-
Roberto Cravero	D	13-01-64	30	3	178	14
Thomas Doll	M	09-04-66	20	2	51	9
Giuseppe Favalli	D	08-01-72	32	1	91	2
Valerio Fiori	G	27-04-69	11	-19	116	-128
Diego Fuser	M	11-11-68	33	10	149	28
Paul Gascoigne	M	27-05-67	22	4	22	4
Angelo Gregucci	D	10-06-64	12(2)	1	124	8
Luca Luzardi	D	18-02-70	25	1	25	1
Dario Marcolin	M	28-10-71	15(9)	-	52	4
Maurizio Neri	F	21-03-65	2(2)	-	65	6
Fernando Orsi	G	12-09-59	23	-32	81	-114
Karl-Heinz Riedle	F	16-09-65	22	8	84	30
Claudio Sclosa	M	28-02-61	20(11)	-	253	4
Giuseppe Signori	F	17-02-68	32	26[5]	64	37
Giovanni Stroppa	M	24-01-68	20(15)	1	84	7
Aron Winter	M	01-03-67	30	6	30	6

MILAN	Pos	D.O.B	Apps	Gls	Serie A Total Apps	Serie A Total Gls
Demetrio Albertini	M	23-08-71	29(5)	2	59	5
Francesco Antonioli	G	14-09-69	9	-7	13	-7
Franco Baresi	D	08-05-60	29	-	355	11
Zvonimir Boban	M	08-10-68	13(1)	-	30	2
Alessandro Costacurta	D	24-04-66	31	-	145	2
Fernando De Napoli	M	15-03-64	4(3)	-	253	11
Roberto Donadoni	M	09-09-63	20(5)	1	230	18
Stefano Eranio	M	29-12-66	21(8)	2	107	8
Alberigo Evani	M	01-01-63	18(9)	-	261	17
Filippo Galli	D	19-05-63	1(1)	-	182	3
Enzo Gambaro	D	23-02-66	11(5)	-	69	-
Ruud Gullit	M	01-09-62	15(2)	7	117	35
Gianluigi Lentini	M	27-03-69	30(2)	7	120	17
Paolo Maldini	D	26-06-68	31	2	228	13
Daniele Massaro	F	23-05-61	29(15)	5	329	52
Stefano Nava	D	19-02-69	14(2)	-	35	-
Jean-Pierre Papin	F	05-11-63	22	13[1]	22	13
Frank Rijkaard	M	30-09-62	22	2	142	16
Sebastiano Rossi	G	20-07-64	27(2)	-25	160	-147
Dejan Savicevic	M	15-09-66	10	4[1]	10	4
Aldo Serena	F	25-06-60	1(1)	-	255	86
Marco Simone	F	07-01-69	13(5)	5	101	23
Mauro Tassotti	D	19-01-60	27(1)	-	346	8
Marco Van Basten	F	31-10-64	15(1)	13	147	90

NAPOLI	Pos	D.O.B	Apps	Gls	Serie A Total Apps	Serie A Total Gls
Luca Altomare	M	14-01-72	14(4)	-	14	-
Cristian Baglieri	F	23-03-74	1	-	1	-
Giorgio Bresciani	F	23-04-69	11(8)	-	129	26
Fabio Cannavaro	D	13-09-73	2	-	2	-
Angelo Carbone	M	23-03-68	27(6)	-	100	2
Antonio Careca	F	05-10-60	24(1)	7	164	73
Carlo Cornacchia	D	04-05-65	3(3)	-	48	7
Giancarlo Corradini	D	24-02-61	31(5)	-	297	8
Massimo Crippa	M	15-05-65	29(4)	1	179	12
Gaetano De Rosa	M	10-05-73	3(3)	-	3	-
Marco Ferrante*	F	04-02-71	4(2)	-	14	-
Ciro Ferrara	D	11-02-67	31	4	220	10
Daniel Fonseca	F	13-09-69	31(1)	16[2]	81	34
Giovanni Francini	D	03-08-63	25(1)	1	274	3
Giovanni Galli	G	29-04-58	32	-49	455	-403
Massimo Mauro	M	24-05-62	10(7)	-	307	15
Sebino Nela	D	13-03-61	23	-	304	16
Fausto Pari	M	15-09-62	13(3)	-	286	7
Roberto Policano	M	19-02-64	30(3)	7	139	24
Gianni Sansonetti	G	28-01-65	2	1	3	-1
Massimo Tarantino	D	20-05-71	30(12)	-	45	-
Jonas Thern	M	20-03-67	27	-	27	-
Paolo Ziliani	D	10-06-71	2(1)	-	5	-
Gianfranco Zola	M	05-07-66	33	12[1]	105	32

*Ferrante sent on loan to Parma in November.

Key:
G Goalkeeper **D** Defender **M** Midfield **F** Forward
( ) Apps as sub **[ ]** pens

MORE SERIE A RECORDS

The Brazilian, José Altafini, made the most Serie A appearances for an overseas player: 459.

Maurizio Iorio has played for the most Serie A clubs (9). From 1977 to 1993, the striker wore the jerseys of Foggia, Torino, Ascoli, Roma, Verona, Fiorentina, Brescia, Inter and Genoa.

On 9 March1980, Pescara's Gianluca Pacchiarotti became the youngest ever Serie A goalkeeper, making his debut aged 16 years, 6 months and 9 days in Pescara's 1-0 defeat at Perugia.

On 23 February 1992, Michelangelo Rampulla became the first Serie A goalkeeper to score from open play. He equalised with a last minute header for Cremonese in a fixture at Atalanta.

Dino Zoff holds 4 Serie A records:
1) The goalkeeper made the most Serie A appearances: 570 (from 1961 to 1983).
2) He kept a clean sheet for the longest duration: 903 minutes for Juventus in the 1972/73 season.
3) Zoff made the highest number of consecutive Serie A appearances: 332 (from 1971 to 1983).
4) On 15 May 1983, he played his final Serie A match (Juventus-Genoa 4-2), aged 41 years, 2 months and 17 days, thus becoming the oldest player to retire from Serie A football.

The volatile Argentinian, Omar Sivori, holds the record for receiving the highest number of career sendings-off in Serie A, totalling 33 days suspension: 10 (1958 to 1969).

Dario Bonetti has been suspended more times than any other player in Serie A history. The central defender has received a total of 39 days suspension in his career with Brescia, Sampdoria, Roma, Milan, Verona and Juventus (1981 to 1990).

Just after World War 2, the Triestina goalkeeper Giacomo Blason received a life ban from Italian football after he struck the referee during a Serie A fixture against Torino. The sentence was later reduced to six months, which is still a Serie A record.

Key:
G Goalkeeper D Defender M Midfield F Forward
( ) Apps as sub [ ] pens

PARMA

	Pos	D.O.B	Apps	Gls	Serie A Total Apps	Serie A Total Gls
Luigi Apolloni	D	02-05-67	31	-	95	-
Faustino Asprilla	F	10-11-69	26(7)	7	26	7
Marco Ballotta	G	03-04-64	29(1)	-23	35	-34
Antonio Benarrivo	D	21-08-68	20	-	49	-
Sergio Berti	M	17-02-69	4(2)	-	4	-
Tomas Brolin	F	29-11-69	22(4)	4[1]	89	14
Stefano Cuoghi	M	08-08-59	22(3)	2	137	4
Alberto Di Chiara	D	29-03-64	30	1	223	15
Cornelio Donati	D	18-01-58	2(2)	-	31	-
Marco Ferrante	F	04-02-71	11(9)	-	15	-
Marco Ferrari	G	21-08-66	1(1)	-	2	-1
Gianluca Franchini	D	11-09-72	4(2)	-	4	-
Georges Grun	D	25-01-62	27	2	93	8
Gianluca Hervatin	F	01-01-74	8(6)	-	8	-
Salvatore Matrecano	D	05-10-70	20(7)	1	48	1
Alessandro Melli	F	11-12-69	28(2)	12	87	31
Lorenzo Minotti	D	08-02-67	33	3	99	13
Aldo Monza*	M	20-08-69	1(1)	-	18	-
Marco Osio	M	13-01-66	23(2)	7	102	17
Gabriele Pin	M	21-01-62	33(3)	-	177	11
Fausto Pizzi	M	21-07-67	20(5)	5[2]	59	11
Ivo Pulga	M	20-06-64	12(9)	-	57	-
Giovanni Sorce*	M	04-07-69	1(1)	-	24	1
Claudio Taffarel	G	08-05-66	6	11	74	-69
Daniele Zoratto	M	15-11-61	27	-	118	-

*Monza sold to Cosenza in November. *Sorce sold to Messina in November.

PESCARA

	Pos	D.O.B	Apps	Gls	Serie A Total Apps	Serie A Total Gls
Salvatore Alfieri	D	26-10-69	18(5)	-	18	-
Massimiliano Allegri	M	01-08-67	31	12[5]	32	12
Vincenzo Aureli	F	20-01-73	2(2)	-	2	-
Edy Bivi	F	11-01-60	21(15)	3[1]	93	20
Stefano Borgonovo	F	17-03-64	28(2)	9	171	42
Giacomo Ceredi	M	21-10-66	12(1)	-	12	-
Giuseppe Compagno	F	25-08-67	22(5)	-	35	-
Emiliano De Juliis	D	08-02-71	15(4)	-	15	-
Giacomo Dicara	D	27-04-70	24	-	64	1
Elio Di Toro	M	28-01-75	2(1)	-	2	-
Carlos Dunga	M	31-10-63	23	3	168	13
Massimo Epifani	M	25-10-74	3(2)	-	3	-
Stefano Ferretti	M	21-03-60	6(1)	1	68	1
Fabio Marchioro	G	01-04-68	24	-46	24	-68
Antonio Martorella	F	19-02-70	7(4)	1	7	1
Frederic Massara	F	11-11-68	27(2)	3	27	3
Roger Mendy	D	08-02-60	16	1	16	1
Salvatore Nobile	D	02-01-64	29	2	158	6
Ottavio Palladini	M	29-11-71	27(12)	6	27	6
Vittorio Pinciarelli	M	02-03-72	1(1)	-	1	-
Ubaldo Righetti	D	01-03-63	14(1)	-	159	1
Gianluca Rosone	D	09-11-74	2(2)	-	2	-
Marco Savorani	G	31-03-65	10	-29	18	-42
John Sivebaek	D	25-10-61	27(4)	1	27	1
Baka Sliskovic	M	30-05-59	18(1)	1	41	9
Mauro Zironelli	M	21-01-70	10	-	18	-

ROMA

	Pos	D.O.B	Apps	Gls	Serie A Total Apps	Serie A Total Gls
Aldair Dos Santos	D	30-11-65	28	2	90	7
Silvano Benedetti	D	05-10-65	30(1)	3	146	6
Walter Bonacina	M	10-07-64	32(3)	-	172	9
Claudio Caniggia	F	09-01-67	15	4	119	33
Amedeo Carboni	D	06-04-65	9	-	153	3
Andrea Carnevale	F	12-01-61	25(10)	7	245	66
Giovanni Cervone	G	16-11-62	27	28	136	-116
Antonio Comi	D	26-07-64	24(6)	2	232	17
Patrizio Fimiani	D	03-01-73	3(1)	-	3	1
Luigi Garzya	D	07-07-69	29(1)	-	130	1
Giuseppe Giannini	M	20-08-64	29	9[2]	244	45
Thomas Haessler	M	30-05-66	26	6[2]	90	10
Sinisa Mihajlovic	M	20-02-69	29	1	29	1
Roberto Muzzi	F	29-01-71	24(12)	1	50	5
Fabio Petruzzi	D	24-10-70	6(2)	-	7	-
Giovanni Piacentini	M	29-04-68	29	-	89	-
Ruggiero Rizzitelli	F	02-04-67	26(1)	7	160	30
Dario Rossi	D	14-11-72	5(2)	-	6	-
Fausto Salsano	M	18-02-62	25(16)	-	246	20
Antonio Tempestilli	D	08-10-59	9(6)	-	225	7
Francesco Totti	M	27-09-76	2(2)	-	2	-
Giuseppe Zinetti	G	22-06-58	6(1)	10	157	-152

SAMPDORIA

	Pos	D.O.B	Apps	Gls	Serie A Total Apps	Serie A Total Gls
Mauro Bertarelli	F	15-09-70	26(22)	2	26	2
Ivano Bonetti	M	01-08-64	13(4)	1	141	6
Roberto Bucchioni	D	02-02-73	2	-	2	-
Renato Buso	F	19-12-69	15(9)	1	138	23
Enrico Chiesa	M	29-12-70	27(9)	1	28	1
Eugenio Corini	M	30-07-70	24(2)	4[2]	75	5
Vladimir Jugovic	M	30-08-69	33	9	33	9
Srecko Katanec	M	16-07-63	4	-	83	11
Giovanni Invernizzi	M	22-08-63	26(5)	1	207	7
Marco Lanna	D	13-07-68	31	1	123	2
Attilio Lombardo	M	06-01-66	34	6	134	20
Roberto Mancini	F	27-11-64	30	15[5]	334	94
Moreno Mannini	D	15-08-62	27	-	270	9
Giulio Nuciari	G	26-06-60	5	8	17	-27
Gianluca Pagliuca	G	18-12-66	29	40	164	-144
Stefano Sacchetti	D	10-08-72	21(1)	-	21	-
Michele Serena	M	10-03-70	34(10)	1	64	4
Pietro Vierchowod	D	06-04-59	29	1	384	24
Des Walker	D	26-11-65	30(3)	-	30	-
Nicola Zanini	M	26-03-74	1(1)	-	2	-

TORINO

	Pos	D.O.B	Apps	Gls	Serie A Total Apps	Serie A Total Gls
Carlos Aguilera	F	21-09-64	31	12	127	45
Antonio Aloisi	D	28-08-68	9(6)	-	99	3
Enrico Annoni	D	01-07-66	25	-	137	4
Pasquale Bruno	D	19-06-62	24	-	224	3
Walter Casagrande	F	15-04-63	24(4)	4	106	26
Sandro Cois	M	09-06-72	17(4)	-	18	-
Ivano Della Morte	M	13-10-74	1(1)	-	1	-
Raffaele Di Fusco	G	06-10-61	-	-	20	-10
Daniele Fortunato	M	08-01-63	29(4)	1	126	10
Luca Fusi	M	07-06-63	31	-	275	3
Luca Marchegiani	G	22-02-66	34	-38	112	-101
Roberto Mussi	D	25-08-63	29(3)	2	102	3
Paolo Poggi	F	16-02-71	21(14)	3	21	3
Marcelo Saraleg	M	19-02-66	32(1)	7[2]	90	20
Raffaele Sergio	D	28-09-66	27(1)	1	117	2
Andrea Silenzi	F	10-02-66	25(12)	3	64	9
Marco Sinigaglia	M	29-02-68	2(2)	-	7	-
Gianluca Sordo	M	02-12-69	7	2	70	3
Andrea Sottil	D	04-01-74	9(6)	-	9	-
Giorgio Venturin	M	09-07-68	33(1)	-	96	1
Christian Vieri*	F	12-07-73	1(1)	-	7	1
Alvise Zago	M	20-08-69	8(5)	-	26	-

*Vieri sent on loan to Pisa in November.

UDINESE

	Pos	D.O.B	Apps	Gls	Serie A Total Apps	Serie A Total Gls
Abel Balbo	F	01-06-66	32	21[5]	60	32
Marco Branca	F	06-01-65	29(1)	8	126	30
Alessandro Calori	D	28-08-66	32	1	56	2
Luca Compagnon	M	11-08-72	2(1)	-	2	-
Renzo Contratto	D	05-12-59	6(5)	-	310	-
Piotr Czachowski	M	07-11-66	11(4)	-	11	-
Stefano Desideri	M	03-07-65	22	3	191	32
Francesco Dell'Anno	M	04-06-67	30	2	44	2
Nicola Di Leo	G	07-01-60	3	-6	70	-104
Paolo Di Sarno	G	01-06-68	30	-41	30	-41
Giuliano Giuliani	G	29-09-58	1	-1	212	-207
Marek Kozminski	D	07-02-71	22(6)	2	22	2
Andrea Mandorlini	D	17-07-60	11(1)	-	291	14
Antonio Manicone*	M	27-10-66	9(4)	1	29	2
Manuel Marcuz	M	06-05-72	1(1)	-	1	-
Massimo Mariotto	M		12(8)	-	12	-
Lorenzo Marronaro	F	16-01-61	15(13)	-	69	7
Luca Mattei	M	10-11-64	32(8)	1	171	7
Marco Nappi*	F	13-05-66	2(2)	-	46	6
Alessandro Orlando	D	06-06-70	29	-	43	1
Stefano Pellegrini	D	06-07-67	27	-	85	2
Alessandro Pierini	D	22-03-73	11(4)	-	11	-
Fabio Rossitto	M	21-09-71	31(1)	-	33	1
Roberto Sensini	M	12-10-66	33	1	66	3

*Nappi was sold to Spal in September.
*Manicone was sold to Inter in November.

PHOTO CREDITS

We are grateful to the following for permission to reproduce copyright photographs: PROFESSIONAL SPORT/FARABOLAFOTO Front cover (Vialli, flag), Back cover (crowd, stadium), 1, 2, 3, 4, 10, 11, 15, 18, 19, 22 (police), 23, 24, 25, 26 (Samp-Lazio), 30 (Baggio), 32 (Van Basten), 34, 37 (Rossi), 38 (Inter), 40, 41, 43, 49 (Coppa Italia), 50, 52, 53 (1970 squad, Riva), 55, 56, 58, 60 (Seno), 61, 63, 64, 65 (1904 squad, Ruotolo), 68, 69 (European Cup, Suarez), 72 (Boniperti, Sivori), 73 (Boniperti), 74, 76 (Piola), 77 (1934 squad, Fuser), 78, 79, 80, 81, 84, 85, 89 (1962 squad), 91, 92 (Di Chiara), 93 (Berti, Melli profile), 94, 95, 96, 97, 98, 99, 100 (Morello), 101, 103, 105 (Conti, Giannini), 106, 107, 108 (Vialli), 109 (1956 action, Vierchowod), 110, 112, 113 (Loik, Lentini), 114, 116 (Giuliani), 118, 119, 121, 122, 123, 124, 125, 126, 127, 132, 133, 137. BOB THOMAS SPORTS PHOTOGRAPHY 6, 42 (Parma), 44, 45, 48, 49 (Caniggia), 54, 59, 60 (Kolyvanov), 69 (Matthaus, Zenga), 72 (Scirea), 73 (Rossi), 76 (Chinaglia), 77 (Gascoigne), 86, 88, 89 (Maradona), 93 (Melli main shot), 100 (Carnevale), 102, 104, 108 (Cerezo), 109 (Mancini), 116 (Causio), 129, 130, 131, 134, 135. BOB THOMAS SPORTS PHOTOGRAPHY/RICHIARDI Back cover (Baggio) 14, 15, 22 (Napoli fans), 26 (Fonseca), 28 (Tacconi), 29 (Signori), 30 (Derby), 31, 32 (Vialli), 35, 36 (Milan-Atalanta), 37 (Rossi, Inter-Napoli), 38 (Asprilla), 39, 42 (Baresi), 46, 49 (Porrini), 51, 53 (Francescoli), 60 (Baiano), 62, 65 (Eranio), 66, 67, 70, 73 (Platini), 82, 89 (Zola), 90, 92 (Grun), 105 (Voller), 111, 113 (Pulici), 117. CHRYSALIS TELEVISION 27, 28 (Papin), 29 (Cesar), 30 (police), 33, 36 (Ferron), 37 (Trapattoni), 47, 75. ACTION IMAGES Front cover (Gazza, Van Basten). SOLO SYNDICATION 8. The Publishers would like to thank Collette Perlin at Professional Sport and Dave Joyner and Stuart Forster of Bob Thomas Sports Photography for their help and patience with the picture research; Ray Driscoll for editorial research; Brian Tremble for sourcing video images; and Printout for producing video grabs.